Understanding
Personal, Social, Health *and* Economic Education *in* Primary Schools

Education at SAGE

SAGE is a leading international publisher of journals, books, and electronic media for academic, educational, and professional markets.

Our education publishing includes:

- accessible and comprehensive texts for aspiring education professionals and practitioners looking to further their careers through continuing professional development
- inspirational advice and guidance for the classroom
- authoritative state of the art reference from the leading authors in the field

Find out more at: **www.sagepub.co.uk/education**

Understanding Personal, Social, Health *and* Economic Education *in* Primary Schools

Nick Boddington | Adrian King | Jenny McWhirter

Los Angeles | London | New Delhi
Singapore | Washington DC

Los Angeles | London | New Delhi
Singapore | Washington DC

SAGE Publications Ltd
1 Oliver's Yard
55 City Road
London EC1Y 1SP

SAGE Publications Inc.
2455 Teller Road
Thousand Oaks, California 91320

SAGE Publications India Pvt Ltd
B 1/I 1 Mohan Cooperative Industrial Area
Mathura Road
New Delhi 110 044

SAGE Publications Asia-Pacific Pte Ltd
3 Church Street
#10-04 Samsung Hub
Singapore 049483

Commissioning editor: James Clark
Editorial assistant: Rachael Plant
Production editor: Nicola Marshall
Copyeditor: Gemma Marren
Indexer: Martin Hargreaves
Marketing manager: Catherine Slinn
Cover design: Naomi Robinson
Typeset by: C&M Digitals (P) Ltd, Chennai, India
Printed and bound by
CPI Group (UK) Ltd, Croydon, CR0 4YY

© Nick Boddington, Adrian King and Jenny McWhirter 2014

First edition published 2014

Apart from any fair dealing for the purposes of research or private study, or criticism or review, as permitted under the Copyright, Designs and Patents Act, 1988, this publication may be reproduced, stored or transmitted in any form, or by any means, only with the prior permission in writing of the publishers, or in the case of reprographic reproduction, in accordance with the terms of licences issued by the Copyright Licensing Agency. Enquiries concerning reproduction outside those terms should be sent to the publishers.

Library of Congress Control Number: 2013946791

British Library Cataloguing in Publication data

A catalogue record for this book is available from the British Library

ISBN 978-1-4462-6875-9 (P)
ISBN 978-1-4462-6874-2

This book is dedicated to Noreen Wetton, practitioner, researcher and friend, whose memory inspired the writing of this book.

CONTENTS

About the authors   viii
Acknowledgements   x

  1 Introduction   1

Part 1   15

  2 Understanding effective practice in PSHE education   17
  3 Understanding school ethos – what is taught and what is caught? 46
  4 Understanding how to start where children are   64
  5 Understanding emotional development and emotional
     intelligence   82
  6 Understanding the pedagogy of PSHE education   95
  7 Understanding how to select PSHE education teaching
     material and resources   127

Part 2   143

  8 Understanding safety and risk education   145
  9 Understanding sex and relationships education   164
 10 Understanding how to address bullying behaviour in
     PSHE education   189
 11 Understanding medicine and drug education   208
 12 Understanding personal finance education   235

Part 3   243

 13 Understanding assessment in PSHE education   245

Appendix 1: PSHE education and safeguarding   273
Appendix 2: PSHE education and the school policy framework   275
Appendix 3: 'Little alien' – photocopiable activity plan   277

Index   279

ABOUT THE AUTHORS

Starting his career as an art and mathematics teacher working in both primary and secondary schools in north London, **Nick Boddington** joined the Advisory Service where he specialised in the teaching of sensitive issues including SRE, HIV, bullying and drug education. One of the first Ofsted Inspectors to be trained, he left the Advisory Service as Lead Senior Adviser for Children's Wellbeing for Essex to take up his current position as Subject Adviser with the national PSHE Association. Nick is committed to a model of PSHE that places children's individual and unique understanding of their world and their own enquiry at the centre of learning. He is co-author of a number of government documents, academic texts and teaching resources committed to improving the quality of PSHE education. He has spent over 25 years championing the importance of placing high quality PSHE at the centre of the school curriculum.

Adrian King has been a teacher in both primary and secondary schools and was Health Education Co-ordinator for Berkshire Local Authority from 1985 to 1998. Since then he has been an independent consultant, trainer and author. In 2004 Adrian was the consultant engaged to write *Drugs: Guidance for Schools* for the Department for Children, School and Families. He has been Membership Secretary of the National Health Education Group since 1986 and has also been an elected official for both the Drug Education Forum and the Drug Education Practitioners' Forum. Adrian is committed to improving the quality of PSHE education for young people, working to ensure it addresses their needs, and respects both their rights and their responsibilities.

Dr Jenny McWhirter is the Research Associate for the PSHE Association and has been interested in the health and wellbeing of children and young people since working as a part-time youth worker in the 1980s. She has been researching effective approaches to PSHE education for more than 25 years. At Southampton University she managed an MSc in Health Education with Health Promotion and developed a special study in PSHE and Citizenship for the secondary PGCE programme. Her research includes many aspects of PSHE education, including personal finance, asthma and drug education. After leaving academia in 2003, Jenny worked for DrugScope and later RoSPA, as an education advisor. Jenny has been Chair of the Drug Education Forum and the Drug Education Practitioners' Forum. She was a member of the NICE Programme Development Group 'Strategies to prevent unintentional injuries among the under-15s'. Jenny's current research includes effective responses to drug and alcohol hidden harm.

ACKNOWLEDGEMENTS

Our thanks to: Celia Allaby, pfeg; Mike Ashton, Editor of Drug and Alcohol Findings; Andrew Brown, Mentor UK; Eleanor Formby, Sheffield Hallam University; Andrew McWhirter, Claudia Pridmore and Lucy Hills (critical friends); staff and children of Banyan and Palm classes, Brindishe Green Primary School, Lewisham; Nicola Overland, Justine Mathews, Jacqui Tyler, and members of the Student Council of Moulsham Junior School, Essex; Nicola Speechly-Watson (formerly Curriculum Development Adviser with Essex Local Authority); Katherine Weare, Emeritus Professor, School of Education, Southampton University.

Also, our thanks to the following organisations: Elsevier; the PSHE Association; and the Royal Society for the Prevention of Accidents.

Finally, we would like to thank the editorial staff at Sage Publications for their help and support.

CHAPTER 1

INTRODUCTION

Aim

To introduce PSHE education.

Learning objectives

Through reading and reflecting on the content of this chapter you will begin to:

- understand PSHE education and how it relates to the rest of the curriculum
- recognise the contribution PSHE education makes to children's personal development
- have an opportunity to reflect on your personal experience of PSHE education to date and consider how you can develop as an effective practitioner.

Introduction

This book has been written for students in primary teacher education and newly qualified teachers (NQTs).

It aims to give you a general grounding in the theory underpinning Personal, Social, Health and Economic (PSHE) education, some practical approaches, and the evidence that supports these approaches. You will find some chapters that deal specifically with effective approaches to teaching, learning and assessment in PSHE education, plus some chapters that deal with particular topics for which you may feel underprepared – and what are sometimes called 'sensitive issues', such as sex and relationships education and drug education – and also safety education and personal finance education. Each chapter will encourage you to consider the evidence for effective practice, and to reflect on what you observe and how you are putting this into practice in *your* classroom.

As you embark on your professional career you may have a good idea about what you will be teaching: English (and possibly Welsh), maths, science, geography, history, religious education, perhaps French or another modern foreign language and physical education. You know you will be a class teacher, with responsibility for the safety and well-being of the children in your class while you are teaching, and with some responsibility, with more senior colleagues, for their pastoral care.

It's possible you already have some understanding of how children develop, and some of the different ways they learn. You will develop teaching skills which will help you to maximise the learning for the children, according to their different needs. Importantly you will learn how to assess their learning needs and plan for the next steps. This book will help you understand how Personal, Social, Health and Economic education fits into all this. It will help you to see how PSHE education makes a link between all the different parts of your responsibilities as a primary school teacher and the personal and social development of the children in your care.

Getting started

We believe PSHE education is an exciting and challenging part of a primary school teacher's role. It may be that your training has not included a great deal about PSHE education so far, or you might be thinking like some of these students we asked about PSHE education:

> Is that the same as SMSC?

> I remember that was the only lesson when we got to say what we thought about things that were happening to us.

> PSHE – that was a waste of a lesson when I was at school.

> I didn't get much from my training in PSHE – luckily my mentor was really into it. In my first school I helped plan a health week.

We also asked some experienced primary school teachers what they thought about PSHE education:

> At first I was unsure about teaching some of PSHE education like sex and relationships and 'economic' education ... I didn't even know what that was!

> I am not a fan of PSHE ... I am not a counsellor – my job is to teach!

> We have a PSHE theme each term, focusing on a different aspect all through the school.

> I use PSHE education to get my class ready to learn.

Ask some of your fellow students and colleagues what their experience of PSHE education has been – and keep an open mind while you read on.

So what is PSHE education?

Before answering this question it's important to recognise that this subject has different acronyms in different schools. You will meet PSHE teachers, Personal and Social Development (PSD) teachers, teachers of Personal, Social, Cultural, Moral, Spiritual and Citizenship (PSCMSC), Lifeskills teachers and even Personal, Economic, Social and Health Education (PESHE) teachers. We have chosen to use the term 'PSHE education' to refer to the subject (and occasionally PSHE if the terminology becomes especially cumbersome). This recognises recent developments principally in England's curriculum for ages 11–16 years which identify common concepts underpinning both personal wellbeing and economic and financial wellbeing. The PSHE Association has developed a programme of study which includes economic education for children in full-time education, and for this reason we have followed their lead.

> PSHE education is a planned programme of learning though which children and young people acquire the knowledge, understanding and skills they need to manage their lives now and in the future. As part of a whole school approach, PSHE education develops the qualities and attributes pupils need to thrive as individuals, family members and members of society. (PSHE Association, 2013)

Taking a closer look at these statements we can see that PSHE education is – and should be – *personal*. For a student or recently qualified teacher this can seem one of the most daunting aspects of the subject. You may wonder if this means you are expected to take on the personal issues for every child in the class. How do you keep your own personal views about such issues as drugs or sex and relationships apart from your teaching? What do parents expect of a curriculum which is intended to develop personal understanding, attitudes and skills?

What *personal* means in the context of PSHE education is 'relevance to the *person*'. Starting from where children are (see Chapter 4) you can make the teaching of the most sensitive issues appropriate and relevant to the children you are teaching this year – who will, of course, be different from the children you will teach next year and every year thereafter! *Personal* also emphasises the importance of identity to children and their health and wellbeing. Learning to know oneself is an important psychological task, beginning in childhood and continuing beyond adolescence, into adult life.

PSHE education plays an important part in developing children's *intra-personal* skills and attributes so that they are resilient in the face of adversity, can manage change, and have a realistic sense of their own worth and capability.

And finally, *personal* means drawing on the children's existing knowledge and experience, so that they can relate what they are learning in the classroom to their real lives, real families and real communities. One of the most important parts of any lesson in PSHE are those moments where children have the opportunity to reflect on what they have learned to do or say, perhaps as part of a group activity, and think about what it means to them *personally*, as individuals.

PSHE education is also *social*. This means it is fundamentally about relationships, whether with friends and staff at school, or with family members. Relationships between people underpin every aspect of our lives, for good and bad. Some relationships can always be relied upon to be strong and nurturing, some may be fun but brief, and others, sadly, may have the potential to damage children's health and wellbeing. The relationships children develop with their peers during primary school may last a lifetime; they may get children into trouble by encouraging dangerous risk taking or be a real source of support and encouragement in difficult circumstances. The attitudes, understanding and *interpersonal* skills they can develop through effective PSHE education will help them to enjoy the best and deal with the worst of life's challenges.

The skills children develop in PSHE education can also prepare them for the relationships they will make in the adult world, including the workplace. Where else in the curriculum can they learn to negotiate, co-operate and take responsibility for their own decisions? These so-called 'soft skills' are as much sought after by employers as academic or technical qualifications.

Health provides some of the most complex and interesting content for PSHE education. What can be more relevant to a primary school child than how their body works, why they are growing so fast, what is happening on the inside that no one can see? Of course, there are strong cross-curricular links here with the biological aspects of the science curriculum. But in PSHE education health is so much more than biology. It's about what goes on your body and in your body; about what you can do today that you couldn't do before, and the responsibility this brings; it's about how you feel about your body growing and changing and about whom you can talk to about those feelings.

This is a good moment to ask 'What is health?' For some, health is simply the absence of disease, for others it is about achieving your full potential, whatever your physical, mental and emotional capabilities and limitations might be. There are clearly many factors which contribute to a person being healthy: biological, environmental, mental and emotional, as well as social and financial. These factors can contribute to real health inequalities: where those who grow up in poverty and in workless families – or whose diet is inadequate, or who have jobs where they have little or no control over their activities, or where class, gender or race prevent access to the best of health care – live shorter, less healthy lives than others.

In Chapter 4 you will find some suggestions for finding out what the children in your school think about being healthy – and about whose responsibility it is to keep them healthy.

Economic education is a relative newcomer to PSHE practitioners and has clear links with the maths curriculum among others. However, those primary teachers who have included personal finance and economic education in their PSHE curriculum have soon recognised children's enthusiasm for learning which goes beyond arithmetical knowledge and understanding. They have discovered children's thirst for learning about money and what money means in their lives.

You may ask why economic education is included in PSHE education and not just in maths. But the link with feelings is just as great as it is with sex and relationships education. How do you feel just before you open your credit card bill? Or when you get an unexpected gift of money? The decisions we make about our personal finances are linked to our feelings – and our identities as risk takers – as well as our capability in arithmetic.

And finally ... *education*. The word 'educate' comes from the Latin homonym 'I lead forth' or 'I raise up'. From this you can see that while education is the means by which knowledge, skills, culture and values are passed from one generation to another, it is not a passive process. It is often said that children do not come to school *tabula rasa* or as empty vessels to be filled with knowledge. Just as children are not empty vessels, they are not sponges – they do not simply absorb information, but make sense of it in relation to what they already know and understand (for more on this constructivist view of education see Chapter 2). By the time they arrive at school they have four (or more) years of experience on which to base their understanding of the world. That experience may lead them to draw some surprising (sometimes amusing!) conclusions about school and other new things they encounter. From a teacher's point of view this may seen like 'non-sense', but it is never, ever, 'nonsense'!

Figure 1.1 'I don't understand – all I did was ask him to come with me to the Head's room'

So, everything you learn about children's cognitive and emotional development, everything you discover about how children learn and how to teach and assess their learning, applies to PSHE education. However, there are some approaches to teaching and learning which are particularly important in PSHE education, which you may not use as frequently in other aspects of the curriculum. These will be explored in more depth in Chapters 2 and 6.

The other thing which is important to recognise about education is that it is happening all the time: not just in lessons, but in assembly, in the playground – and on the way to and from school. Neither do schools have the privileged status with regard to education in its broadest sense. Children are being educated informally in the family, through the media, especially social media, and in the wider community. As the definition of PSHE education above tells us, PSHE education may simply be the only *planned* part of school life where children can, with your help, make sense of the many influences and experiences they are living through.

Why is PSHE education important?

As we have begun to explore, PSHE education helps children and young people to identify, understand, celebrate and manage the many personal, social and economic challenges they will face, while they are at school and in the future. Through PSHE education primary school-age children can begin to acquire the knowledge and understanding and to put into practice many of the skills they need as they (and their communities) grow and change, so that they can be safe, healthy and economically secure.

What can children be expected to achieve through PSHE education?

The aims of PSHE education are to help children and young people to develop the knowledge, understanding, attitudes and skills to keep themselves healthy and safe, and to contribute to the health, safety and wellbeing of others.

Effective PSHE education facilitates learning, so that children and young people can draw on their talents and skills, and on the resources provided by their families and communities, to achieve their full potential.

Some will claim that PSHE education develops self-esteem, self-worth, self-efficacy and resilience, and there is good enough evidence to suggest that PSHE education can contribute to all of these attributes. It is important to remember, however, that PSHE education is not the only aspect of school which impacts on these important personal development outcomes. While PSHE education contributes to children's personal development it is not a form of inoculation against all the excitements or difficulties of life.

What can PSHE education *not* be expected to achieve?

Despite what some people expect, it's important to point out that the aim of PSHE education is not to determine how children should behave or what lifestyle, career or financial choices they should make in the future. PSHE education is about the provision of knowledge and the development of skills and attitudes that enable children and young people to make effective choices and take opportunities which will help them to live happy, healthy, successful lives, now and in the future. PSHE education helps children to develop their decision making skills; it does not set out to predetermine what those decisions should be.

Making effective choices includes enabling children and young people to recognise and assess the benefits and risks of their actions, and to act on their best intentions, whatever the pressures to do otherwise. This means that PSHE education is about influencing young people's attitudes and developing their skills to manage different influences and pressures, as part of their personal development.

What does PSHE education have in common with other school subjects?

As you will see, PSHE education has a body of knowledge, and is based on well-known and -understood theories and concepts for which there is good evidence. It includes a clear set of skills and competences. Like other subjects in the curriculum, PSHE education can be differentiated according to a child's needs and abilities. It can be assessed in a range of ways, depending on what is being taught. (See Chapter 13).

How does PSHE education relate to other school subjects?

PSHE education provides the opportunity for pupils to reflect on the personal and social elements of some topics which are learned in other areas of the curriculum. For example the effects of exercise on the body may be part of physical education, but how we feel about our bodies may have a bigger influence on whether we decide to take part in sport or not.

Teaching science provides opportunities to discuss the effects of tobacco on the lungs and heart but it is in PSHE education where children can reflect on what this information means in their lives, what influences people to start smoking, and how smoking affects them, their friends and families and their communities. Through PSHE education, children can also be encouraged to think about the personal, financial aspects of smoking and the alternative uses for the money spent on tobacco.

PSHE education also enables children and young people to use skills they have developed elsewhere in the curriculum, which are transferable to other aspects of their learning. For example planning a healthy meal on a budget will draw on their arithmetical skills as much as their knowledge of healthy eating.

Importantly, PSHE education can provide an opportunity for pupils to reflect on issues which do not arise as part of the formal curriculum, for example understanding themselves, their interests and needs, managing challenging relationships in and out of school, understanding their personal response to risk, and recognising the contribution they make to the wider community.

How is PSHE education different from the other school subjects?

PSHE education deals with real life issues which affect children, young people, their families and their teachers. If taught well it engages with the social and economic realities of children's lives, and draws on the values, experience, attitudes and emotions they bring to their education as well as their knowledge and understanding. Because of this, it is often said that PSHE education starts where children are. (This does not mean, however, that the teacher does not need to plan where they may go from this starting point!) Each chapter of this book begins with an example of how you can start where children are, and Chapter 4 goes into more depth about this important aspect of effective practice in PSHE education.

Some of the traditional topics within PSHE education, such as drugs, sex and relationships and safety education may have a moral, social or political context, which is more apparent than in other subjects such as maths or French. However, teachers of English, religious studies, geography and history also have to deal with important and complex moral and political issues. What is different about PSHE education is that the moral and political is also *personal*; personal for teachers, parents and carers and also for the children and young people. This means that what is learnt in PSHE education can have an immediate application in the lives of children and young people. It also means that some aspects of PSHE education can be challenging and also exciting for teachers.

Importantly, PSHE also draws on a body of knowledge about health and economic behaviour, not common elements of a teacher's training or professional development.

Whole school approach

This may seem obvious, but PSHE education is most effective when it is part of a whole school approach. We will examine the rationale and evidence for this in Chapter 3. We have already seen, however, how what is learnt in the curriculum for PSHE education relates to the pastoral care of the children and to the expectation that they will be learning in a safe and nurturing environment.

The best example of a whole school approach is the Healthy Schools movement. In England, Healthy Schools enjoyed cross-government support for many years and continues to be supported by the Department for Education through its Healthy Schools toolkit (Department of Education, 2013). Some local authorities also provide support for schools to become Healthy Schools in the form of co-ordinators or training.

You may find yourself on teaching practice or teaching in a school which has Healthy School status in one form or another. If so it will be part of a huge movement across Europe and other parts of the world to help schools focus some of their precious time and effort on creating a physical and policy environment in which healthy choices are the easy choices, for pupils and staff. This means that school staff work together with pupils, parents and community partners to identify priorities for action which will create a healthy, safe place to work and learn. Ideally, these priorities will complement those in the local community so that those healthy choices are also easier to implement outside of school.

The alternative to a whole school approach, where what is taught about health, safety and wellbeing is in conflict with school and community policy, makes it more difficult for children and their families to act on their intentions to select and maintain healthy lifestyle choices.

Is PSHE education *too* personal?

Some teachers who are new to PSHE education fear that they may get in 'too deep' with this subject. You might be concerned about questions children may ask which are about your personal behaviour, or find yourself using examples from your own life. You might wonder if you have to be the perfect role model, who does not drink, smoke or overeat. The answer is that this is all about finding the balance between the personal and professional that works for you. Some teachers are comfortable with questions about their family and things they like to do out of school. It helps the children to see you as a real person and not someone who exists only to teach them, but who has a real life beyond the school gates. On the other hand, while you may be happy to disclose you have a Friday afternoon doughnut habit, it would not be appropriate to disclose drug taking or other risky behaviour you may have been involved in as a student.

Setting the boundaries between what is acceptable to ask or say in the classroom and what is not acceptable is an important part of PSHE education in itself and something the children and you need to agree at an early stage, perhaps in the form of a learning agreement or contract. Ultimately, you and the children should always have the right to 'pass' or not answer a question – something else which makes PSHE education unique! We will go into this in more depth in Chapter 3 and again in Chapter 6.

The other concern expressed by teachers is whether the content of PSHE education might provoke strong emotions, which might be difficult (or inappropriate) to manage in the classroom or might prompt a child to disclose they are being harmed by a member of their family or the community. This is a matter for you and the staff of your school to consider carefully. Good planning for PSHE education, along with good pastoral knowledge of the children in your class, should mean you are prepared to minimise the emotional impact of these rare events, while maintaining the children's entitlement to know and understand what is happening to them and to be able to ask for your help when it is needed. The alternative would be a curriculum designed to *prevent* children from seeking adult help, which would be morally and educationally inadequate.

 Consider

Now you have read this chapter, ask yourself: What kind of school did you go to? Was PSHE education part of your curriculum? How did your school encourage you to make healthy choices? Were you aware of efforts to consult pupils or parents about being and staying healthy? Did you notice conflict between what you were taught about being healthy (for example healthy eating) and the overall approach to this issue in school (the range of food and drinks available in the school)?

> What were the relationships like in the schools you attended? Were you treated with respect, as capable of fulfilling your potential as an individual? Were you encouraged to treat others with respect?
>
> Now ask yourself about schools where you have done observations or teaching practice. Was PSHE education valued by senior staff as part of the overall contribution a school can make to the personal development of the child? Was it well structured and resourced, or were there times when you were unsure how PSHE education fitted into the curriculum and policies of the school? There is so much to do and see when you enter school as a professional that you can be forgiven if these questions have never occurred to you until now! Make time to consider these questions in the school where you are working, and the possible implications of your reflections for the pupils attending the school.

Chapter summary

Primary school is a very special time in a child's life. They enter school, some just four years old, barely out of babyhood – and leave on the cusp of adolescence. During their time at primary school they may encounter many of life's challenges for the first time, including bereavement, family breakdown, financial worries or serious illness. They will also make their first friendships, experience their first tastes of achievement in learning new and fundamental knowledge and skills, enjoy their first competitive sport and maybe even spend their first nights away from home on school visits. Good PSHE education will help you and the children in the class to manage all these many and varied challenges.

Further reading

The current programmes of study for PSHE education can be downloaded from the Department of Education website: www.education.gov.uk/schools/teachingandlearning/curriculum (accessed 8 October 2013).

(Continued)

(Continued)

Ofsted (2013) 'Personal, Social, Health and Economic (PSHE) Education Survey Visits' in 'Generic grade descriptors and supplementary subject-specific guidance for inspectors on making judgements during visits to schools'. Available at: www.ofsted.gov.uk/resources/generic-grade-descriptors-and-supplementary-subject-specific-guidance-for-inspectors-making-judgemen [sic].
A clear description of what Ofsted is looking for in PSHE education when inspecting schools.

Ofsted (2013) 'Not yet good enough: Personal, social, health and economic education in schools'. Available at: www.ofsted.gov.uk/resources/not-yet-good-enough-personal-social-health-and-economic-education-schools (accessed 8 October 2013).
Part A focuses on the key inspection and survey findings. Part B describes the characteristics of PSHE education that are outstanding and those aspects that require improvement or are inadequate. Part B can be used to evaluate the quality of PSHE education in a school.

References

Department of Education (2013) www.education.gov.uk/schools/pupilsupport/pastoralcare/a0075278/healthy-schools (accessed 24 January 2014).

PSHE Association (2013) www.pshe-association.org.uk/content.aspx?CategoryID=335 (accessed 28 January 2014).

PART 1

2 Understanding effective practice in PSHE education	17
3 Understanding school ethos – what is taught and what is caught?	46
4 Understanding how to start where children are	64
5 Understanding emotional development and emotional intelligence	82
6 Understanding the pedagogy of PSHE education	95
7 Understanding how to select PSHE education teaching material and resources	127

In this part we offer advice to students and newly qualified teachers about what PSHE education is, its rationale and how to teach it. There are important principles that apply to all PSHE education, no matter what the content. We set these out, together with advice on how the school ethos needs to work hand-in-hand with PSHE education. We explore suitable teaching methods and offer guidance for selecting appropriate and high quality teaching materials that will help you meet the needs of the children you teach.

CHAPTER 2

UNDERSTANDING EFFECTIVE PRACTICE IN PSHE EDUCATION

Aim

To introduce ten principles for effective practice in PSHE education.

This chapter is structured around a series of questions, all of which are intended to help you understand effective approaches to teaching and learning in PSHE education.

Learning objectives

By reading and reflecting on the content of this chapter you will:

- know the rationale underpinning effective approaches to PSHE education
- understand why some approaches are more effective than others
- be able to take account of the ten principles for effective PSHE education in your planning
- be able to create opportunities for your pupils to take decisions which will enable them to act on their intentions.

Getting started

This chapter reviews theories and some of the evidence underpinning the ten guiding principles of effective practice in PSHE education.

> **Consider**
>
> Before reading this chapter ask yourself where your own understanding of effective teaching and learning comes from. What key principles guide your practice in the primary school classroom? The similarities and differences between effective primary practice and effective PSHE education may surprise and, we hope, reassure you.

What do we need to know about children and young people to teach PSHE education effectively?

There are many theories of teaching and learning, all of which rely on an understanding of how children and young people develop, cognitively, morally and socially (see Berk, 2007; Gray and MacBlain, 2012; Gross, 2010; Muijs and Reynolds, 2011, for more detailed discussion of child development). Theories of child and adolescent development also have some basis in the development of the human brain and the extent to which that development is predetermined (nature) or shaped by experience (nurture) (Battro et al., 2008). Drawing on these sources, in this section we consider how our knowledge and understanding of child development has helped to shape PSHE education practice in the last 20 years.

What is learning?

According to the PSHE Association's definition, learning is the process through which 'children and young people acquire the knowledge, understanding and skills they need to manage their lives, now and in the future' (PSHE Association, 2013).

Some authors define learning more narrowly in terms of knowledge and skills (Gray and MacBlain, 2012: 2) while others define learning in terms of behaviour change (see Gross, 1996: 155). Whether learning should be defined in terms of behaviour change is an important question

EFFECTIVE PRACTICE IN PSHE EDUCATION   19

which goes to the heart of teaching and learning in PSHE education. We have already argued in Chapter 1 that PSHE education does not set out to predetermine the decisions children may make, or the behaviours they may adopt. Your view on this will almost certainly influence how you approach teaching and learning in your PSHE education lessons.

 Consider

It is readily acknowledged that smoking tobacco is bad for our health. The rates of smoking among adults have been falling steadily over the last 20 years, but once other factors are accounted for, girls are more likely to report being smokers than boys (Gill et al., 2012). More women are developing lung cancer than ever before (Cancer Research UK, 2012). Our education about smoking provides children with an understanding of the physical and psychological effects of smoking, the financial cost, knowledge about who smokes and why, skills to identify and resist influence and pressure to become a smoker, supported by sources of advice for smokers and their families. Should it also include the instruction to children that they should never smoke tobacco? Should we imply that those who have had this information and still become smokers will have only themselves to blame if they later develop smoking related illnesses? What effect would we expect if we did?

How do children learn? A philosophical approach

Philosophers have wrestled with this question throughout human history. Aristotle believed learning occurred through the repetition of simple exercises, while Socrates held the view that when a child was conceived he or she contained all the knowledge and skills needed for adult life, but these were 'lost' during birth. Importantly, Socrates also believed that this knowledge could be reacquired through the processes of questioning and enquiry. In the seventeenth century John Locke introduced the idea that the newborn mind is a blank slate (or *tabula rasa*) on which experience and repetition can be written. In his view learning should be enjoyable, but inevitably some learning is also painful – as we find out when we step on a sharp object!

Locke was a major influence on the thinking of another philosopher of the eighteenth century: Jean-Jacques Rousseau. Rousseau believed that all children are born 'good' and argued for developmentally appropriate education which was experiential. He reasoned that children learned best when they could experience the physical, social and moral consequences of their behaviour and that the tutor or teacher should construct an environment where that learning could occur safely.

Like Rousseau, the US philosopher John Dewey was also a liberal reformer. Writing at the end of the nineteenth and beginning of the twentieth century, Dewey was concerned with social reform through democracy and the active participation of citizens in shaping their own destiny. He was influenced by other liberal educators including Froebel and Montessori and developed pedagogy with the child at the centre who takes an active role in shaping and participating in the curriculum. Dewey's view of education reads much like the definition of PSHE education adopted by the PSHE Association:

> to prepare him for the future life means to give him command of himself; it means so to train him that he will have the full and ready use of all his capacities. (Dewey, 1897: 6)

Another social reformer working around the same time and who had practical experience of teaching (albeit mainly adults) was John Ruskin. He favoured personalised learning which was appropriate for the individual needs of the learner.

> One man is made of agate, another of oak; one of slate, another of clay. The education of the first is polishing; of the second, seasoning; of the third, rending; of the fourth, moulding. It is of no use to season the agate; it is vain to try to polish the slate; but both are fitted, by the qualities they possess, for services in which they may be honoured. (Ruskin, 1853)

The thinking of these liberal philosophers and reformers continues to influence the way we approach teaching and learning in the twenty-first century, supported increasingly by more empirical studies of child development, experimental studies in teaching and learning and, of course, our growing understanding of the developing brain.

Theories of learning

Early theories of learning were based on studies of the behaviour of laboratory animals. Pavlov famously noticed that dogs began to salivate when the technicians who fed them entered the room. He experimented with other, more neutral stimuli, such as the sound of a bell, which became associated with the reward of food. The theory of classical, or Pavlovian, conditioning was modified and extended by Skinner to operant conditioning which more closely simulated the real world. In operant conditioning a spontaneous but useful response could be both encouraged (with a positive reinforcement) and discouraged (with a negative reinforcement or punishment). The crucial difference is that in classical conditioning it is what happens before the observed behaviour which determines whether the behaviour is repeated, whereas in operant conditioning, it is what happens after the behaviour which is relevant.

Other psychologists showed that both classical conditioning and operant conditioning can be effective in modifying some behaviours in children, and the behaviourists' approach, as it became known, is still in use in education today. For example, operant conditioning is the basis of the use of reward and punishment systems in schools. The behaviourists' view of learning also concurred with Aristotelian views of education that learning was based on repetition and association and encouraged rote learning, for example of times tables and poetry.

 Consider

How would a behaviourist approach teaching and learning in PSHE education? Is there a place for rote learning in the twenty-first-century curriculum? What are the advantages and disadvantages of this approach?

What do we need to know about cognition to teach PSHE education effectively?

The early behavioural psychologists paved the way for 'cognitive' psychologists who tried to understand the mental processes behind learning. When a dog learned to associate a sound stimulus with food and respond with a specific behaviour, or a cat learned how to get out of a box, what was the link between 'knowing' and 'doing'? In the 1930s, Tolman, a student of Skinner, showed that experience could lead to learning which, although not immediately expressed as observable behaviour, when rewarded, would lead to a rapid behavioural response. Rats placed in a maze soon learned how to find the food box if it contained food. Their 'cognitive' map of the maze worked just as well if the rats had to walk or swim through the maze, so the behaviour was not specific to their internal map of the maze. Rats placed in the same maze with no reward did not learn to go directly to the food box but continued to wander around apparently aimlessly. However, if the same rats were then rewarded with food they learned where to find it more quickly than the first group, suggesting their apparently aimless wandering had provided them with a mental map of the maze they could then draw upon when needed.

These forms of learning, known as S-R or stimulus–response learning can be compared with another form of learning known as insight learning. These ideas are based on studies of chimpanzees by Kohler, a cognitive scientist. Kohler observed that chimpanzees used sticks placed outside their cages to stretch to bananas which were out of reach. The connection between the stick and the banana did not occur as a result of a random series of events, but after period of failure, followed by 'reflection'. However, some would argue that insight learning is an extension of S-R learning because both sticks and bananas were already part of the chimpanzee's experience. Other experiments with chimpanzees by Harlow and others showed how by repetition of a familiar task using different stimuli, a chimpanzee could learn how to learn. In other words the chimp had developed a set of rules to solve a new but familiar puzzle – a bit like doing a new Sudoku or crossword.

 Consider

Children are taught how to cross the road safely in streets close to their school. The rules of 'stop at the kerb, look all around, listen and walk straight across the road' are learned and applied to all similar roads, whether near the school, near their home or when out and about with friends and family, so that they can soon do so in all weathers and in all lighting conditions. The more experience they gain the more they can adapt the rules they have learned to their situation, for example the necessity in some circumstances to cross between parked cars – which they are often expressly taught not to do, but which can be unavoidable in some urban environments.

Increasingly cognitive scientists have used sophisticated experiments with human subjects to discover how children develop mental or cognitive maps of mathematical concepts and reading.

What do we need to know about child development to teach PSHE effectively?

Unlike the behaviourists, and early cognitive psychologists, the developmental psychologists Piaget, Vygotsky and Bruner based their theories directly on their studies of children. Piaget carried out intensive observations of his own children, proposing his famous 'stage theory' of a child's cognitive development, where thinking develops from concrete to abstract forms in fixed, linear and irreversible stages. Other 'stage theories' flourished including Kohlberg's theory of moral reasoning. Piaget also proposed that children's understanding is actively constructed by assimilating new information into existing 'schema', accommodating or modifying the schema until the new information fits. Although criticised for being based on small samples of children from a particular culture, and on a deficit model of a child – that is, what a child cannot do, rather than what they can – Piaget's theories continue to influence teaching and learning, especially in the early years where play and discovery learning go hand in hand.

Importantly for PSHE education, Piaget and other constructivists suggest that children's reality is different, although not inferior, to an adult's reality and that to understand a child's point of view you must first understand their reality. Another key figure among the constructivists is Jerome Bruner, an American psychologist who also believed that children build new understanding on what they have already mastered, through enquiry and intuition. Rather than a stage-based approach he suggested that children, and adults, learn in broadly similar ways using three forms of representation: 'action' based, 'image' based and 'language' based. In Bruner's view a learner of any age can understand most concepts if the material is organised appropriately, with more and more specific activity, images and language to 'scaffold' the learning as they progress. Bruner's ideas have led to the notion of a spiral curriculum where teaching is planned so that the learner can build on their prior knowledge and understanding more easily.

 Consider

The spiral curriculum has been very influential in all areas of the curriculum. Where did you first hear this term? How have you used the idea in your planning, for example in mathematics or science education? How could you use this in PSHE education?

It can also be seen that a constructivist approach has much in common with the ideas of Rousseau, Froebel and Montessori who believed learning should follow a child's natural development. To return to the question at the beginning of this chapter – according to a constructivist approach,

learning is the search for meaning. (Muijs and Reynolds, 2011: 88)

Taken together these ideas suggest that PSHE education should be based on active and discovery learning, with the teacher in the role of 'facilitator', and not just in the early years.

Bruner also shared views similar to other twentieth-century developmental psychologists such as the Russian, Vygotsky, in stressing the importance of culture and social interaction in learning. Like Piaget and the other constructivists, Vygotsky adopted a child-centred approach to learning and believed that children actively construct their reality based on existing understanding. Vygotsky did not fully support the idea of a staged approach to development, arguing that tasks which are too challenging could lead learners to regress to 'earlier' forms of learning.

In PSHE education Vygotsky's idea of the 'zone of proximal development' has become influential. Contrary to Piaget's view, that learning happens at fixed stages in a child's development and cannot, therefore, be accelerated, Vygotsky proposed that it is possible to help a child to learn more quickly if you can assess their starting point, which includes their capacity to learn. A teacher can then plan to provide appropriate activity and support so that the child can progress to the next level of understanding. However, a Vygotskyan teacher would support the learning by encouraging collaboration with more knowledgeable peers rather than give instruction.

For social constructivists like Vygotsky the social context in which learning takes place is more important than the learning material, and this idea is also important for PSHE education. Teachers, family members, peers, the wider community and the media all contribute to the learner's development though formal and informal learning.

 Consider

How might a social constructivist's approach to drug education differ from that of a behaviourist? What kind of strategies for teaching and learning would they adopt?

Other social psychologists including Bandura and, later, Bronfenbrenner have also stressed the importance of environmental factors in children's learning. Bandura showed through observation and experiment that children imitate behaviour they observe in others, particularly if they identify with the people whose behaviour they are modelling. Bandura's theories are commonly used to explain socially unacceptable behaviour such as aggression or attention seeking in young children. Bandura also proposed that as a result of early social experiences children develop strong beliefs about their abilities to do well and achieve success in particular situations. Known as self-efficacy, this factor can have a strong influence on children's motivation to tackle challenging tasks, since they 'know' in advance whether or not they will succeed, either of which can become a self-fulfilling prophecy. For PSHE education, this means that it is of great importance to model and reward efforts to practise the behaviours we are encouraging through our approach to teaching and learning.

Bronfenbrenner's ideas have been very influential in the development of approaches to combating disadvantage among very young children. His ecological theories of child development were fundamental to the introduction of the Headstart programme of early years education in the USA, which in turn influenced the Sure Start programme in the UK.

While Bandura's work is mainly focused on the individual child, Bronfenbrenner emphasises the ever changing context in which development takes place: family, school and the wider society in which the child lives, as well as the events and transitions taking place as they mature. For PSHE education, Bandura, Bronfenbrenner and other social psychologists offer a way to understand how to support the development of resilience in children and young people, through the development of individual skills and attributes and by creating environments in which they can learn to manage change successfully.

 Consider

Is PSHE education concerned with developing the capacity of children and young people to manage their lives effectively, or a vehicle for social reform?

What does all this mean for PSHE education?

Many of the approaches to teaching and learning in PSHE education are based on a blend of behaviourist, constructivist and social constructivist approaches, which:

- start where children are, with their knowledge, understanding and experiences
- scaffold the learning with developmentally appropriate but increasingly complex activity, imagery and language as part of a spiral curriculum
- encourage reflection to promote the assimilation of learning
- use collaborative approaches (small group work)
- employ positive language, reinforcement, modelling and rewarding the behaviours you wish to encourage
- recognise the influence of family and wider society.

In the rest of this chapter we will continue to develop these ideas, drawing on evidence and theory from other disciplines which have also helped to inform our understanding of effective practice. At the end of this chapter these ideas are summarised in the form of ten principles for effective practice in PSHE education.

What do we need to know about learning styles to teach PSHE education effectively?

The idea that different people learn best in different ways began to assert itself in the 1970s and 1980s with the work of David Kolb. Kolb was concerned mainly with organisational psychology and therefore with how adults learn. He saw experiential learning as a holistic, integrative approach which incorporated the understanding of many of his predecessors, who tended to argue for one or other model of learning (Kolb, 1984). Kolb argued that learning takes place through concrete experience, reflective observation (watching others), abstract conceptualisation (creating theories that explain observations) and active experimentation (problem solving and decision making). In Kolb's view these were stages through which all learners move with time. Some psychologists suggest that learners gradually rely on, and so develop a preference for, particular learning styles (see Muijs and Reynolds, 2011) and others suggest that particular professions attract those with certain learning styles, implying that knowing someone's learning style can determine their suitability for those professions.

Other typologies of learning styles are based on the different senses employed for learning, for example Visual, Auditory, Kinaesthetic learning or VAK (Dunn and Dunn, 1978).

Proponents of these theories have developed approaches to teaching which reflect the various typologies of learning. For example a teacher might choose a range of teaching strategies to ensure that children in the class can all access the learning equally, whatever their learning style.

There is something appealing and intuitive about these theories, which make sense at one level. Some children, and adults, do seem to learn by rote better if they can also be physically active at the same time; some children recall information for exams better if they can listen to instrumental music they heard while learning (Angel et al., 2010).

Critics of these approaches argue that people use different approaches to learning for different subject areas. For example auditory learning might be very important for the acquisition of a foreign language while tactile or kinaesthetic learning might be more important for acquiring practical skills such as crossing the road or making bread. More importantly, there appears to be no empirical evidence that preferred learning styles can be measured in any reliable way (Pashler et al., 2008).

Perhaps an understanding that there can be different learning styles should remind teachers to offer a variety of approaches in the classroom, which in turn will prevent children from becoming bored by the teacher's preferred teaching style!

What do we need to know about intelligence to teach PSHE education effectively?

It is all too apparent that health and wellbeing are not determined by 'intelligence'. Clever people, those who achieve national and international recognition for their achievements in science, mathematics, engineering or the arts, have problems with money, substance misuse and relationships and become ill just like the rest of us. Traditionally intelligence has been measured by the Intelligence Quotient (IQ) (see Gross, 2010, for an overview). IQ tests measure a range of intellectual capacities from spatial and numerical reasoning to memory and verbal reasoning. Some people perform better in some of these 'primary mental abilities' than others, but many psychologists argue that there is an underlying factor which correlates positively with the individual tests, known as 'g'. Attempts to define and measure IQ are of great social and political importance. If a test can predict which 11-year-olds will become the doctors, engineers, plumbers and shop assistants of the future, then their education could be tailored to suit their different abilities. (More examples of self-fulfilling prophecies, perhaps?) Critics of such tests argue that their predictive value, especially when carried out at the age of 11 years, is not high enough to differentiate children on the basis of this alone. IQ tests have also been criticised for being biased in terms of race, gender, social class and culture (Gould, 1996).

This controversy has contributed to an ongoing search for measures which describe intelligence in different ways, which capture more about the forms of intelligence used in the world outside school, such as the 'ability to deal with relative novelty'. One of the most well-known theories of intelligence was developed by Howard Gardner in the 1980s (Gardner, 1983). In his view intelligence is a collection of independent but interacting intelligences. According to Gardner each intelligence can be measured using standardised psychometric tests; resides in a specific region of the brain, which is identifiable by studying patients with brain damage; and can be observed in extreme forms by 'idiots savants', who despite severe disability can achieve remarkable feats.

Gardner's intelligences include: linguistic, logical mathematical, spatial, musical, bodily kinaesthetic and – importantly for PSHE education – *inter*personal and *intra*personal intelligence.

Around the same time the idea of emotional intelligence was also developing. This could be seen as separate from but complementary to 'conventional' intelligence. Goleman observed that in business, leaders with similar intellectual ability could be differentiated on the basis of their Emotional Quotient or EQ (Goleman, 1995) and it has been suggested that those with a high EQ perform better than those with a low EQ (Weare, 2004). It is important to note that the ideas underpinning EQ have come from observations with adults rather than children, whose brains continue to develop throughout their school years and beyond.

The work on multiple intelligences, and specifically emotional intelligence, has led to the development of a range of resources for schools which focus on social and emotional development as a way of improving a wide range of outcomes, for example Social and Emotional Aspects of Learning for Primary Schools (SEAL) which was implemented in schools across England with support from the Department for Children, Schools and Families, now the Department for Education (DfE). A small scale independent evaluation of SEAL suggested some positive findings for children with regard to a range of beneficial social outcomes which were sustained over several weeks (Humphrey et al., 2008). SEAL resources have been archived by the DfE but are still accessible through the Teachfind website (see p. 88).

We will look again at EQ when we review social and emotional well-being in Chapter 3.

What do we need to know about brain development to teach PSHE education effectively?

This section has drawn on a collection of essays arising from a seminar 'Mind, Brain and Education' held in 2003 (Battro et al., 2008). Compared with the philosophical or psychological approaches to understanding children's learning, described above, our understanding of brain development is in its infancy. Until relatively recently much of what we understood about the brain and learning was based either on animal studies where parts of the brain were deliberately damaged, or on observing the effects of brain injury on human behaviour. Some studies were also carried out during brain surgery, when the patient was not anaesthetised. (The brain itself has no pain sensors!)

However, great strides have been made in the last 30 years, assisted by non-invasive techniques for studying the brains of living people such as: functional magnetic resonance imaging (fMRI), magneto-encephalography (MEG) and optical topography (OT) (Koizumi, 2008). Each technique has its strengths and weaknesses and the results are often combined. While fMRI and MEG require the individual to be motionless, OT enables neuroscientists to study the brains of infants and children while they are going about their normal activities, and has recently been used to demonstrate that adults with 'locked in syndrome' are conscious.

For educationalists the important questions are not about how the brain develops but, rather, how this knowledge can help us to make sense of theories of cognition, child development, learning styles and multiple intelligences, or help us to relate to the work of the philosophers whose work we continue to respect despite the passage of time.

Many people believe we can begin to make these links and this has spawned a plethora of novel resources for schools, which could loosely be described as brain based learning. However, some of the leading researchers in the field have urged caution in leaping to conclusions about curriculum development, based on our, as yet imperfect, understanding of the relationships between brain development and learning (Fischer, 2008).

There is still a lot to learn about the link, for example, between cognition (understanding), the specific area of the brain which is activated when learning or performing a specific task, and whether a child demonstrates that learning reliably in the future in an unfamiliar setting. Some evidence points clearly to the work of the behaviourists: groups of neurones become associated with one another through synaptic connections which are reinforced through repetition. According to Singer: 'Neurons wire together if they fire together' (Singer, 2008: 100).

As the brain matures these processes become irreversible. This is why early experience is so important to 'normal' development. This observation also leads some neuroscientists to suggest that there are critical periods in brain development when the neuronal structure is optimised to develop a specific function. The development of language is a good example of this. Numerous studies have shown that babies make all the sounds heard in all human languages but that gradually they selectively pay attention to and mimic the speech sounds in their immediate environment, especially maternal speech. They acquire a vocabulary and use recognisable grammatical rules to make new sentences they have never heard spoken before. Gradually the ability to learn new languages becomes more and more difficult (although some people appear to learn how to learn and become fluent in many languages).

Interestingly, neuroscientists make a clear distinction between learning and education, using knowledge of how the brain works to explain not just how we learn about maths or reading, but also human attributes such as love and hate: 'Learning is the process of making neuronal connections in response to external environmental stimuli, while education is the process of controlling or adding stimuli and of inspiring the will to learn' (Koizumi, 2008: 167).

It is clear there is much more to learn about the role the brain plays in education.

> **Consider**
> We often hear the term 'teaching and learning' used in curriculum planning. What does brain science tell us about teaching and its relationship to what is learned?

What do we need to know about childhood to teach PSHE education effectively?

After all this discussion of child development, learning theory and brain development, it is important to reflect that we should not think about children as brains, or even as learners, isolated from the rest of their lives in the community. We must remember that while children are at school they are also in a very important phase of their overall development: a phase which we know as childhood.

The limits of childhood are not determined by biological factors (according to some, brain development continues up to the age of 30, which is beyond even the broadest definition of childhood!). The definition of childhood varies from culture to culture and across time. Hence childhood is described as a social construct, dependent for its meaning on the interactions of a particular group of people, rather than an objective or inherent reality. Indeed, childhood is a relatively new construct, arising in the seventeenth century with the industrial revolution and the emerging awareness of adults of the need to protect children from the effects of heavy work and the harsh conditions in the factories.

PSHE education in primary schools is taught to children between the ages of 4 and 11 years (or 12 years in Scotland). This means that however childhood is defined, children of primary school age are included and so are affected by what we understand by this term.

> **Consider**
>
> What does childhood mean to you? How is it shaped by the culture in which you have grown up? Is it a time of innocence, freedom and play? Or a time of forced labour, prostitution and military service? Or a time of economic dependence or economic exploitation?

By the late twentieth century sociologists began to question notions of childhood and whether the study of childhood in some ways disempowered children as actors or 'agents' in their own lives (Moran-Ellis, 2010). The idea of childhood, with its early focus on protecting children, had become, for some, a means of objectifying and demeaning children. This can be seen to some extent in the research into child development described earlier in this chapter. Psychological research tended to be done 'on' children as subjects, rather than 'with' children, as participants, as if they had no insights of their own to bring to the discussion, even when the aim of the research was to understand children's needs.

A 'new sociology of childhood' emerged which had parallels with the social constructivist movement in psychology. Indeed, the work of Vygotsky and Bronfenbrenner, among others, was influential in shaping this new approach, placing children at the centre of studies of childhood, through methodology more familiar in anthropology, ethnography, history and geography than from psychology or sociology. Allison James and Alan Prout, leading sociologists in this field, argued that we should see children as agents in the here and now and not as future adults (James and Prout, 1990).

> **Consider**
>
> In PSHE education, learning is the process through which 'children and young people acquire the knowledge, understanding and skills they need to manage their lives, now and in the future'. How does this definition reflect the new sociology of childhood?

The view of childhood in the UK in the early twenty-first century can be described as confused. According to Moran-Ellis (2010: 189), politically, children are seen simultaneously as 'in danger' (and so must be protected) and 'a danger' (and so we must be protected from them). This has led to social policies and practices which have contributed to children in the UK being ranked lowest overall for 'wellbeing' of 21 developed countries (UNICEF, 2007). A closer look at these rankings shows that while the UK is placed twelfth for health and safety, it is placed twenty-first for family and peer relationships, suggesting our motivation and efforts to keep children physically safe do not match those which would keep children emotionally safe.

What do we need to know about risk and protective factors to teach PSHE education effectively?

It is well known that some children are more likely than others to have problems now and in the future. The features of their lives which make them more vulnerable are known as risk factors. Similarly, some children appear to be relatively untouched by the same risk factors and appear to benefit from protective factors, which, interestingly, are not always the reverse of risk factors (Jessor et al., 1995, 1998).

It is important to remember that risk and protective factors do not *predict* outcomes for children and young people but are factors which are correlated with more or less positive outcomes. Some children grow up in very adverse circumstances and lead happy, healthy and successful lives. Others appear to have many advantages and yet experience serious problems. Also risk factors are not static; they can change according to the broader social and economic situation in which the child is growing up. This suggests that education may be able to influence the outcomes for vulnerable young people, although not only in conventional ways, through knowledge acquisition (Cleveland et al., 2008).

Risk and protective factors can be divided into several domains (Cleveland et al., 2008):

- individual (for example, knowledge or skill)
- school (for example, policy, connectedness to school)
- peer group (for example, attitudes and social norms)
- family (for example stability, parental rules)
- community (for example, crime rates, neighbourhood attachment).

Risk factors also vary according to the problem, so risk factors for bullying are different from those for child abuse, although there are some which are common to both. Some problems can themselves become risk factors and can lead to a child becoming vulnerable to other problems. For example, young people who have serious problems with substances such as alcohol may report that they were bullied when they were younger, or suffered abuse or neglect at the hands of adults.

Similarly protective factors are not static and can vary from one problem or issue to another. However, protective factors which promote resilience – such as stable, supportive relationships with significant adults, achievement which is recognised and valued by school or the community, and engagement in a range of activities – are often cited as protective for a range of potential problems such as drug misuse and bullying. According to Cleveland et al. (2008) different protective factors can be important for children of different ages, with family and community factors being of greater value to younger children, and peers and school having greater impact for adolescents.

How can an understanding of health-related behaviour help us to teach PSHE education effectively?

Much of what we understand to be effective practice in PSHE education is rooted in an understanding of health, health promotion, health-related behaviour and public health, which aim to improve the health and wellbeing of individuals and communities (for an introduction to health promotion see Naidoo and Wills, 2009).

The health and longevity of the population of the western democracies has improved considerably since the end of the nineteenth century. Economic development and public health measures aimed at the whole population, such as better housing and working conditions, cheaper food, improved sanitation, vaccination and other advances in medicine, have all played their part. Improving health has led to longer, more economically active lifestyles for a large majority of the population, but not for everyone, with the poorest still experiencing the worst health (Doran et al., 2004). Genetic differences also influence our health and wellbeing. Finally, we have to consider too the influences on individual health-related behaviour for those who have real choices about diet and exercise.

PSHE education often focuses on the issue of individual behaviour, but as you will see in Chapter 3, how the whole school addresses the needs of the children and its community is also a powerful influence. Just as biology is fundamental to much of our understanding in public health and medicine, the social sciences too such as psychology, anthropology, economics and sociology have also increased our understanding of health and health-related behaviour.

Human behaviour is complex and changes throughout the life course. There are several models and theories which can help to describe our health-related behaviour. The models and theories also help to predict what will happen if we try to influence the way individuals behave. In this section we describe some of the better-known models and their implications for PSHE education.

Remember, in PSHE education we are trying to create the circumstances where the healthy and safe choice is the easy choice, and to enable young people to act on those choices. We are not trying to predetermine their behaviour or the choices they should make.

The Health Belief Model

This is one of the oldest and simplest models of health-related behaviour. Its basic premise is that we need a stimulus to change unhealthy behaviour

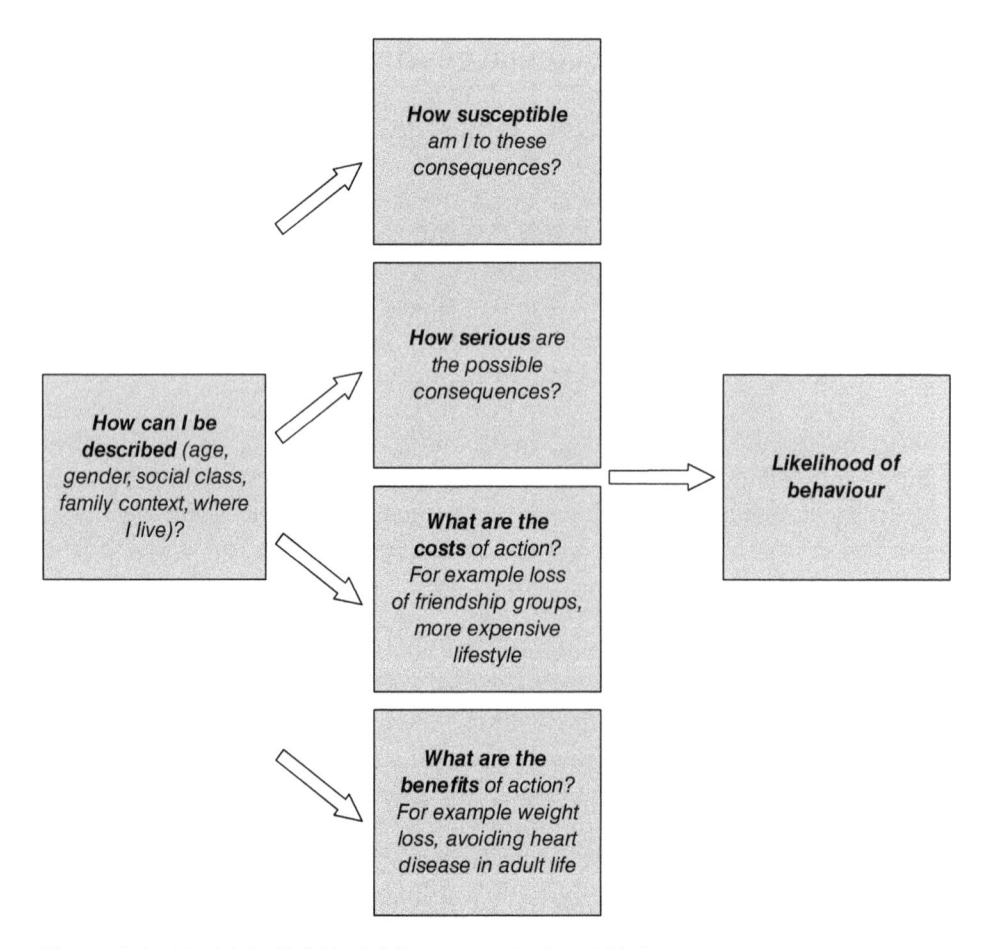

Figure 2.1 Health Belief Model (based on Becker, 1984)

to healthy behaviour. The model assumes that each person knows and understands the benefits of changing their behaviour (for example giving up smoking) and then makes a rational decision based on the costs and benefits of the change.

Key to the model is that an individual:

- is motivated to change
- believes their present behaviour represents a threat to their health
- believes the benefits outweigh any costs
- feels competent to carry out their decision.

Various other factors are known to influence or modify how people respond. These include:

- demographic factors such as age, gender and ethnicity
- psycho-social factors such as personality, social class, peer and other social norms
- structural factors such as knowledge of the possible outcomes, availability of advice and services, prior experience or experience of close family members or friends.

It is important to note that the Health Belief Model is a model to explain health-related behaviour, not a behaviour change model. Nevertheless, the Health Belief Model is the basis of many past educational campaigns and approaches. This is because it seems to suggest that providing knowledge about, or creating fear of, a disease or illness can help groups of people to avoid poor health outcomes. However, in practice, we know that knowledge is necessary but not sufficient to change individual behaviour, so educational approaches based only on information are unlikely to result in better health outcomes.

Fear arousal, which might increase our perceived susceptibility to disease, is also not very effective in changing behaviour, especially among young people. One reason for this is that young people have less experience to call on when comparing the information they are given with their own behaviour. They may not have experienced ill health themselves or in their immediate family. Young people also tend to demonstrate 'optimistic bias', because they may not immediately understand how the information applies to them. For example, young people often overestimate what they might earn in the future, and underestimate what basic services and goods cost. Non-smokers may think they are not likely to have heart disease, even though they are overweight and take no exercise. This phenomenon gives the false impression that young people think they are invulnerable – and this in turn can lead adults to exaggerate the magnitude of the problem, or to use scare tactics to emphasise the risks. We return to this in Chapter 11 (drug education).

A similar problem arises with a moralistic approach to health issues. Children find it difficult to see how someone they know to be 'good', such as a parent, can also do something 'bad', such as provide unhealthy food or drive without a seatbelt. So approaches to PSHE education which attempt to make people feel guilty are also likely to fail.

Another criticism of the Health Belief Model is its relative simplicity. Health-related decision making is much more complex than a series of rational calculations based on factors over which you may have no immediate control.

Where the Health Belief Model has been most successful is as a part of 'motivational interviewing'. This approach encourages individuals, rather than groups, to recognise the risks to their health, but focuses on the benefits of changing behaviour and helps people to consider what would help them to change. There is an emphasis on empowering people to make small, manageable changes which can be built upon as confidence grows. Brief motivational interviews with vulnerable young people who are beginning to have problems with drugs have been shown to be very effective, when carried out by trained workers (NICE, 2007).

Theory of Planned Behaviour

As its name implies, this theory suggests that health choices are planned and carried out on a rational basis. However, this theory also recognises that our beliefs affect our intentions and these intentions can to some extent predict whether or not we will turn our intentions into action. While a moment's reflection confirms that we do not always behave as we intend, the Theory of Planned Behaviour suggests that the strength and stability of the beliefs underpinning our intention are crucial. This means that beliefs which have been held and reinforced over a long period, which are held by other people in the same social group, and which coincide with other related beliefs are more likely to influence our behaviour, positively or negatively. As this is a theory of behaviour change it has little to say about the maintenance of existing healthy behaviour which applies to children of primary school age, the overwhelming majority of whom have not yet

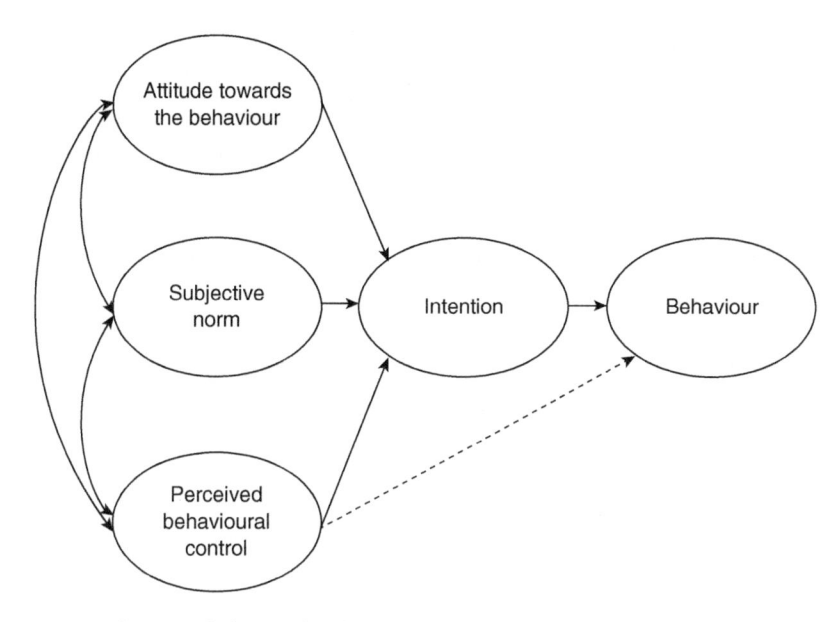

Figure 2.2 Theory of Planned Behaviour

Source: Ajzen, 1991: 182

started to adopt risky behaviours such as smoking, drinking alcohol or using illegal drugs.

One of the most important things we can learn from the Theory of Planned Behaviour is the importance of social norms in influencing our intentions. Social norms are what we believe to be acceptable values, beliefs and behaviours. They are the often unwritten, sometimes even unspoken, rules by which we conduct our everyday lives. Social norms vary from culture to culture, but also from generation to generation within a social group. Some social norms are communicated explicitly through the law, or by a formal religious custom, but some forms of communication are more subtle, such as how we dress, what words we use and what topics of conversation are acceptable.

Adolescents seem to be particularly alert to the social norms among their age group and may feel compelled to conform, as they may believe that not conforming will result in them being shut out or ostracised by their peers. However, some reviewers suggest that so-called 'peer pressure' is a far less powerful factor in risky behaviour among young people than has been thought (Coggans and Watson, 1995) and may be more appropriately described as 'peer influence'.

It is important to realise that social norms are often informal and some are more accurately described as perceived social norms. For example, young people may believe that most people in their age group regularly use illegal drugs. However, this norm may be influenced by a few prominent members of their peer group, by the media – and by the exaggerated fears generated in PSHE education lessons! Carefully constructed and properly administered anonymous surveys demonstrate that most young people of school age in the UK do not use illegal drugs – and that the proportion who do is falling. According to Gill et al. (2012) cannabis use among young people aged 11–15 years in England has almost halved from 13.4 per cent in 2001 to 7.6 per cent in 2011. As far as substance misuse is concerned, it seems that the actual norm is very different from the perceived norm.

The Theory of Planned Behaviour tells us that making sure children and young people know how few of their peers use illegal drugs will strengthen the beliefs underpinning a young person's intention not to use drugs themselves. It also suggests that PSHE teachers should challenge perceived norms where they may have a damaging influence.

Primary school-age children might have a very exaggerated and misplaced belief about secondary school pupils' use of drugs, for example, which may need to be addressed. Young people who believe, erroneously, that most of their peers use illegal drugs would therefore also observe that most do not suffer any ill health consequences. As a result they may dismiss any information about the potential harm caused by illegal drugs as exaggeration, whereas they have simply overestimated drug use among their peers. Thus it is the responsibility of PSHE education to provide information that is not only relevant but also objective, accurate and balanced. Challenging perceived norms by encouraging discussion and reflection of the facts about young people's drug use is a normative approach to drug education and this has been shown to be effective in several studies (Stead and Angus, 2004).

If we reflect on the Theory of Planned Behaviour, challenging perceived norms about healthy behaviour can have two benefits. It can reinforce the majority who have made healthy choices and help to change beliefs that may contribute to unhealthy choices.

Health Action Model

The Health Action Model (Green and Tones, 2010; Tones, 1987) focuses on the interaction between an individual's beliefs, their environment and the contribution education can make to their intentions to act in a given

EFFECTIVE PRACTICE IN PSHE EDUCATION 39

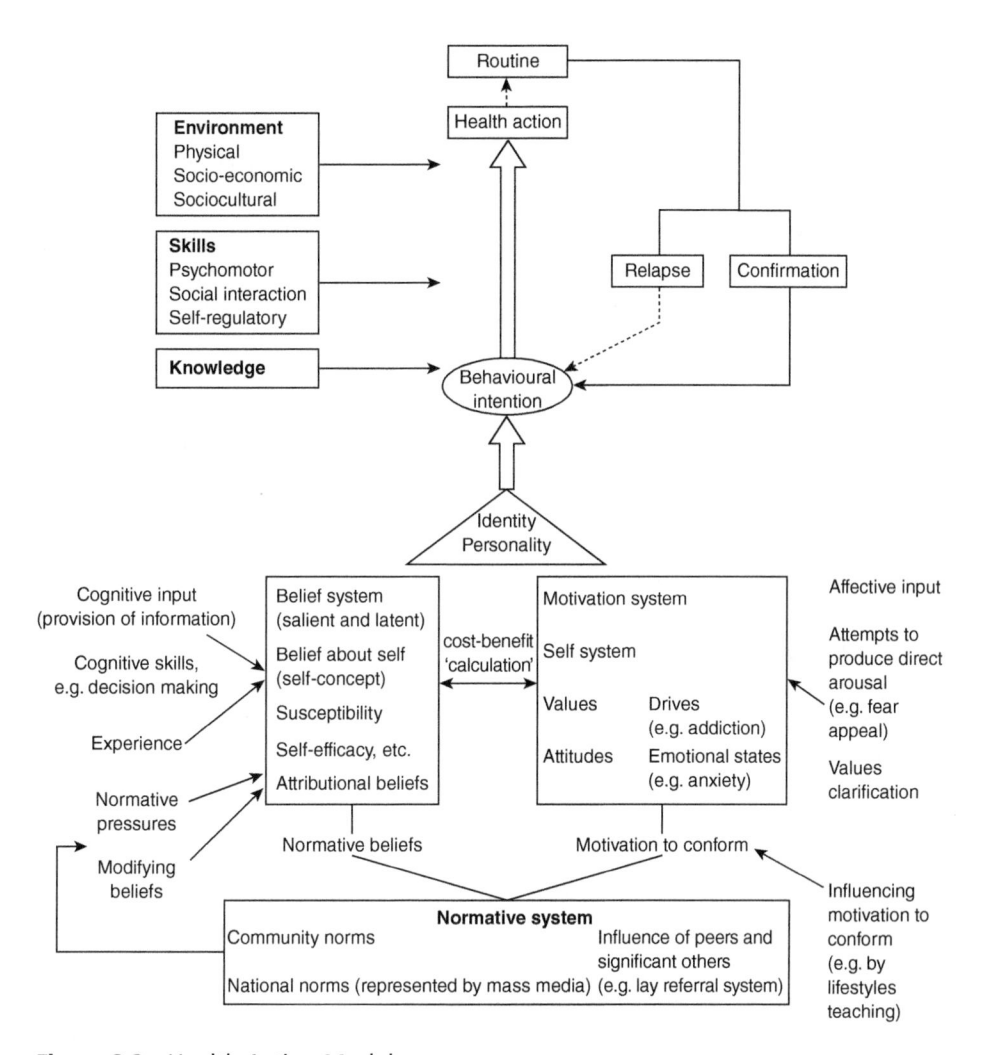

Figure 2.3 Health Action Model
(adapted from Tones, 1987, and Green and Tones, 2010)

way. It draws on well-known models including the Health Belief Model and the Theory of Planned Behaviour, among others (see Green and Tones, 2010).

Although this model is not as well known as the others it is included here because the Health Action Model is particularly useful for planning in PSHE education. Various versions have been published over a period of 20 years with Figure 2.3 based on two – one older and one more recent. At the base of this model are the norms of our community, family and peers, which have a powerful effect on our motivation and beliefs about health behaviour. The lower right-hand side shows how emotional arousal can influence our intentions. This typically occurs via high profile roadshows and media campaigns intended to make us fearful of the consequences of unhealthy behaviours, while in PSHE education it may be through Theatre in Education, as well as in lessons, which enable young people to reflect on and clarify their values with respect to health behaviour. This 'affective input' is balanced by the lower left-hand side of the model which suggests that efforts to help young people to feel good about themselves (self-worth) and to feel capable and confident in carrying out their decisions (self-efficacy) will also help them to form healthy intentions. Fear arousal without this balancing is unlikely to be effective in changing behaviour (Ruiter et al., 2001).

The upper left-hand side of the Health Action Model suggests that the policies of a school should be congruent with the health behaviour we are asking young people to demonstrate. Within this setting children and young people should have structured opportunities to practise the social, emotional and physical skills they need to recognise their feelings, make choices and decisions and be able to take risks in a safe and supportive environment. This could be through role play, team building and physical challenges which test their competence and may not just be in PSHE education but also in opportunities for adventurous and challenging activities. Classroom activities can never be exactly like the real world, but should always provide an opportunity for young people to reflect on their actual experience. Schools can also provide real opportunities for young people to make and sustain responsible choices in a range of practical ways, and in doing so demonstrate they can help to influence the health, social and economic wellbeing of themselves and others through their choices.

Whole school approaches to health and wellbeing provide the best evidence for the effectiveness of this part of the model. There is growing evidence that 'healthy' or 'health promoting' schools contribute to the development of confident individuals who are competent in their decision making and are resilient in the face of adversity (Stewart et al., 2004; Stewart-Brown, 2006). Interestingly there is also emerging evidence that healthy schools can provide the context for improved academic outcomes (Murray et al., 2007; Symons et al., 1997) (see also Chapter 3).

The upper right-hand side of the model acknowledges that even when we try to behave in healthy ways we don't always succeed, but that what we learn from failure *and* success can help us to do better next time. This draws on the trans-theoretical model of change developed by Prochaska and DiClemente (1983, 1984) as part of their work in understanding adult addictive behaviour.

Overall, what the Health Action Model really shows us is that in PSHE education there is no magic bullet. It shows that knowledge, social norms, some idea of personal susceptibility, our experience, our environment, our skills in decision making, our confidence in carrying out our decisions and our resilience in the face of setbacks all matter when it comes to whether or not we form healthy intentions and can act on those intentions. This suggests that using a range of approaches to teaching and learning in PSHE education, combined, will be more effective than focusing on one or another as some of the other models suggest.

Chapter summary

In this chapter we have attempted to bring together philosophy, psychology, neuroscience and sociology to inform our understanding of children, learning, teaching and how this can impact on health-related behaviour. All of this material (and more!) can be explored in more depth in more specific texts we have recommended.

Some of what we have covered will be very familiar and some new and, potentially, challenging. Whatever your starting point there is a lot of information to consider every time you plan a PSHE education lesson. To help with this, in 2009, the PSHE Association reviewed similar information and distilled it down to ten principles for effective PSHE education. It is worth noting that the ten principles apply to whole school planning for PSHE education, and not to each and every lesson. The aim is to achieve a balanced approach through formal and informal education, with the guidance of your PSHE co-ordinator, the help of external contributors and opportunities for learning outside the classroom.

Ten principles for effective PSHE education

1. Start where children and young people are: find out what they already know and understand, are able to do and are able to say. For maximum impact involve them in the planning of your PSHE education programme.
2. Plan a 'spiral programme' which introduces new and more challenging learning, while building on what has gone before, which reflects and meets the personal developmental needs of the children and young people.
3. Recognise that the PSHE programme is just one part of what a school can do to help children and young people to develop the knowledge, skills, attitudes and understanding they need to fulfil their potential. Link the PSHE programme to other whole school issues such as Healthy Schools, information, advice and guidance and to pastoral support, providing a setting where the healthy and safe choices become the easy ones. Encourage staff, families and the wider community to get involved.
4. Offer a wide variety of teaching and learning styles within PSHE education, emphasising interactive learning and the teacher as facilitator.
5. Encourage young people to reflect on their learning and the progress they have made, and to transfer what they have learned to say and to do from one school subject to another, and from school to their lives in the wider community.
6. Provide opportunities for children and young people to make real decisions about their lives, to take part in activities which simulate adult choices and, where they can, demonstrate their ability to take responsibility for their decisions.
7. Take a positive approach which does not attempt to induce shock or guilt but focuses on what children and young people can do to be healthy, stay safe, enjoy and achieve, make a positive contribution and achieve economic wellbeing.
8. Provide information which is realistic and relevant and which reinforces positive social norms, such as saving for the future or not using illegal drugs.
9. Provide a safe and supportive learning environment where children and young people can develop the confidence to ask questions, challenge the information they are offered, contribute their own experience, views and opinions, and put what they have learned into practice in their own lives.
10. Embed PSHE education within other efforts to ensure children and young people have positive relationships with adults and feel valued, and those who are most vulnerable are identified and supported.

> **Consider**
>
> Can you relate each principle to one or more sections of this chapter? Is there anything missing from the ten principles that you would include? Why?

Further reading

Dowling, M. (2010) *Young Children's Personal and Social Development*. London: Sage.
Provides a useful overview of personal and social development for early years practitioners.

McWhirter, J. (2009) *Personal, Social, Health and Economic Education: From Theory to Practice*. London: PSHE Association. Available at: www.pshe-association.org.uk/10principles (accessed 28 January 2014).
A review of evidence relevant to PSHE education similar to that covered in this chapter, from which the 10 principles were derived.

Miller, D. and Moran, T. (2012) *Self-esteem: A Guide for Teachers*. London: Sage.
This book will help you develop classroom strategies for developing intrapersonal skills which enhance self-esteem.

References

Ajzen, I. (1991) 'The theory of planned behaviour', *Organisational and Human Decision Processes*, 50: 179–211

Angel, L.A., Polzella, D.J. and Elvers, G.C. (2010) 'Background music and cognitive performance', *Perceptual and Motor Skills*, 10 (3C): 1059–64.

Battro, M., Fischer, K.W. and Lena, P.J. (eds) (2008) *The Educated Brain*. Cambridge: Cambridge University Press.

Becker, M.H. (1984) *The Health Belief Model and Personal Health Behaviour*. Thorofare, NJ: Charles B. Slack.

Berk, L.E. (2007) *Infants, Children and Adolescents*. Needham Heights, MA: Allyn and Bacon.

Cancer Research UK (2012) www.cancerresearchuk.org/cancer-info/cancerstats/types/lung/smoking/lung-cancer-and-smoking-statistics#cancer (accessed 14 May 2013).

Cleveland, M.J., Feinberg, M.E., Bontempo, D.E. and Greenberg, M.T. (2008) 'The role of risk and protective factors in substance abuse across adolescence', *Journal of Adolescent Health*, 43 (2): 157–64.

Coggans, N. and Watson, J. (1995) 'Drug education: approaches, effectiveness and delivery', *Drugs: Education, Prevention, and Policy*, 2 (3): 211–24.

Dewey, J. (1897) 'My pedagogic creed', *The School Journal*, 54 (3) (16 January): 77–80.

Doran, T., Drever, F. and Whitehead, M. (2004) 'Is there a north–south divide in social class inequalities in health in Great Britain? Cross-sectional study using data from the 2001 census', *British Medical Journal*, 328: 1043–5.

Dunn, R. and Dunn, K. (1978) *Teaching Students Through Their Individual Learning Styles*. Reston, VA: Reston Publishing.

Fischer, K.W. (2008) 'Dynamic cycles of cognitive and brain development: measuring growth in mind, brain and education', in M. Battro, K.W. Fischer and P.J. Lena (eds), *The Educated Brain*. Cambridge: Cambridge University Press, pp. 127–50.

Gardner, H. (1983) *Frames of Mind: Theory of Multiple Intelligences*. New York: Basic Books.

Gill, V., Hawkins, V., Mandalia, D. and Whalley, H. (2012) *Smoking, Drinking and Drug Use Among Young People in England in 2011*, ed. E. Fuller. London: Health and Social Care Information Centre.

Goleman, D. (1995) *Emotional Intelligence: Why It Can Matter More Than IQ*. New York: Bantam Books.

Gould, J. (1996) *The Mismeasure of Man*. New York: W.W. Norton & Company.

Gray, C. and MacBlain, S. (2012) *Learning Theories in Childhood*. London: Sage.

Green, J. and Tones, B.K (2010) *Health Promotion: Planning and Strategies*. London: Sage.

Gross, R. (1996) *Psychology: The Science of Mind and Behaviour*. London: Hodder and Stoughton.

Gross, R. (2010) *Psychology: The Science of Mind and Behaviour*. London: Hodder and Stoughton.

Humphrey, N., Kalambouka, A., Bolton, J., Lendrum, A., Wigesworth, M., Lennie, C. and Farrell, P. (2008) *Primary, Social and Emotional Aspects of Learning (SEAL): Evaluation of Small Group Work*. London: DCSF. RR064.

James, A. and Prout, A. (eds) (1990) *Constructing and Reconstructing Childhood: Contemporary Issues in the Sociological Study of Childhood*. London: Falmer Press.

Jessor, R., Van Den Bos, J., Vanderryn, J., Costa, F.M. and Turbin, M.S. (1995) 'Protective factors in adolescent problem behaviour: moderator effects and developmental change', *Developmental Psychology*, 31 (6): 923–33.

Jessor, R., Turbin, M. and Costa, F. (1998) 'Protective factors in adolescent health behaviour', *Journal of Personality and Social Psychology*, 75 (3): 788–800.

Koizumi, H. (2008) 'Developing brain: a functional imaging approach to learning and educational sciences', in M. Battro, K.W. Fischer and P.J. Lena (eds), *The Educated Brain*. Cambridge: Cambridge University Press, pp. 166–80.

Kolb, D. (1984) *Experiential Learning: Experience as the Source of Learning and Development* Englewood Cliffs, NJ: Prentice Hall.

Moran-Ellis, J. (2010) 'Reflections on the sociology of childhood in the UK', *Current Sociology*, 58: 186–205.

Muijs, D. and Reynolds, D. (2011) *Effective Teaching: Evidence and Practice*. London: Sage.

Murray, N.G., Low, B.J., Hollis, C., Cross, A.W. and Davis, S.M. (2007) 'Coordinated school health programs and academic achievement: a systematic review of the literature', *Journal of School Health*, 77 (9): 589–600.

Naidoo, J. and Wills, J. (2009) *Foundations for Health Promotion (Public Health and Health Promotion)*. London: Bailliere Tindall.

National Archives (2005) 'Social and Emotional Aspects of Learning (SEAL): improving behaviour, improving learning'. http://webarchive.nationalarchives.gov.uk/20110809101133/nsonline.org.uk/node/87009 (accessed 9 October 2013).

NICE (2007) *Interventions to Reduce Substance Misuse Among Vulnerable Young People (PH4)*. http://guidance.nice.org.uk/PH4 (accessed 9 October 2013).

Pashler, H., McDaniel, M., Rohrer, D. and Bjork, R. (2008) 'Learning styles: concepts and evidence', *Psychological Science in the Public Interest*, 9 (3): 105–19.

Prochaska, J.O. and DiClemente, C.C. (1983) 'Stages and processes of self change of smoking: toward an integrative model of change', *Journal of Consulting and Clinical Psychology*, 51: 390–5.

Prochaska, J.O. and DiClemente, C.C. (1984) *The Trans-theoretical Approach: Crossing Traditional Boundaries of Therapy*. Homewood, IL: Dow Jones Irwin.

PSHE Association (2013) www.pshe-association.org.uk/content.aspx?Category ID =1043 (accessed 8 October 2013).

Ruiter, R.A.C., Abraham, C. and Kok, G. (2001) 'Scary warnings and rational precautions: the psychology of fear appeals', *Psychology and Health*, 16 (6): 613–30.

Ruskin, J. (1853) *The Stones of Venice*, Volume 3. London: Smith, Elder & Co.

Singer, W. (2008) 'Epigenesis and brain plasticity in education', in M. Battro, K.W. Fischer and P.J. Lena (eds), *The Educated Brain*. Cambridge: Cambridge University Press, pp. 97–110.

Stead, M. and Angus, K. (2004) *Literature Review into the Effectiveness of Drug Education*. Edinburgh: Scottish Executive Education Department.

Stewart, D., Sun, J., Patterson, C., Lemerle, K. and Hardie, M. (2004) 'Promoting and building resilience in primary school communities: evidence from a comprehensive "Health Promoting School" approach', *International Journal of Mental Health Promotion*, 6 (3): 26–33.

Stewart-Brown, S. (2006) *What Is the Evidence on School Health Promotion in Improving Health or Preventing Disease and, Specifically, What Is the Effectiveness of the Health Promoting Schools Approach?* (Health Evidence Network Report). Copenhagen: WHO Regional Office for Europe. Available at: www.euro.who.int/document/e88185.pdf (accessed 21 May 2013).

Symons, C.W., Cinelli, B., James, T.C. and Groff, P. (1997) 'Bridging student health risks and academic achievement through comprehensive school health programs', *Journal of School Health*, 67: 220–7.

Tones, K. (1987) 'Health promotion, affective education and personal-social development of young people', in K. David and T. Williams (eds), *Health Education in Schools*. London: Harper Row.

UNICEF (2007) *Child Poverty in Perspective: An Overview of Child Well-being in Rich Countries*, Innocenti Report Card 7. Florence: Innocenti Research Centre. Available at: www.unicef.org/media/files/ChildPovertyReport.pdf (accessed 21 May 2013).

Weare, K. (2004) *Developing the Emotionally Literate School*. London: Paul Chapman Publishing.

CHAPTER 3

UNDERSTANDING SCHOOL ETHOS – WHAT IS TAUGHT AND WHAT IS CAUGHT?

Aim

To set out the difference between personal and social development and personal, social, health and economic education, and to explain the concept of the 'health promoting school'.

Learning objectives

By the time you finish this chapter you will:

- understand the importance of the school culture in the personal and social development of pupils
- understand the concept of the health promoting school
- have strategies for exploring this concept with pupils
- understand the contribution of PSHE education to the school's overall culture and ethos and vice versa.

Key ideas underpinning this chapter

- Pupils' personal and social development is being influenced by all of the micro and macro interactions and experiences that happen in their school day
- There are practical ways of positively influencing these.

Getting started

The following activity, based on Wetton and McCoy (1998), is aimed at a classroom teacher (or student on teaching practice).

> **Teaching activity**
>
> Ask a group of children to draw a picture of themselves coming into school on a day when they feel really good about it. Now ask them to write down all the things that are making them feel really good about coming into school.
>   Ask a group of children to draw a picture of themselves coming into school on a day when they feel not so good about it. Now ask them to write down all the things that are making them feel not so good about coming into school.
>   Now ask them to draw a picture of someone making it feel better. Write beside them who they are. How are they making things better?
>   (With younger children invite a small group, in each case, to draw a picture and then talk to you about what it is they have drawn.)

What did the children share with you? It can be surprising to notice what makes children feel good and not so good about coming to school. Sometimes it can be elements of the curriculum or aspects of learning but usually it is about relationships with their friends and their teachers. Who helped to make things better and how did they describe what they did? If we want children to feel positive about learning, first they need to feel positive about where they are learning. Their drawings may have provided insight into what can *routinely* turn a bad day at school into a good one.

PSHE or PSD?

Personal, social and health education is often confused with personal and social development. The first is the subject: the discrete curriculum time where the focus is given to the exploration of an issue or the development of a skill that has been identified as particularly important to children's future lifestyle.

The second is a little more nebulous: it is the accumulation of all of the experiences, planned and unplanned, that a pupil receives as part of their wider education and that contributes to their personal development and their social skills. Perhaps one way of thinking about it is that we have a subject in the curriculum called English but the development of literacy and spoken English is not confined to English lessons. PSD can be defined as the outcome of PSHE education plus the rest of the formal and informal curriculum.

So is personal and social development simply the sum of the planned experiences such as team working in physical education, or communication skills developed through English? It is more than that. There is a subtler and perhaps more powerful type of learning that contributes to our personal and social development.

You might think of it as a target – a centre bull's eye plus inner and outer rings. At the centre is PSHE education, the subject. In the inner ring

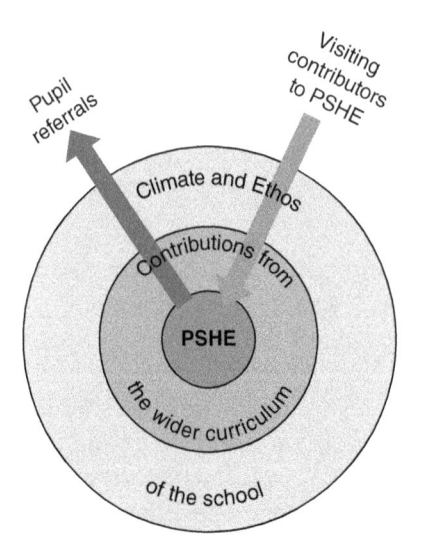

Figure 3.1 PSHE education is at the heart of children's development, but is not alone

is the wider curriculum, the contribution made by other subjects. So, for example, English helps children develop their communication skills and vocabulary of feelings, while science contributes to pupils' understanding of the importance of being safe with medicines. Wrapped around this in the outer ring are the school's climate and ethos, which influence all the other moment-by-moment experiences that help to shape the children. Visitors may contribute to the PSHE education programme. Sometimes, a child may need outside help and referral.

Unconscious learning through modelling

Have you ever done something or said something that made someone point out, 'Do you realise your mum [or your dad] does that?!' Perhaps it is a mannerism that you have 'picked up' or an exclamation that they use. This can often be followed by the feeling of horror as you realise that you are beginning to turn into your parents or carers.

What is interesting is not what you said or did but how you learnt to do it. It almost certainly was not something you intended to learn. You probably did not sit in front of mirror practising a particular expression or deliberately and repeatedly rehearse a statement or saying. We use the expression, 'It is just something I must have picked up'. What we are experiencing is learning through modelling, the unconscious learning that our brains are constantly engaging in and that sometimes reveals itself at embarrassing moments.

There is some evidence that an area of the brain known as 'mirror neurons' drives modelling. Have you ever seen someone, perhaps someone you care about, hit themselves – perhaps they bang their elbow against something and before you even have time to think your own hand jumps to your own elbow? Perhaps you notice your own face tenses, you find yourself rubbing your own elbow and even saying out loud, 'Oh, I bet that hurt!'

Learning through modelling, especially feeling someone else's pain without having to experience a similar injury ourselves, could have been a very effective mechanism for survival. Mirroring someone else's behaviour and learning from it would have saved a considerable amount of our own distress in having to learn from first-hand experience.

Our capacity to learn in this way could also be at the centre of empathy. As social creatures, feeling others' distress and caring for them would have protected the group and hence ourselves. It seems that most people's brains are 'hard wired' to be kind. This is expressed as prosocial behaviour when it develops in the youngest children.

The hidden curriculum

Consider all the experiences a child has during a school day. All the language they hear, the human interactions, the messages they get from the environment around them, and then imagine the unconscious learning that is taking place. Learning is not restricted to the learning objectives of a lesson: children are learning all the time and from everything they experience. This is a powerful element of the rationale for PSHE education, to use routinely the 'resource' of the other children in the class, and not attempt to restrict useful input to what the teacher says or does.

Our personal and social development is not only a product of the 'taught' curriculum but also 'caught' through all of the hundreds of interactions that we experience throughout our lives. One commonly used term for this in the field of education is 'the hidden curriculum' – an area that has been explored since the start of the twentieth century.

Two definitions are useful here. The first, from Roland Meighan (Meighan, 1981: 314):

> The hidden curriculum is taught by the school, not by any teacher ... something is coming across to the pupils which may never be spoken in the English lesson or prayed about in assembly. They are picking up an approach to living and an attitude to learning.

The second, from Michael Haralambos (Haralambos et al., 2004: 702):

> The hidden curriculum consists of those things pupils learn through the experience of attending school rather than the stated educational objectives of such institutions.

In fact if the educational objectives are in conflict with the experiences of the child, then they may be learning not to 'do as I say' but to 'do as I do'.

Great teachers and great schools understand this process and attempt to manage not only the planned curriculum but also, as far as it is within their control, the entire experience of the child in the school, sometimes called the school's 'ethos' or 'culture'.

> ### Consider
> Try to recall a moment from your own primary school days when something happened that made you feel really uncomfortable.

> It may be an event you can easily recall, even if you now would rather forget it again! Would it have been as significant an event to everyone else?
>
> What can appear to be trivial events to others can have a powerful effect on us as recipients. We may find that what to others may seem a 'throw away' comment can have a powerful impact on our self-belief and willingness to confidently engage with an aspect of learning.

Is there a subject you feel you are not very good at? If there is, try to recall the moment when you first learnt that you were not very good at it. Many people find that there is moment they remember when they first doubted they could do a subject; that moment often involves embarrassment or even a feeling of humiliation. Children's belief in their ability can be very fragile and a single event, or even a single word, can strengthen or weaken it. It is important to recognise that an event that can appear small or trivial to others can be significant to a child. It is sometimes said that we are shaped as much by the micro events in our lives as the macro events.

Being given the opportunity to star in the school play can be hugely beneficial for a child's self-esteem, but so can a simple smile across a classroom with a softly spoken 'well done' from a teacher if it is offered at just the right moment.

Understanding the Health Promoting School

Imagine two children walking towards two school entrances on their first day. One child sees a door with a sign stuck behind the glass that they are told says, 'Wipe your feet!' The other sees children's drawings of smiling faces stuck behind the glass with a caption they are told says, 'Welcome to our school!' Even before the child has entered the building they have learnt something about their new school.

How would a health friendly school differ from a health promoting school? A health friendly school might provide healthy options at lunchtime or healthy snacks at break. A health promoting school would encourage young people to recognise the importance of healthy eating in the curriculum and most importantly make the connection between the learning and the food that is on offer. A health friendly school might

> **Personal activity**
>
> Imagine a health negating school – one that seems to go out of its way to create the unhealthiest ethos, apparently ignoring everything that might damage children's self-esteem. What would you expect to see, hear, smell and feel as you walked around such a school?
>
> Now think about a health friendly school – one that takes care not to damage self-esteem. What would you expect to see, hear, smell and feel that was different as you walked around this school?
>
> Now think about a health promoting school – one that tried hard to bolster and nurture children's feelings of wellbeing at every opportunity. What would you expect to see, hear, smell and feel as you walked around such a school?

request only healthy food in packed lunches while a health promoting school might offer information sessions for parents, explaining the importance of healthy lunches, suggesting what might go into one and suggesting cheaper sources of fruit and vegetables. Children might be encouraged to grow some of the fruit and vegetables used in school dinners, perhaps in a school allotment.

A health promoting school makes the healthy choice the easy choice and this includes policies which encourage healthy choices, learning about a balanced diet and its relationship to health, to help motivate sensible eating choices. Although we have used healthy eating in our example above, a health promoting school attempts to find every opportunity to promote children's physical, emotional and social health, hand in hand with relevant education to promote understanding and competence.

Now imagine enlisting the help of children, teachers, parents and carers and school governors in researching, identifying and prioritising ways of improving children's health, giving them a collective responsibility for bringing about change and then involving them in the evaluation. We now have a 'whole school approach' to school improvement using a broad definition of 'health' to focus the developments. This is sometimes referred to as taking a 'settings' approach. Put simply there is little point in teaching about something in the classroom (for example bullying, active listening or healthy eating) unless the child's experience in the school is reflecting and reinforcing this learning.

The European Network of Health Promoting Schools (ENHPS)

Based on research undertaken during the 1980s, in 1990 the European Commission, the Council for Europe and the World Health Organization set up the European Network of Health Promoting Schools (ENHPS). Their document outlining the project states:

> The health promoting school aims at achieving healthy lifestyles for the whole school population by developing supportive environments conducive to the promotion of health. It offers opportunities for and requires commitment to the provision of a social and physical environment that is safe and enhances health. A health promoting school uses its management structures, its internal and external relationships, its teaching and learning styles and its methods of establishing synergy with its social environment to create the means for pupils, teachers and all those involved in everyday school life to take control over and improve their physical and emotional health. It uses health promotion as a device to improve the whole quality of the school setting. Success here will better equip schools to enhance learning outcomes. (Burgher et al., 1999: 4–5)

The last sentence is particularly important in making the connection between children's health in its broadest sense and their capacity to learn. ENHPS identifies ten principles that underpin a health promoting school:

1. Democracy

The health promoting school is founded on democratic principles conducive to the promotion of learning, personal and social development, and health.

2. Equity

The health promoting school ensures that the principle of equity is enshrined within the educational experience. This guarantees that schools are free from oppression, fear and ridicule. The health promoting school provides equal access for all to the full range of educational opportunities. The aim of the health promoting school is to foster the emotional and social development of every individual, enabling each to attain his or her full potential free from discrimination.

3. Empowerment and action competence

The health promoting school improves young people's abilities to take action and generate change. It provides a setting within which they, working together with their teachers and others, can gain a sense of achievement. Young people's empowerment, linked to their visions and ideas, enables them to influence their lives and living conditions. This is achieved through quality educational policies and practices, which provide opportunities for participation in critical decision making.

4. School environment

The health promoting school places emphasis on the school environment, both physical and social, as a crucial factor in promoting and sustaining health. The environment becomes an invaluable resource for effective health promotion, through the nurturing of policies that promote wellbeing. This includes the formulation and monitoring of health and safety measures, and the introduction of appropriate management structures.

5. Curriculum

The health promoting school's curriculum provides opportunities for young people to gain knowledge and insight, and to acquire essential life skills. The curriculum must be relevant to the needs of young people, both now and in the future, as well as stimulating their creativity, encouraging them to learn and providing them with necessary learning skills. The curriculum of a health promoting school also is an inspiration to teachers and others working in the school, and acts as a stimulus for their own personal and professional development.

6. Teacher training

The training of teachers is an investment in health, as well as education. Legislation, together with appropriate incentives, must guide the structures of teacher training, both initial and in-service, using the conceptual framework of the health promoting school.

7. Measuring success

Health promoting schools assess the effectiveness of their actions upon the school and the community. Measuring success is viewed as a means of support and empowerment, and a process through which health promoting school principles can be applied to their most effective ends.

8. Collaboration

Shared responsibility and close collaboration between ministries, and in particular the ministry of education and the ministry of health, is a central requirement in the strategic planning for the health promoting school.

The partnership demonstrated at national level is mirrored at regional and local levels. Roles, responsibilities and lines of accountability must be established and clarified for all parties.

9. Communities

Parents and the school community have a vital role to play in leading, supporting and reinforcing the concept of school health promotion. Working in partnership, schools, parents, NGOs (non-governmental organisations) and the local community, represent a powerful force for positive change. Similarly, young people themselves are more likely to become active citizens in their local communities. Jointly, the school and its community will have a positive impact in creating a social and physical environment conducive to better health.

10. Sustainability

All levels of government must commit resources to health promotion in schools. This investment will contribute to the long-term, sustainable development of the wider community. In return, communities will increasingly become a resource for their schools.

> **Consider**
>
> Think about a school with which you are familiar. How does the school promote the health and wellbeing of the staff?

The National Healthy Schools Programme (NHSP)

Given the first principle, 'democracy' it might be a surprise to you that many of the early adopters of the health promoting school approach were countries which at the time had no democratically elected government. It was not until 1999 that England adopted the NHSP, which was established by the Department of Health and the Department of Education as part of the 'Children's Plan' (DCSF, 2007). This, however, took a different approach from the concept of a healthy school, and instead of developments being driven by each school's own agenda it provided a set of national criteria that schools needed to meet, based around four themes:

- Personal, Social and Health Education, including sex and relationships and drugs education. These come under PSHE lessons for Years 7, 8

and 9 and can be included in religious studies classes. It provides young people with knowledge, understanding, skills and attitudes to make informed decisions about their lives.
- Healthy Eating includes healthy and nutritious foods being made in school canteens and available in schools as well as enabling young people to make informed decisions about healthy food.
- Physical Activity encourages young people to do physical activity as well as being given opportunities to be physically active. It helps understanding of how physical activity can make people healthier, and can improve life as well as being part of it.
- Emotional Health and Wellbeing, including bullying, how to express feelings, build confidence and emotional strength as well as supporting emotional health through counsellors and chaplains. It is the promotion of positive emotional health and wellbeing.

By December 2009 more than 97 per cent of schools were engaged in this work and 75 per cent had achieved 'Healthy School' status.

Building in pupil responsibility and the pupil voice

Did you have a close friend at primary school? Do you remember those days when they were away perhaps because of sickness? Playgrounds can be very lonely places for some children who lack friends or find it difficult to make friends, and being on your own can make both break and lunchtime very long experiences. For some children this is a regular occurrence and many schools respond to this by organising play activities, and staff that supervise are mindful of children who appear to be isolated. Increasingly, children who have undergone training as 'play leaders' lead many of these activities and help to draw in their socially isolated peers.

A further opportunity to increase children's responsibility in supporting a health promoting school climate is the introduction of peer mediators. These are children who have undergone detailed training in conflict resolution. Some will intervene if a row is breaking out, but once programmes have been established many children will approach a peer mediator to help resolve a disagreement before it becomes a conflict. Though not realistic at early ages, by 10 or 11 years peer mediators can be trained and can become very useful. Their tendency to relate well to their peers, with similar levels of language and general understanding, make for a valuable resource both for children their own age and those younger.

These are both examples of handing ownership and responsibility to children. In reality teachers or other adults responsible for supervision are closely monitoring these types of activity. Sensitive training to develop good listening skills is vital. With such young people, it is also vital to get the balance right between offering real opportunities to experience responsibility while monitoring their activity carefully, and providing support when necessary both to mediators and those of their 'customers' that need more skilled, adult help.

Student councils

School councils, or more accurately student councils, are a strong example of providing an opportunity for 'pupil voice' to help shape the school improvement. Many schools make use of their student council to identify areas for improvement as part of the whole school approach required for recognition as a 'Healthy School' (see Chapter 4 for an example of a possible survey about healthy school meals).

Different schools use their student councils in different ways. They operate most effectively where they are built into the school's processes and are not an activity that happens outside of the day-to-day running of the school. In most cases each class elects their student council representatives but it is important for teachers to facilitate their work with their class, especially with younger pupils.

Many schools provide opportunities for student council representatives to talk with the class they represent as part of the planned school day. Some student councils focus quite narrowly on issues that only affect children while others contribute to larger issues affecting the entire school. It is important that children understand there are decisions that they cannot make and that there are boundaries around what can be changed.

Others adopt a slightly different approach using their student council to organise work that will have an impact outside of the school, for example organising fund raising events to support a local charity. This outward looking activity, valuable though it may be in its own right, has more to do with pupils collectively undertaking acts of civic responsibility than a democratic approach to school improvement.

There is no reason why the student council should not meet with representatives of the school's governing body, and some schools schedule this. Many meet local politicians and use this opportunity to feed back how children in their community feel about issues.

The most important issue with student councils is to be clear exactly what purpose the school intends it to serve. It is very easy for student councils to lose their credibility with pupils if they feel their expressed views are undervalued or ignored. Student councils need a lot of facilitation and monitoring by teachers although once they are established this becomes easier as children become more practised in exercising their responsibilities. There is no lower age limit to involvement. Imaginative school staff will find ways to involve the very young in saying what they like and what they don't like about their school, and making suggestions about what might change. The activity at the beginning of this chapter, investigating what can turn a bad-looking school day into a good one, is just such a way to involve young infants.

A particular issue in primary schools is the range of maturity and ability across the year groups. It is important to ensure that all members of the student council have an equal voice in their activities and that older pupils do not dominate proceedings.

Into practice

The following activity is aimed at teachers and student teachers.

> **Personal activity – investigate a student council**
>
> - How was it set up?
> - How are representatives selected? By teachers? By pupil election? Both?
> - What is their remit? Is it 'inward facing' – helping school review and school improvement? Or 'outward facing' – undertaking projects beyond the school gates?
> - How do adults facilitate the workings of the student council?
> - How do members communicate with other pupils?
> - Can all pupils stand for election?
> - Do they have real responsibility and power?
> - Do they have a budget – if so, how much and how are decisions made over spending it?
> - How do the children feel about their council? How do the children not directly involved feel about their representatives?

Some schools use similar techniques to others we have explored in this book to create an agenda for their school council. For example:

Ask the children to consider the following request:

> 'A detective needs help. They have heard about something called a 'healthy school' – a really good school where everyone feels really happy to come into school and be the very best they can be – but the detective doesn't know what to look for. They need help to find a 'healthy school'. They ask the children in a school a bit like this one.

You could then ask:

- What would those children tell the detective to look for?
- How would children describe a school like that to the detective?
- What words would they use?
- What do they think people in a school like that will be saying to one another, doing with one another?

You could then ask the children (thinking about the healthy school the detective now understands):

- Do you feel our school is a lot like that? A little like that? Not much like that?
- What could we all do to make our school like that?
- What could any of you do differently that would help?
- What could the grown-ups in our school do differently to help?

In this way the pupil voice can help create an agenda and also create shared ownership of school improvement. These activities and those that follow are expanded in *Confidence to Learn* and *Feeling Good: Raising Self-esteem in the Primary School Classroom* (see Further reading at the end of this chapter).

Looking at the fine detail

It might be tempting to think that the concept of the healthy school is all about looking at the 'big things' a school does. For example, changing the food in school meals or 'zoning the playground' (creating areas on a playground to encourage a wide variety of activity). This would be a mistake. The health of a healthy school lies just as much in its micro interactions. Think about some of these situations or locations. How could they be 'health promoting' in terms of developing relationships, self-esteem and encouraging greater engagement in learning?

> ### 💭 Consider
>
> What would be a health promoting:
>
> ... ten minutes before school starts?
> ... first five minutes of the school day?
> ... registration?
> ... assembly?
> ... learning objective?
> ... communication in the classroom?
> ... way to assess children's learning?
> ... playground?
> ... breaktime?
> ... display of children's work?
> ... last five minutes of the school day?
>
> And what would each look, sound and feel like?

It might be challenging to think about a display of work being health promoting beyond the obvious celebration of their work.

Here are four ways children's work can be selected for display:

- the child chooses, based on his or her own criteria
- the child chooses based on your criteria (or external criteria)
- you choose based on the child's criteria
- you choose based on your criteria.

None is right or wrong, there is a place at the right time for each. What is important is to explore the criteria. For example, a child may have very definite reasons why they want to share a piece of art with others. We need to be careful that we find ways to celebrate all children's achievements, not just those who are successful in attaining a particular set of external standards. It is important to separate attainment from achievement. For some children modest attainment can in fact be a huge achievement. (If in doubt think – attainment is how high you can climb up a mountain. Achievement takes into account all the ability and circumstances around the challenge – for a highly experienced climber, getting half way up is probably not much of an achievement, but for a disabled person the same attainment might be a huge achievement.)

We can enrich a wall display. What if you added a title 'We have been learning about ...'. If we imagine it is a science display you could add a notice that says, 'The scientists that produced this work are ...' because scientists are what the children were at the time. We can all be scientists; it isn't restricted to just those who are employed as scientists. You could make the display interactive by asking the children to identify a question that they could ask of other children who might pass by the display. You could then add to the display, 'One of questions we wanted to ask was ... One of us found the answer ... Can you see who it was and what they found out?' You will know if this has worked because a greasy finger mark will appear on the answer as the children that pass by show their friends by pointing it out. Try always to make sure displays celebrate children's achievements and encourage their peers to learn from this. They could so easily be treated as 'just decoration' – a chance missed.

Next time you walk into a school entrance look at the display boards and ask yourself if they display the best work of children with a variety of abilities or do they display the most gifted or able children's work?

Even something as simple as 'visitors' badges' given to adults visiting the school can be designed or even produced by the pupils. Through this activity you can discuss why visitors' badges are important to keep everyone safe. And you can show children that they can share this responsibility with you by helping you explore what might be put on a badge to identify legitimate visitors and make them feel welcome. (One child suggested – 'I am a visitor – if I look lost please find a teacher to help me'!)

Even taking the register can be made more interesting. Instead of simply calling out if a child is present or not, how about asking them what colour they feel this morning, or what animal they feel like? How about how they feel today on a scale of one to ten? If a child says they feel ten, then ask them why and perhaps celebrate it. If a child says one then store it away and ask them in private if they want to talk about why they feel a one today. Other, empathic children may want to offer their support, too, during the day.

The last five minutes of the school day can be an opportunity to reflect on the day. For example, ask your pupils:

- 'Who has learnt something that they didn't know before? If your hand is up tell the person beside you what it was.'
- 'Who has learnt something that surprised them?'
- 'Who mucked something up today? Was it something you can put right tomorrow, or is it like spilt milk: all you can do is say sorry and clean it up?'

- 'Who helped, or was helped by, someone else today? Tell them how they helped you and quickly say thank you to them.'
- 'If we could start today all over again, can anyone tell us something they would do differently?'

We could ask children what jobs they had today: 'Who has been a scientist? An engineer? A mathematician? A musician? An artist? A counsellor? A councillor?' Imagine a child going home from school and being asked by their parents what they have been doing today and replying, 'I was a scientist, an engineer, a researcher, a team manager and when my friend got upset and didn't know what to do, a counsellor!' Helping children to develop this vocabulary enriches their language but more importantly values their behaviour.

In a health promoting school, try to find ways to use the last five minutes of the school day that will encourage the children to want to come back to school as soon as possible.

Chapter summary

In this chapter we have explored the various factors that can affect a school's ethos, and the profound effects ethos has on the children (and staff) in the school. We set out the importance of consistency – exhortations to care for others and behave in positive ways are undermined unless the school models the same care and behaviours. We also showed how ethos can be addressed and improved, and how to seek insightful, meaningful contributions from the children themselves.

Further reading

Wetton, N. and Cansell, P. (1993) *Feeling Good: Raising Self-esteem in the Primary School Classroom*. London: Forbes.
  Practical approaches to raising self-esteem. A reminder of the crucial role of self-esteem in the confident, happy learner.
Wetton, N. and McCoy, M. (1998) *Confidence to Learn*. Edinburgh: HEBS.
  Short book published in Scotland and issued to all Scottish primary schools on the importance of children becoming confident in their ability to learn.

References

Burgher, M.S., Barnekow Rasmussen, V. and Rivett, D. (1999) *The European Network of Health Promoting Schools – The Alliance of Education and Health*. Brussels: International Planning Committee of the European Network of Health Promoting Schools. Available at: www.schoolsforhealth.eu/upload/TheENHPStheallianceofeducationandhealth.pdf (accessed 11 October 2013).

DCSF (2007) *The Children's Plan: Building brighter futures*. London: Department for Children, Schools and Families.

Haralambos, M., Holborn, M. and Heald, R. (2004) *Sociology: Themes and Perspectives*. London: Harper Collins, 2004.

Meighan, R. (1981) *A Sociology of Educating*. London: Holt, Rinehart and Winston.

National Healthy Schools Programme – Tools and Planning Aids. Department for Education. Available at: www.education.gov.uk/schools/pupilsupport/pastoralcare/a0075278/healthy-schools. (accessed 10 January 2014)

Wetton, N. and McCoy, M. (1998) *Confidence to Learn*. Edinburgh: HEBS.

CHAPTER 4

UNDERSTANDING HOW TO START WHERE CHILDREN ARE

Aim

To introduce approaches to finding out children's unique starting points in PSHE education.

Learning objectives

By reading and reflecting on the content of this chapter you will:

- know some ways to start where children are in PSHE education
- understand how to carry out simple classroom based research
- know how to use classroom based research to plan your teaching and learning strategies
- be able to create opportunities for your pupils to be active participants in their own learning in PSHE education.

Getting started

In this chapter we hope to show you how important it is – but also how easy – to start where children are in PSHE education, and how you can use what you learn to be a really effective teacher of PSHE education.

> **Teaching activity**
>
> Ask a small group (or a whole class) of children to draw a quick picture of a healthy person. Be careful not to give any introduction to what being healthy means to you – you want to know what the children in your class know and understand before you have done any teaching. Then ask them to tell you all the things this person does to make themselves healthy and keep themselves healthy. Record the children's responses on the white board or flip chart, or orally, using a digital recorder.
>
> Next, with the help of the children, group their answers in categories, for example food, exercise, play, hygiene, relationships, and emotional wellbeing (the latter can often be surmised from the smiles on the faces of the healthy people). Celebrate the children's knowledge and discuss why these are all important to being healthy. Plan how to address any misunderstandings or gaps in their knowledge in future lessons.

This person is healthy because her and her children do there daily exersise and they eat there 5-a-day!

Figure 4.1 This ten-year-old girl has a good understanding of physical activity as a route to health

Source: Brindishe Green Primary School, Lewisham, ten-year-old girl

Health warning: Starting where children are in PSHE education is addictive! Your transition from class teacher to classroom researcher could begin here!

In this deceptively simple activity, you have just done your first piece of classroom based PSHE research! You also know a lot about the children's understanding of health, which you could use to plan every aspect of PSHE education from relationships education, to drug and even environmental education. You will also have some clues too about what they don't yet know, what they half know and what they have misunderstood. All of this will be enormously helpful when you are planning what they will be learning to do, say and think, to keep themselves healthy now and in the future.

Introduction

In Chapter 2 we reviewed some of the philosophy and theory that underpin effective practice in PSHE education. The PSHE Association has distilled this understanding of effective practice into ten principles, the first of which is: 'starting where children are'. Social constructivists, sociologists and public health practitioners all agree that a person- (or child-) centred approach is an appropriate and effective way to promote learning about health and wellbeing.

There are many different ways to start where children are in PSHE education, some of which we will describe below. The challenge for many new teachers is finding manageable ways to do this with young children, without setting endless tests, or intruding, unprepared, into some very personal aspects of a child's life. It can also be a challenge to know how to make the best use of the information you have collected. To begin with, we will describe the origins of one of the first reliable methods which enabled teachers and researchers to see health from a child's point of view, known as 'draw and write'.

The origins of draw and write

In the 1980s a team of researchers at Southampton University were tasked with the responsibility of developing a curriculum for health education for primary school children (Williams et al., 1989a, 1989b). The team had access to questionnaires which had been developed for use by children aged nine years or older (Balding, 1985). Like many questionnaires this one consisted of a series of closed questions, each with a fixed set of responses. Almost 10,000 of the children in the sample were four to eight years old. The questionnaire effectively excluded all children who were unlikely to be able to read or interpret the questions reliably enough to choose one of the predetermined responses. The team also suspected that the answers to the closed questions would not fit what the younger children would answer if they were given a free choice. At this time there was a prevailing view that children as young as four to eight years would not know much about health (or anything else!) and that what they would know would be wrong. There was an option of interviewing a small sample of children, but this would be unlikely to be representative of the views of large numbers of children from different communities.

One of the team, Noreen Wetton, an early years specialist, had the idea of asking children to:

- draw a picture of a healthy person and
- write around the picture (or whisper to an adult 'scribe') what makes the person healthy and keeps them healthy.

Following a small pilot study, the research team trained teachers in all their sample schools how to carry out this novel research so that:

- children were not prompted in any way and
- sharing (copying!) each other's answers was minimised.

Figure 4.2 Children frequently include sport as a way to keep healthy

Source: Williams et al., 1989a: 37

The researchers also encouraged teachers to be as inclusive as possible, for example by:

- telling the children that there were no wrong answers – all their ideas were right
- encouraging children not to worry if they did not know how to spell the words correctly and
- involving 'scribes' for children unable or unwilling to write for themselves, who were instructed to write down exactly what the child said without attempting to teach or hint at a 'better' answer.

In draw and write studies, only the written word is analysed, although as Figures 4.2 and 4.3 show, sometimes the drawing removes any ambiguity!

As this was part of a research study the children were asked not to put their names (or the date) on the paper, but to write if they were a boy or a girl and their age in years. The latter proved particularly challenging for children who were about to have a birthday!

Figure 4.3 Boys often focus on physical fitness

Source: Brindishe Green Primary School, Lewisham, ten-year-old boy

Figure 4.4 Having a good memory is also part of being healthy

Source: Brindishe Green Primary School, Lewisham, ten-year-old girl

Figure 4.5 This image from the original research in 1989 captures what many children think being healthy means to them

Source: Williams et al., 1989a: 57

The results of the research were remarkable, and have been replicated in lots of schools in the UK and beyond. The children demonstrated that they knew more than their teachers (and the researchers) expected about being healthy, including many of the current priorities. But their views went way beyond what the original questionnaire had anticipated. For example, after 'food' and 'exercise' more children wrote about 'play' being something which makes people healthy than any other category.

Having friends was also more frequently mentioned than health professionals such as doctors and dentists. Clearly the children's view of health was not dominated by the 'medical model' of many so-called experts.

By doing the research with children across the whole age range for primary schools it was also possible to see developmental changes: the age at which children were able to generalise about health and health-related behaviour (moving from lists of individual food items such as peas, cabbage, apples and oranges to 'fruit and vegetables' for example).

The technique became known as 'draw and write', and has since been used to investigate children's understanding of a wide range of health issues, some of which we will describe in this chapter and throughout the book. The open ended nature of the technique has also encouraged researchers and practitioners to use draw and write with older pupils (McWhirter et al., 2004) and even with adults (Mortimer, 1997).

Pros and cons of draw and write
Pros:

- Draw and write is open ended so children are able to respond as they wish, and does not 'put ideas in their heads'.
- It is inclusive: children can ask a scribe to write for them, and children with learning difficulties or whose first language is not English can participate if an interpreter is available to scribe for them.
- Draw and write resembles an everyday classroom activity and does not feel like a test.
- You can analyse the findings with your class, sharing their ideas in a way that encourages them to contribute to your planning.
- The findings can be shared with external contributors to your PSHE programme such as school nurses and fire and rescue services so that they can start where the children are too.
- It is a form of assessment *for* learning and can be repeated as assessment *of* learning.

Cons:

- This method cannot be used when children are unable to handle a pencil. Other methods are recommended on p. 76.
- Interpretation and analysis of draw and write for large samples can be complex and time consuming. Some researchers have published their analysis frameworks which can be used as a guide.
- Like other forms of classroom based research there are practical, ethical and research issues to be considered (see below). Backett-Milburn and McKie (1999) have written a more detailed critique of the method, but many of their criticisms apply equally to other methods used in school based research, suggesting it is the context and not the method which has to be considered carefully.

Ironically, some children find the open ended nature of draw and write quite challenging. They think that there must be a *right* answer, if only they can second guess the teacher. If you think the children in your class will feel like this, take a look at Chapter 7 where we discuss how to create a classroom environment or climate where children feel comfortable about being asked, and responding to, open ended questions in PSHE education.

> 💭 **Consider**
>
> **Doing classroom based research**
>
> Before looking in more detail at draw and write and other techniques for starting where children are in PSHE education, there are several important factors to be taken into consideration before you embark on what might be considered to be small scale classroom based research (also known as 'practitioner based enquiry') with your class.
>
> First, what is the purpose of your enquiry? Is it for planning one lesson or a scheme of work for half a term? In this case your work need not be considered research, but you should think carefully about how you will record and represent what the children tell you, e.g. in classroom displays. Are children's responses identifiable by others because of their handwriting? If the children have shared personal information about family life should their contributions be anonymised?
>
> Has your PSHE co-ordinator asked you to collect information from your class which is going to be pooled with other data from other classes
>
> *(Continued)*

> *(Continued)*
>
> in the school, with the idea of helping with whole school planning? Are you doing some research as part of your training or as part of a Master's module or dissertation? If the latter, have you thought carefully about who else has access to the information you will be collecting? For example, you will need to anonymise the data if it is going to be shared with adults outside the school. Remember that, as in all forms of social research, the children's participation should be voluntary, so if this is a research activity and not just for your own planning, then you should provide the children with an alternative activity they can do quietly while you collect your data from those who do wish to participate.
>
> Second, what do you want to know? Will the questions you ask elicit appropriate answers? (Note we don't say: will they elicit the 'right' answers? – they will always be the right answers as far as the children are concerned, no matter how ambiguously the initial question is worded). Do your questions hint at a 'right' answer or, as happens more often, inadvertently suggest a different response from the ones you were expecting?
>
> Third, how many children do you need to involve so that you are able to meet the children's needs? If planning for a whole school, for example, it might be sufficient to ask a sample of children to take part, rather than every child in the school, or you could take a sample of responses at random from a larger group.
>
> Fourth, are you asking about one of the many so-called sensitive issues – drugs, sex and relationships? Is your question likely to give a child an opportunity to disclose (either intentionally or unintentionally) something which suggests they may be at risk of significant harm? How will you monitor and respond to responses of this kind?
>
> Finally, have you thought about how you are going to analyse the information you collect: formally on spreadsheets or informally as a series of 'key messages' which summarise the main issues?
>
> Take some time to think through the answers to these questions. Speak to your PSHE co-ordinator and teacher with responsibility for safeguarding. If you are a student talk it through with an experienced education researcher at your university or with your mentor if you are an NQT. Remember that your overall purpose is to find out what the children already know and understand so that you can plan effectively to meet their needs. In so doing you will really engage the children in the topic.

Examples of draw and write you can use in PSHE education

The very first draw and write used in PSHE education became known as 'A picture of health' for obvious reasons. Before long the same researchers were being asked to develop new examples which could be used to explore children's understanding of other aspects of PSHE education. In Chapter 8 we describe two draw and write techniques you can use to plan safety and risk education for your class (McWhirter and South, 2004; Williams et al., 1989b). In Chapter 9 we will show how draw and write can inform your planning for sex and relationships education. Chapter 11 looks at one of the best known draw and write techniques, 'A world of drugs' (Williams et al., 1989b). In Chapter 12 we refer to a draw and write which can help you to start where children are in personal finance education, and in Chapter 13 we describe how you can use draw and write to assess children's learning in PSHE education.

Before going on to look at other methods, we should reflect on the subject of 'sensitive issues' and draw and write. One of the most sensitive issues in PSHE education in the 1980s was drug education (see Chapter 11). No one was sure what primary school aged children knew – or needed to know – about drugs, but there was public concern about an apparent increase in the use of heroin and other addictive drugs among adults. Should drug education begin as early as primary school, before children have independent access to legal or illegal drugs? What should drug education consist of and how can we do this kind of research without 'putting ideas in their heads'?

Similar concerns continue to be expressed today, and particularly with respect to sex and relationships education. Faith groups have strong and deeply held views about how and when children should learn about sexual matters, and some object strongly to school based sex education, mistakenly assuming sex education is all about sexual intercourse and not first and foremost about love and loving relationships. Chapter 9 explores some of these issues in more depth.

Consider

What are sensitive issues for you when thinking about teaching your class? Make a note of some of your thoughts, and continue to do so as you answer the questions that follow.
Next ask yourself:

- What are sensitive issues for parents?
- What are sensitive issues for governors and senior managers in your school?
- What are sensitive issues for the children in your class?

(Continued)

> *(Continued)*
>
> Compare the notes you have made in answer to each of these questions. How similar/different are they?
>
> Now consider what makes these topics sensitive to each group? Parents tend to be concerned most about matters as they affect *their* child. Governors and senior managers are concerned with the reactions of parents, but also community leaders, policy makers and Ofsted – how will the local press represent the school if there is a problem?
>
> Children, who are constantly growing and changing, may have concerns which superficially may appear trivial: having freckles, being liked, getting into trouble for something they have not done. They may also have major concerns they are not able to express, such as a parent who is depressed, using alcohol or drugs, going through a family break-up or in financial difficulty.
>
> Now look back at your own list. As the class teacher you have to deal with everyone else's sensitive issues as well as your own. No wonder we sometimes fear opening what may be a can of worms.

In our experience draw and write can help overcome fears about teaching sensitive issues in the classroom, precisely because it starts where children are, and what they are ready for, rather than where adults are, and what they fear children may *not* be ready for. Children are free to interpret the questions how they wish and to disclose more, or less, about what happens at home or in relationships out of school.

Some draw and write techniques use a method known as distancing when asking about what might be a sensitive issue. Distancing is a useful technique in PSHE education generally (see Chapter 7). In draw and write it means asking the children to illustrate a story about fictitious characters who are about their own age and who live in their neighbourhood. The questions gradually focus on more specific issues and eventually seek a more personal response. In 'A world of drugs' (Williams et al., 1989b) the story is about two children who find a bag of drugs while on their way home from school. The children are asked to draw and write about what is in the bag, the person who dropped it and what that person intended to do with the contents of the bag. As with other draw and write techniques, no definition of drugs is given, so what the children draw and write about is based on their own interpretation of the word. Only after these initial questions are the children asked what they would do if they had found the bag of drugs (see Chapter 11 for the full instructions). As the class teacher you will know how many of the questions to ask, at what pace and if the questions are becoming too personal for the children in your class. As a student you should discuss this with your mentor who may know the children better than you.

Our advice is that children need an opportunity to be heard, especially when they may fear the issue is too sensitive to raise directly with an adult. In addressing any sensitive issue it is important to create a safe and supportive environment where children feel confident you will respond constructively to their concerns (see Chapter 6).

Draw and talk

This is an adaptation of draw and write which works extremely well with nursery age children or children with a learning difficulty or physical disability that means they are unable to write. It is obvious that they will need a scribe, but it may still be useful to ask them to draw while they are thinking about how to answer. Sometimes the drawing is immature (it should never be called a scribble!) but to the child it will have meaning. Toddlers will 'write' a shopping list in this way but can't be fooled, pointing out which mark on the paper means potatoes or bread if you happen to mention them twice!

This approach was used to good effect to explore nursery school-aged children's understanding of the effects of sun on their skin (McWhirter et al., 2000). Nursery staff wanted to know how to explain why children should wear sunscreen, hats and long-sleeved tops outdoors in the sun, without frightening them with inappropriate information about skin cancer. As the nursery was in Southampton, near the sea, the children were asked to draw a picture of a family 'on the beach on a very hot, very sunny day'. Then they were asked to talk to the researcher about what the grown-ups were doing to make sure the children were safe, 'on the beach on a very hot, very sunny day'. Children described lots of appropriate adult behaviour including staying safe by the water, keeping safe from 'strangers' and from bad dogs ('bad dogs' is a dominant theme for young children in all discussion about safety). Lots of children pointed to their pictures and spoke about sunshades, sunhats and sunscreen. One child mentioned 'salad cream' and demonstrated how this was rubbed in to stop sunburn! The researcher simply noted the responses on the child's drawing for analysis later.

The staff were surprised and pleased about the children's knowledge and used what they learned to plan the rest of the work for the term on the topic of 'Being out and about', reinforcing sun safety messages in a range of environments.

Other ways of starting where children are in PSHE education

The choice of method for starting where children are will always depend on what you want to know. Draw and write can tell you about children's understanding and attitudes towards drugs and drug users, while a questionnaire might be more suitable to find out about their drug (including medicine) use. In the primary school, the more the approach resembles other classroom activities, the more relaxed you and the children will be when taking part and so the more useful their responses will be for your planning.

Quizzes

If you want to know the accuracy of children's knowledge of a PSHE topic then multiple-choice quizzes can be used. You need to be confident that the children will not be put off by something resembling a test and that you can record their answers faithfully. Some schools use handheld remote devices with their interactive white boards to record and analyse answers (see also Chapter 6 on pedagogy).

Bubble dialogue

This is a variation on draw and write which works best when children are confident to write for themselves. In this case you do part of the drawing, which could be the outline of two faces or the backs of two heads, with speech or thought bubbles. It is usual to start the 'conversation' with a statement to complete. For example, in a survey about school meals the conversation between the friends could begin, 'The dinners at my school are healthy because ...' and the second child could respond with, 'I know what you mean but I think they would be even healthier if ...'.

Circle time

If the children are accustomed to circle time discussion this can be a good medium. You might be familiar with circle time as a means to raise

> 'The dinners at our school are healthy because...'

> 'I know what you mean but I think they would be even healthier if...'

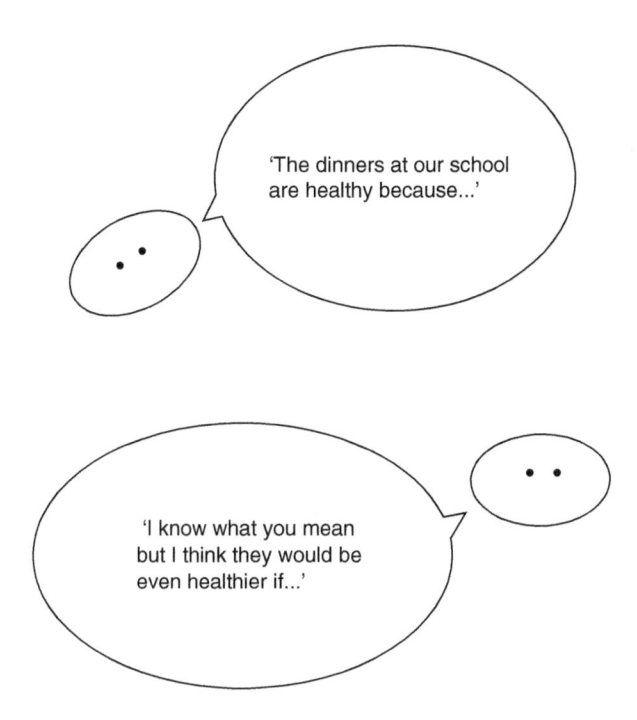

Figure 4.6 Example of a 'bubble dialogue'. Children can complete the faces of the two characters and give their ideas about healthy school meals as part of a consultation

emotional or relationship issues with children but it can also be used to generate starting points for a range of topics in PSHE education. You can choose an appropriate object to pass around the circle to generate and manage the discussion. For example, a Year 2 teacher started a topic in economic education by passing round a baby doll which was wearing just a nappy. The children were asked what they would need to do to make sure the baby was warm and healthy and their responses included clothes and blankets. The teacher continued by asking where the clothes might come from and if from a shop how they would be paid for. She soon had a range of ideas about money, including cash, credit and debit cards, loyalty cards and vouchers to explore with the children in future lessons (support materials relating to this example can be found online at: www.pfeg.org/learning-about-money-primary-classroom-support-materials).

Focus groups

Focus group interviews or discussion require some skill to set up but can be very productive, especially in finding out children's understanding and opinions about complex issues where questionnaires would not be appropriate or writing would be too challenging. Focus group discussions could be used to explore children's ideas about what makes a school a healthy place to learn and work, for example. This approach has also been used successfully to explore children's understanding of accidents (Green, 1997). An example of a subject for a focus group discussion with Year 5 and 6 pupils could be how exercise keeps you healthy, leading on to questions about competitive sport. Do children think that competitions make it more or less likely that they will take part in activities to help them stay healthy if there are winners and losers?

With young children it is a good idea to keep the group size small, and for some topics you might find single-sex groups useful, as long as the follow-up work you do is in mixed groups. You may want to select members of the groups according to other characteristics depending on the topic. While it would be unwise to put children in the same group if they do not get along, you should also avoid free choice based on friendship groups, as this means they are more likely than not to share similar views.

As with other open ended techniques used in curriculum planning and development, the point of a focus group is to collect as many ideas as possible rather than to find the 'right' answer or reach a consensus. You should emphasise that there are no wrong answers both at the start and during the discussion.

Your role is to ask the questions, which should be easy to answer at the beginning, become more focused on your topic in the middle section and conclude with clarification and summing up. It can be helpful to have a stimulus activity to get you started. This could include talking about a relevant object, some photographs, or asking the children to do a drawing to bring to the discussion. You will need a video or digital recorder to enable you to review the discussion later. The time span will depend on the age of the children and their ability to concentrate on one activity. For more on the use of focus groups in classroom based research see Vaughn et al. (1996).

The sign of a good focus group is when the participants no longer wait for the next question and respond individually, but enter into a discussion among themselves on the topic you have initiated. In this way they will generate more ideas than they might while working individually, as in draw and write, but there will be group interactions to manage. Shy pupils, those who most fear being wrong or saying something 'silly', may find it harder to contribute in a group. Equally more vocal pupils will dominate the conversation if allowed to do so. Both effects will limit the range of ideas and views the group can generate. If this is the case try using paired discussion based on friendship groups.

Paired discussion

This approach works well when children are used to open ended questions or have a lot to say about a topic, which means a group can get lively and difficult to manage, or where quiet children find it hard to contribute as part of a larger group. The result is a longer, deeper and more sustained interaction which can really help you see things from the children's point of view.

Ask children to discuss a topic in pairs. Provide a quiet but not isolated space, where you can keep an eye on them without having to be part of the conversation once they get started. As with focus groups and the circle time activity, you may need a stimulus to get the discussion started, or a few carefully worded, open ended questions may be enough. You can remain with them or leave them to discuss while their conversation is recorded using a video camera or digital recorder. Your role is not to guide or direct the conversation. You may need to encourage the flow of discussion initially, but you should be able to leave them to talk, once started, moving on to get another pair talking. When this works best it will seem, when you play back the recording, as if you are eavesdropping on a private conversation (Mayall, 2000). This approach has been used with teenagers when sensitive issues are being discussed (Highet, 2003) but can be used equally well with younger children.

Photography

Now that we have digital cameras it is a relatively straightforward matter to ask children to photograph or video-record aspects of their environment which they might associate with a topic in PSHE education. In Chapter 8 we describe how you can use photography to initiate learning about safety and risk in a range of familiar and unfamiliar environments.

In all these examples the children should know what the purpose of the activity is – whether planning for teaching or 'research', the findings of which will be shared with others. Older pupils may be really interested in why teachers do research so be prepared to answer a few open ended questions if they ask!

Into practice

Think about your next PSHE education session. Try to use one of the suggestions in this chapter to find out where the children are, before you begin teaching. Take a few minutes to reflect on the range of knowledge and understanding the children can already demonstrate. Now think about what you would like them to learn. What are the next steps? How can you scaffold the learning and differentiate the tasks you give the children so that they all have a chance to achieve the learning outcomes?

> **Chapter summary**
>
> All the approaches described in this chapter should give children and young people an opportunity to contribute to the development of their PSHE lessons and programmes. You will be surprised (and hopefully delighted!) by how much they know and how differently from you they see the world you all occupy. There will be gaps in their knowledge that you can help them to fill, and some misunderstandings which you can help them to address, but try not to mistake a difference of view for misunderstanding or stupidity. See the world through their eyes and you will have a chance to learn too.

> **Further reading**
>
> Fraser, S., Lewis, V., Ding, S., Kellett, M. and Robinson, C. (2004) *Doing Research with Children and Young People*. London: Sage.
> *An excellent overview of the philosophy, politics and ethics of doing research with children and young people, including involving young people as researchers.*
> Greene, S. and Hogan, D. (2005) *Researching Children's Experience*. London: Sage.
> *This includes ways to research children's behaviour, so goes beyond the methods for school based research described in this chapter.*
> Wilson, E. (2012) *School-based Research*. London: Sage.
> *A helpful, practical guide to classroom based research.*

References

Backett-Milburn, K. and McKie, L. (1999) 'A critical appraisal of the draw and write technique', *Heath Education Research: Theory and Practice*, 14 (3): 387–98.

Balding, J. (1985) *Health Education Priorities for the Primary School Curriculum*. Exeter: HEA/Schools Health Education Unit, University of Exeter.

Green, J. (1997) *Risk and Misfortune: The Social Construction of Accidents*. London: UCL.

Highet, G. (2003) 'Cannabis and smoking research: interviewing young people in self selected friendship pairs', *Health Education Research: Theory and Practice*, 18 (1): 108–18.

Mayall, B. (2000) 'Conversations with children: working with generational issues', in P. Christensen and A. James (eds), *Research with Children: Perspectives and Practices*. London: Falmer Press, pp. 120–35.

McWhirter, J.M. and South, N. (2004) *Young People and Risk*. Report for Government Office East.

McWhirter, J.M., Collins, M., Wetton, N.M., Bryant, I. and Newton Bishop, J.A. (2000) 'Evaluating safe in the sun: a curriculum programme for primary schools', *Health Education Research: Theory and Practice*, 15 (2): 203–17.

McWhirter, J.M., Young, A.J. and Wetton, N.M. (2004) 'In a class of its own: introducing a new tool for understanding adolescents' perceptions of the world of drugs', *Health Education Journal*, 63 (4): 307–23.

Mortimer, F.S. (1997) 'Adults' perception of risk'. Unpublished MSc dissertation, University of Southampton.

Vaughn, S.R., Schumm, J.S. and Sinagub, J.M. (1996) *Focus Group Interviews in Education and Psychology*. London: Sage.

Williams, T., Wetton, N. and Moon, A. (1989a) *A Picture of Health*. London: HEA.

Williams, T., Wetton, N. and Moon, A. (1989b) *A Way In: Five Key Areas of Health Education*. London: HEA.

CHAPTER 5

UNDERSTANDING EMOTIONAL DEVELOPMENT AND EMOTIONAL INTELLIGENCE

Aim

To ensure you understand 'emotional intelligence' and realise the importance of exploring feelings with growing children.

Learning objectives

By the end of this chapter you will:

- have an understanding of the terms 'emotional health', 'emotional wellbeing' and 'emotional intelligence'
- understand the contribution PSHE education offers, in its role as part of the wider curriculum and whole school culture, to developing children's emotional intelligence
- appreciate the nature of progression in developing emotional intelligence.

Getting started

> **Teaching activity**
>
> In Chapter 4 we suggested that you ask children to draw a picture of a healthy person. If you have not done this yet try it now.
> Now look at the children's drawings. How many have smiling faces? How many have drawn pictures of people with their arms raised? Many children instinctively know that there is a relationship between our physical health and our emotional state.

There is no health without mental health. (WHO, 2009)

Have you ever been somewhere where you felt really comfortable, either where you are always able to relax and enjoy others' company, or where you can really focus on achieving outcomes knowing everyone around you is supporting you? Perhaps this is an example of being in a state of *emotional wellbeing*.

Poor emotional wellbeing can lead to mental health concerns such as stress, depression and anxiety, while positive emotional wellbeing can contribute to increased coping ability, self-esteem, performance and productivity (Fredrickson and Joiner, 2002). Emotional health is more than just how a person feels.

Have you ever been in a different situation where either you have found your own emotions are getting in the way of you achieving something, or you have needed to think carefully about what you say and do in order to work successfully with someone else? We might call this an example of a need to behave in an *emotionally intelligent* way either in order to better manage ourselves or better manage a relationship. A planned programme of PSHE education can support the development of these skills.

Emotional wellbeing and emotional intelligence are mutually supportive. Behaving in emotionally intelligent ways can help to create and maintain positive relationships which in turn help create the supportive networks and communities that can underpin our own emotional wellbeing. Children who are better able to behave in emotionally intelligent ways in turn contribute to the maintenance of a school ethos that promotes the mental health and emotional wellbeing of the school community. This in turn models emotionally intelligent behaviour to individual pupils.

> **Consider**
>
> What do you think it means for a child to be 'emotionally intelligent'? What skills would they have? How might this change the way they behave towards other children and adults? What are the benefits to children who learn to behave in emotionally intelligent ways?

Introduction

Our feelings are often critically important in our decision making. We may find ourselves making our decisions based not on what we know about something but on how we feel about what we know. Even if we choose to override our feelings they may have influenced our decision. Some feelings like fear are our brain's way of drawing our attention to something that might hurt us, physically or emotionally. Feelings of pleasure alert us to things that we may want to repeat. Most of us experience a range of feelings and each feeling has intensity. Some can be experienced as little more than mild passing waves, while some can be overpowering and unbearable.

Emotional literacy could be defined as:

> the ability to understand ourselves and other people and in particular to be aware of, understand, and use information about the emotional states of ourselves and others with competence. It includes the ability to understand, express and manage our own emotions and respond to the emotional needs of others in ways that are helpful to ourselves and others. (Weare, 2004: 2)

We are aware that there are differences of view between authors about how to define terms such as 'emotional literacy' and 'emotional intelligence'. This is to be expected in what is, essentially, an emerging field.

One of the most important skills we can teach children is to recognise and name feelings in themselves and in others, and so develop their emotional vocabulary. This vocabulary could be thought of as lying on two dimensions, the range of feelings being one axis and the intensity on the other. For example, feeling safe and feeling scared are different, while uneasy, anxious, scared, frightened and terrified provide a range for the feeling 'scared'. Being able to clearly recognise and communicate our own feelings is an essential element in communication. It is equally important to be able to recognise, appreciate and respond to another's feelings in an emotionally intelligent way (see Chapter 3 on ethos for more on empathy).

The theoretical background

Any model is just that, a model. It is no more the real world than a model of a ship or aeroplane is a real ship or aeroplane. Models can help us deconstruct complex ideas and through testing can be refined to better reflect reality. All of the models below have faced criticism but are helpful for teachers to consider how we might structure learning to support the development of emotional literacy.

So what are the 'emotions'? Plutchik (in Plutchik and Kellerman, 1980) identified eight primary emotions (anger, fear, sadness, disgust, surprise, anticipation, trust and joy) but since we might experience emotions in combination the true number is far larger.

In his book *Frames of Mind: The Theory of Multiple Intelligences*, Howard Gardner (1983) introduced the idea of multiple intelligences: that intelligence is not one attribute but is more like a spectrum of attributes. The question was no longer '*How able is this child?*' but '*How is this child able?*'.

Two intelligences that relate to emotional intelligence are:

- *interpersonal intelligence* – the capacity to understand the intentions, motivations and desires of other people, and
- *intrapersonal intelligence* – the capacity to understand oneself, to appreciate one's feelings, fears and motivations.

There are different definitions of emotional intelligence. Mayer et al. (2001) define it as the ability to perceive emotion, integrate emotion to facilitate thought, understand emotions and regulate emotions to promote personal growth. They identify four abilities:

- the ability to perceive emotions in others and in ourselves
- the ability to use emotions to best fit the task at hand
- the ability to understand emotions, and how they work together and evolve over time, and
- the ability to manage emotions, being able to regulate emotions in ourselves and others.

Goleman (1998) offers a set of competencies:

- self-awareness – knowing our own emotions and their impact on others
- self-regulation – controlling or directing our own disruptive emotions and adapting to change
- social skill – managing relationships to enable other people to achieve a desired outcome
- empathy – recognising and considering others' feelings when making a decision
- motivation – being driven to achieve for its own sake.

Petrides and Furnham (2003) take a different approach. Instead of measuring ability they argue that emotional intelligence is best identified through self-reflection and reporting, organised under four factors:

- wellbeing
- self-control
- emotionality
- sociability.

Finally Bar-On (2006) defines emotional intelligence as being concerned with effectively understanding oneself and others, relating well to people and adapting to and coping with the immediate surroundings in order to be more successful in dealing with environmental demands.

All of these models have faced criticism, and emotional intelligence has proved difficult to measure. Some of the early claims for emotional intelligence in terms of predicting future life chances have been difficult to prove empirically. However, regardless of these criticisms and difficulties, developing the range of qualities and abilities that are encompassed by the term 'emotional intelligence' is clearly desirable simply for day-to-day living.

SEAL – Social and Emotional Aspects of Learning

One of the largest projects to undertake development of emotional intelligence in school children was the government-funded SEAL programme (Social and Emotional Aspects of Learning).

SEAL is not, nor was it intended to be, an alternative to PSHE education. The Department for Education and Skills (DfES, 2007) defined it as 'a comprehensive, whole-school approach to promoting the social and emotional skills that are thought to underpin effective learning, positive behaviour, regular attendance, and emotional wellbeing'.

The SEAL programme offered both a planned programme and opportunities for curriculum enrichment, for example material for assemblies. While it complemented PSHE education it also complemented other subjects, including English. However, a school that replaced PSHE education with SEAL would have been denying children access to much of the learning offered by PSHE education (for example safety, medicines and drugs, healthy eating).

The SEAL programme was intended to develop five main areas:

- self-awareness
- empathy
- social skills
- motivation
- managing feelings.

SEAL developed these through lessons that fell into six broad themes, each covered during a half-term, which were revisited with increasingly complex work each year of the primary school (there was a complementary programme in secondary schools). The themes were:

- new beginnings
- getting on and falling out
- going for goals
- good to be me
- relationships
- changes.

An evaluation of SEAL by Hallam (2009: 313) showed:

> Of the school staff, 90% agreed that the programme had been at least relatively successful overall. All responding head teachers, 87% of teachers and 96% of non-teaching staff agreed that the programme promoted the emotional wellbeing of children, while 82% of teachers agreed that it increased pupils' ability to control emotions such as anger. The interview data indicated that the programme had increased staff understanding of the social and emotional aspects of learning and helped them to better understand their pupils, which changed their behaviour, enhanced their confidence in their interactions with pupils, and led them to approach behaviour incidents in a more thoughtful way.

At the time of writing, the SEAL project had been transferred to a website called teachfind.com, and could be accessed and its resources downloaded by using this link: http://bit.ly/1bNHhkt (accessed 7 January 2014). Under 'See also' on that page we recommend you click the link: 'SEAL curriculum materials: Year by year'.

Into practice

One of the most powerful routes into this work is through children's stories, which is why we have described this so fully in Chapter 6. Reading a story to children can lead to various ways of exploring feelings, by inviting them: to share what they think characters are feeling at different moments; to recall a time when they may have had that feeling; to put their hand where that feeling happens (it can be a revelation when children see how many of their peers experience feelings in the same part of their bodies); or perhaps to show the person beside them how they looked when they had that feeling.

> **Personal activity**
>
> Take a children's book, read it through and consider the feelings it might help you explore with children. (For example, look for *The Second Princess* by Oram and Ross (1995). This is a short picture book about a princess who decides to have her sister murdered by the big bad wolf and the three bears.) Try to identify all the feelings your chosen book could help a class to explore.

We can help children to understand that one feeling can be good or not so good in different circumstances. For example, is fear always a not-so-good feeling? If it helps us to avoid danger it is a great feeling. We encourage not using the word 'bad' to describe feelings that may be uncomfortable – whatever the degree. It isn't the feeling itself that is bad – a word often used for food that is rotten or an act that is wicked. Not-so-good feelings are the ones you *may* not want to feel, or seek, or wish would go away. However, if you experience fear when someone dares you to do something that might be dangerous, this is a good feeling and one you should listen to, but if you experience fear outside a birthday party because you might not know many people inside, perhaps this is a time to take a deep breath and ignore it. The fear of watching the frightening bits of *Dr Who*, or the fear you may feel at the top of the roller coaster, may be desirable and uncomfortable at the same time. Exploring 'fear' offers a rich opportunity to help children to learn about the significance of context and judgement as key factors in understanding a situation where there is strong feeling. Or any feeling.

Three uses of circles

Many schools make use of circles both as a teaching pedagogy for PSHE education and as a means of developing and managing the relationships within the classroom. It is important not to confuse the two. 'Circle time' is probably most commonly associated with Mosley (1998) and is a discrete activity within the curriculum that can help a class develop as a cohesive and supportive community, and if necessary resolve difficulties. Sitting children in a circle can also offer a powerful environment for promoting discussion as part of a planned PSHE education programme. It provides an arrangement that communicates both equality and feelings of safety. In this more intimate setting, children can find it is easier to explore feelings, ideas and situations that they find difficult or uncomfortable. For example, you could explore the feelings of a character in a story by asking each child in the circle, as you read through the story, to offer a word for how a character is feeling at a given moment. In this way, you can choose the best moments to explore, perhaps picking on 'crunch' moments when the class is old enough to grasp this concept, and help the children understand the importance of feelings in helping them decide what to do or say, or sometimes getting in the way of a good decision. The third use is a class Circle of Feelings. Draw a big circle on a large sheet and inside it record the feeling words the children use, as each arises. Leave the circle on permanent display. As new words emerge describing children's or story character's feelings (pleased, nervous), or the strength of that feeling (joyful, terrified), add them to this growing record of the children's emotional vocabulary.

Into practice – a progressive programme of learning objectives

In Chapter 9 on sex and relationships education, we offer a developmental structure for teaching children the skills of developing good relationships with others. This work clearly complements work on children's emotional development. The following outlines a strand on developing feelings drawn from one local authority's programme of study (Speechly-Watson, n.d.) and building on the early learning goals.

Self-confidence and self-esteem:

- respond to significant experiences, showing a range of feelings when appropriate

Dispositions and attitudes:

- be confident to ... speak in a familiar group
- maintain attention, concentrate and sit quietly when appropriate

Self-confidence and self-esteem:

- have a developing awareness of their own feelings and be sensitive to the feelings of others

Making relationships:

- work as part of a group or class, taking turns and sharing fairly, understanding that there needs to be agreed values and codes of behaviour for groups of people, including adults and children, to work together harmoniously

Behaviour and self-control:

- understand what is right, what is wrong and why
- consider the consequences of their words and actions for themselves and others.

Learning objectives for ages five to six years might include children learning:

- about some of the things that help people to feel good about their days
- to identify what makes them feel good about their days
- about some of the things that might make people feel not so good about their days
- a vocabulary of not-so-good feelings
- about what they can do to make themselves feel better when they are feeling not so good
- about how it might feel to be scared or uneasy
- about what they could do if they were feeling scared or uneasy
- that all feelings are okay, but not all behaviours are okay
- a vocabulary of angry feelings
- some appropriate strategies for managing angry feelings
- a vocabulary for feeling good
- to recognise what they are good at.

EMOTIONAL DEVELOPMENT AND EMOTIONAL INTELLIGENCE

During ages six to seven years, learning:

- about some ways to manage feelings of excitement
- a vocabulary to describe feelings of excitement
- some words to describe feelings of disappointment
- about some ways that people manage feelings of disappointment
- how it might feel to lose something
- some strategies for managing feelings of loss
- that an ability to manage a range of feelings is important when working towards a goal
- ways of managing feelings of failure and frustration in order to persevere and stay motivated
- to think about and be sensitive to the feelings of others
- to begin to see things from other people's points of view
- about the effect of people's behaviour (e.g. boasting) on other people's feelings
- about why people boast and strategies for managing these feelings.

During ages seven to eight years, learning:

- a vocabulary for feeling happy
- to identify what makes them feel happy
- about how it feels to be sad
- about how people might behave when they are feeling sad
- ways that they can help when others are feeling sad
- to manage feelings of not being as good as others
- that being able to manage negative emotions positively can help you to achieve what you want
- that feelings (for example, jealousy) can be hidden and why people might hide their feelings
- that hidden feelings can build up, and what the effects of these feelings might be
- ways of recognising angry feelings
- some positive strategies for managing angry feelings
- about what 'confident' looks and feels like.

During ages eight to nine years, learning:

- about the difference between feelings and moods
- about the way that different moods affect them and others
- what they can do for themselves if they are in a bad mood and how they can help others

- how it might feel to be separated from someone/something we care about
- that there are many ways to manage the same feeling
- strategies for managing feelings of loss and separation
- about who can help them to manage uncomfortable feelings
- that people are different – in the way that they see things, do things and in what they are good at
- to feel good about and value themselves and who they are
- about what it means to have hope and why hope is important
- that when people are feeling negative about something, it sometimes helps to look at/think about things in a different way.

During ages nine to ten years, learning:

- about a range of moods and feelings and how they affect behaviour
- about mood swings and how to manage these
- a vocabulary for very strong feelings
- how strong feelings may cause people to act in a way that they would not usually act
- that different people may feel differently and react in different ways to the same situation
- to understand behaviour by thinking about what other people might be thinking/feeling
- that people sometimes feel the need to spend time alone
- where they could go if they were feeling the need to spend time alone
- about feelings that people might encounter while working to achieve a goal
- about skills, qualities and strategies which help people to overcome difficulties in order to achieve a goal
- about how making and achieving targets can make you feel good
- to set simple targets for themselves
- to break a long-term ambition into smaller, achievable goals.

During ages 10 to 11 years, learning:

- that sometimes people have conflicting feelings surrounding an issue or situation
- some strategies for managing conflicting feelings
- that people can be responsible for their own emotional states
- about some of the things that people can do to keep their emotional states 'in balance'
- that there are different ways to communicate feelings
- ways of telling how someone else is feeling

- that change is part of everyone's life experience
- a vocabulary of feelings for change
- some strategies for managing change
- about feelings that children may have about moving to secondary school
- to have strategies for managing their feelings about moving to secondary school
- that preparation can help individuals to cope more effectively with change
- about some preparations that they can make for starting secondary school
- to reflect on and celebrate what they have achieved in Key Stage 2.

Chapter summary

The emotional competence of children – their ability to recognise and manage emotions in themselves and others – is a key to being able to make and sustain good relationships and to manage situations where feelings are strong and germane.

In this chapter we have described how emotional intelligence can be fostered in the classroom, and indicated the nature of progression towards competence.

Further reading

Boddington, N. and Hull, T. (1996) *The Health Promoting School – Focusing on Health and School Improvement.* London: Forbes.
Weare, K. (2004) *Developing the Emotionally Literate School.* London: Paul Chapman Publishing.
Weare, K. (2013) *Promoting Mental, Emotional and Social Health: A Whole School Approach.* London: Routledge.
These three publications consider the importance of a whole school approach to developing children's emotional wellbeing, and how such activity can impact on whole school improvement.
Fredrickson, B.L. and Joiner, T. (2002) 'Positive emotions trigger upward spirals toward emotional well-being', *Psychological Science,* 13: 172–5.
This paper explores the prediction that positive emotions broaden attention and cognition and increase emotional wellbeing.

(Continued)

> *(Continued)*
>
> WHO (1986) *Ottawa Charter for Health Promotion*. Geneva: WHO. Available at: www.who.int/healthpromotion/conferences/previous/ottawa/en/index1.html (accessed 8 October 2013).
> *This Charter defined the fundamental conditions and resources for health.*
>
> WHO (2009) *Mental Health: Strengthening Our Response*. Fact sheet no. 220, September. Geneva: WHO. Available at: www.who.int/mediacentre/factsheets/fs220/en/ (accessed 10 January 2014).
> *This paper strengthens the connection between mental health and our wider overall health.*

References

Bar-On, R. (2006) 'The Bar-On model of emotional-social intelligence (ESI)', *Psicothema*, 18 (supl): 13–25.

DfES (2007) *Social and Emotional Aspects of Learning for Secondary Schools (SEAL) Guidance Booklet*. Nottingham: Department for Education and Skills.

Fredrickson, B.L. and Joiner, T. (2002) 'Positive emotions trigger upward spirals toward emotional well-being', *Psychological Science*, 13: 172–5.

Gardner, H. (1983) *Frames of Mind: The Theory of Multiple Intelligences*. New York: Basic Books.

Goleman, D. (1998) *Working with Emotional Intelligence*. New York: Bantam Books.

Hallam, S. (2009) 'An evaluation of the Social and Emotional Aspects of Learning (SEAL) programme: promoting positive behaviour, effective learning and well-being in primary school children', *Oxford Review of Education*, 35 (3): 313–39.

Mayer, J.D., Salovey, P., Caruso, D.L. and Sitarenios, G. (2001) 'Emotional intelligence as a standard intelligence', *Emotion*, 1: 232–42.

Mosley, J. (1998) *Turn Your School Round: Circle-time Approach to the Development of Self-esteem and Positive Behaviour in the Primary Staffroom, Classroom and Playground*. Wisbech: LDA.

Oram, H. and Ross, T. (1995) *The Second Princess*. London: Collins Picture Lions.

Petrides, K.V. and Furnham, A. (2003) 'Trait emotional intelligence: behavioral validation in two studies of emotion recognition and reactivity to mood induction', *European Journal of Personality*, 17: 39–75.

Plutchik, R. and Kellerman, H. (eds) (1980) *Emotion: Theory, Research, and Experience: Vol. 1. Theories of Emotion*, ed. R. Plutchik and H. Kellerman. New York: Academic Press.

Speechly-Watson, N. (n.d.) Planning tool for PSHE&C. Chelmsford: Essex Local Authority.

Weare, K. (2004) *Developing the Emotionally Literate School*. London: Paul Chapman Publishing.

WHO (2009) *Mental Health: Strengthening our Response*. Fact sheet no.220, September. Geneva: WHO. Available at: www.who.int/mediacentre/factsheets/fs220/en/ (accessed 10 January 2014).

CHAPTER 6

UNDERSTANDING THE PEDAGOGY OF PSHE EDUCATION

Aim

To set out some common teaching methods suitable for PSHE education.

Learning objectives

While reading this chapter you will:

- understand the crucial difference between methods most suitable for PSHE education and those more suited to academic subjects
- appreciate the rationale for involving children in their PSHE learning
- explore the role of the teacher as facilitator
- understand the power and potency of using story and drama to aid learning
- become familiar with other active teaching methods.

Getting started

> ### 💭 Consider
> Think about this statement: In order to be ready to teach a subject to children, you need to have studied it thoroughly and to have all the information at your fingertips.
>
> Now consider: Do you know all you need to about every element of PSHE education? What if a child asks a question in a PSHE lesson and you don't know the answer?

A change of emphasis

There are significant differences between teaching PSHE education and teaching most other subject areas – most particularly, academic subjects. Consider a subject where the teacher is well informed and expert, the children much less so, and where the main aim of the teaching is principally to increase the children's knowledge level in that subject. In such situations, the teacher assumes the role of expert, able to impart knowledge, which may often take the form of information. If children ask questions, they expect the teacher to know the answers, or at the very least to know where to find the answers. Mostly, the teacher will indeed know the answer – often a single, unambiguous 'right' answer. In such teaching situations, the children quickly find out that you know more than they do, and learn to accept that what you know is what they need to learn.

Here lies the fundamental difference. In teaching PSHE education, the transfer of knowledge is often far less central though it remains important. More pivotal are:

- the skills the children need to develop, practise and learn to apply
- the confidence they need to make key decisions and carry them out
- sound understanding of their growing role in taking care of themselves in partnership with key others whose role slowly declines as the children grow in capability
- learning to be accountable for their actions and decisions
- becoming proficient at learning from their experience and from the experiences of others
- accepting that in every class or group there is likely to be a range of points of view and attitudes, each of which may be valid
- developing an unshakeable belief in their own worth.

This list is not exhaustive. Once you add the vital ingredient of starting where children are (see Chapter 4) with possibly a whole class full of differing experiences and levels of understanding – a series of lessons confined to information-giving, however expertly conducted, seems less like a good idea. Of course, there generally is important information relevant to each specific PSHE education topic that needs to accompany developmental work. For example, it wouldn't be much use to children to be committed to road safety, and with the confidence to cross the road, if they didn't also know the steps set out in, for example, the Green Cross Code. But equally, consider a young person out and about, who feels unsafe, perhaps lost or unwell, and knows the importance of seeking help when it's needed, but doesn't have the confidence to ask anyone. A range of useful skills and healthy attitudes needs to be underpinned by the knowledge necessary for deciding when, how and why they are to be used, and the likely consequences if they aren't.

This chapter explores how to reduce reliance on your own factual knowledge, and increase both the focus on the skills your class needs to develop, and the attitudes and experiences they need to explore. With that approach in mind it becomes more straightforward to construct lessons that move them forward.

Differences in practice

There are two key steps in this move away from a simple 'provider' role to one that is more of a facilitator.

The first key step is to move beyond the idea of right and wrong answers, and away from any need to feel you are an authority on every area of content you or your class choose to focus upon. When a child asks a question, there may be more than one helpful answer. A question such as 'What should I say when I need help?' needs some thought by the class, not a single formula that may not fit all children nor all situations. How urgent is the need for help? What kind of help is needed? What sort of person may provide such help? You no longer need to be seen as 'having all the answers'; the value can be more lasting to children if they arrive at their own answer, or help each other to consider options and outcomes, and arrive at a group of suitable strategies to deal with particular circumstances. Noreen Wetton often reminded us that children need to discover the words that fit in their own mouths. Sometimes there may appear a single right answer. 'If he hits me, should I hit him back?' You certainly won't want to encourage violence, but rather than providing 'the answer', help the class explore the options, and the consequences, until they see more clearly what makes best sense. Even when there is a simple factual question, it can often be more useful to encourage the young person to become a successful researcher than always to rely exclusively on you as their source of information and wisdom. Others in the class, or those at home, may know. Or, as the children become more adept at information technology, electronic sources may be checked out, though information brought back to the class from any source may still need to be confirmed, as information can go out of date and websites can be unreliable. This means your job is sometimes more that of an arbiter than a fount of wisdom. In a climate such as this, where enquiry itself is valued, it is also entirely appropriate for any member of the class, including you, to be open about not knowing the answer to every factual question. This can reinforce that 'not knowing' is a legitimate starting point for further enquiry, and not a cue to scorn others' ignorance.

More often, though, the most significant questions from children will warrant a less singular or precise answer, and these are the questions that may be most helpful to explore during a lesson, using the whole class as research tool for their own queries. And when the children *don't* ask those important questions that help focus upon the nub of real life situations, about feelings, options, consequences, responsibilities, current class perceptions and limitations? *You* ask them. For example: '(In this situation) what might happen next?'

Open-ended questions and thinking time

The best prompts are often open-ended questions: 'Have you ever been in that position – what did *you* do?', 'Can you tell me a useful or important thing you have learned (from that story, from our discussion)?', 'How could you make use of what you have just learned?' Relevance and learning will frequently differ from pupil to pupil and this is not only appropriate – it is quite inevitable. Acknowledging diversity of response and opinion both recognises and respects individual difference, and encourages children to think for themselves (rather than try to guess what you are thinking or simply say what they think you want them to say).

'Thinking time' is important, too. An obvious pause after a request for a response will tell pupils you are genuinely wanting them to think and then answer. 'I can see you're still thinking about this' can punctuate a pause without adding pressure. A further wait after a helpful-sounding response can underline your desire for several responses, not a single 'right' answer. Thank those who contribute.

Framing the sort of questions that stimulate constructive thought is one of the most important things you can do. It turns your class from a group of passive recipients of wisdom into a community of enquiry, where considering important questions is helpful, exciting, challenging, worthwhile. And it turns the class into a group of young people capable of *finding* answers as well as asking them, which is a powerful confidence booster, as well as a skill that will always be valuable.

> **Consider**
>
> What are the practical differences between didactic, active and interactive teaching methods for you, the teacher? What might be the benefits and disadvantages of each, to the children?

Active methodology

The second key step is to help children be active and interactive in the class. Children's active participation in their own learning is perhaps more important in PSHE education than anywhere else in the school curriculum. There is a sound rationale for young people to be active for much of the time in their PSHE education lessons. Children are far keener on project work in groups, and class debates, than long periods of reading or listening, and can easily become bored on an unbroken diet of worksheets and writing tasks. See Chapter 2, where we explore the background to effective teaching in PSHE education.

PSHE education aims to help children develop a sound understanding of themselves and their lives, and to become competently responsible for their behaviour and their welfare. If they willingly consider important questions that will help develop their judgement, their skills and their competence, they need to feel involved in the very fabric of the PSHE education lessons that aim to bring about this development.

Active means involved!

Perhaps the most obvious benefit is that when learners are active, they are more likely to be closely engaged with the subject matter than when they are solely listeners. Even when you expect children to be listeners, they may not always be listening. The attention span of a healthy five-year-old is quite short, typically 8–10 minutes when enjoying an activity, and shorter than that when not, and having something interesting to do can help actively impede the temptation for a young mind to wander. (Note, though, that if children display symptoms of Attention Deficit and Hyperactivity Disorder, difficulty in concentrating may persist and they may be easily distracted whatever the task.) Relevance of lesson content (see Chapter 4) helps enormously with this engagement, too. The class needs to feel close to the material being explored. While they are very young it is not realistic to hope that they will make the judgement to immerse themselves in something that may become relevant when they are older. As they grow, and their horizons and aspirations widen, they may want to do precisely that, but you will need to use enquiry activities to establish when they are ready for such jumps.

Another advantage is that when the whole class is active, no child need feel left out. Everyone can contribute and, following the activity, taking feedback sensitively helps ensure that these contributions are both heard and valued.

If the children are active 'for much of the time', what about 'the rest of the time'? Activity needs to be balanced with opportunities to reflect, and sometimes to listen. Reflection is important and each lesson needs to allow for some reflection time, perhaps simply to think about an idea, a suggestion, or a question, or to frame one. Reflection time can also provide the chance for the children to think individually about the significance and value of a lesson that has just taken place. Listening, whether to other class members or to you, is also a key feature of PSHE education – a skill to be practised. Information input delivered in a didactic way can be just as important as the exploration of real life situations. The trick is to choose a suitable time when the children are receptive, perhaps at the precise moment they realise they are short of hard facts and that they need some. ('Doesn't anyone have an answer to that? Well, let's see if I can help!'). Make sure the input is highly relevant, short and punchy so that it matches the available attention span. Watch the children to see when attention generally starts to wander. You may find calling for everyone's attention once it has been lost may be less successful than changing the task back to a more active one at that point.

Children's literature can be an excellent source of useful information and a safe way to explore worries and feelings, to consider challenging or otherwise problematic situations, and to reflect on the wisdom or otherwise of particular courses of action. Telling the story becomes a stimulus to involvement, rather than a simple 'I tell and you listen!' approach. There are many ways of actively engaging the audience in the lives of the story's characters and the situations they encounter. Ways to use story are discussed in greater detail later in this chapter.

Interactive work

The engagement of each child with the relevant subject matter under scrutiny is helped by their active involvement, whether that means writing, drawing, thinking, answering, asking, playing, acting, designing or talking. Promoting and reinforcing interaction between the children themselves *as normal practice* in the classroom goes a step further. It is a powerful way to ensure each child recognises the value of the other children in the class as sources of ideas, sounding boards, allies, etc. It can be both fun and fruitful to work in pairs and consider another's ideas as well as your own. Working in a group may compound both the enjoyment and the output and can also helpfully put the spotlight on the relationships within a group and how tasks are undertaken, roles allotted and conflicts managed.

We now set out and describe a variety of teaching methods aimed at stimulating active involvement of the children, and – just as important – interaction. A crucial step, before undertaking any work that may have sensitive or personal content, is to ensure that everyone in the class feels safe and positive, and if not, to put that right.

The value of any activity or discussion is likely to be limited if the children feel they can only safely say things they think you or the class want to hear.

Classroom climate

The key condition for good PSHE education in every class is a constructive 'classroom climate'. We use this term as shorthand for how it feels to be a child in that class. Do I feel comfortable? Do I feel safe to open my mouth and say what I'm thinking? Am I the only one who thinks and feels as I do, or do most of the class think and feel the same as me? Can I say what I think and feel even if I think I'm the only one to feel like this? What if I say something silly? Will the others laugh at me? What if I say something nobody else agrees with – will they shout at me or make me feel small? Is it safe to talk about my mistakes as well as things I've done that I feel proud of? I'm not very clever and I feel a bit afraid …

These kinds of inner questions and feelings are not unique to young people. For new teachers, speaking up at a parents' evening or even a full staff meeting can sometimes feel quite an ordeal. But there is much that can be done to recognise such feelings in young children and help them all to feel safe enough to speak honestly and value each other's ideas and experiences for what they can contribute to helping *everyone* move forward. It is often from mistakes, whether real or projected, their own or others', that they can learn most. A young person with an idea or opinion that is different from everyone else's may provide just the stimulus that is needed to look at something from a different angle. Children confident enough, and skilled and practised enough, to stand up for themselves and speak out, are better prepared for situations later in their child and teenage years when this may be just what is needed.

In the early years, children will be quickly made aware of rules in the school. Places where they are allowed to run and places where they aren't. Times to speak and times to be quiet. Behaviour that is kind and considerate to others, and behaviour that is unfair and unkind, and not allowed. How they treat each other when talking about important ideas in the classroom is a bit different, partly because with the best will in the world, we cannot put rules in place that will determine for certain how children feel. The best rules are those in which the children have some investment; rules that, when broken, will not just make the teacher want to take action to remedy, but will make the children feel indignant too. This is best achieved by helping children to frame their own rules and helping them to feel some responsibility for policing them, with firm but caring responses to anyone stepping over the lines they have set.

Rules. Doesn't the very word sound like something imposed from outside? We think there are better terms to be found. One notable PSHE education programme for older children called them 'Our Keys to Co-operation'. Another possibility is 'Our Class Promises' – moving emphasis away from 'rulers' and 'ruled' to those making the promises. You will find your own way to describe them – or perhaps your class will choose the best term. We'll call them 'promises' for now.

For younger children aged five to seven years, a draw and write exercise will be more inclusive and less verbally focused. If children start early to become familiar with working within the confines of self-imposed and respectful ways of treating others, they will never again need to start entirely from scratch, simply revisiting and refining the pool of promises in the class agreement to reflect their older language and more developed ideas in the light of their experience. The principles are the same whatever the children's ages. The very youngest may not be ready to do this entirely without help from you, but they may be more capable and imaginative than you think, as long as they have a framework for expressing it. That is where a draw and write exercise can help. Almost all children can draw, and most are capable of telling you what they have drawn, even if they cannot write it down. In some exercises of this kind they will need to whisper to you, so as not to influence others. That is not so important in this instance as long as everyone is able to contribute.

Classroom climate – paired drawing and writing task

Sometimes, draw and write exercises are conducted individually, without talking or sharing ideas. On this occasion, when talking and sharing ideas is a crucial factor, it is best done in pairs or groups. There is guidance later on in this chapter about forming groups, but for this activity it is important that the children are with friends they feel comfortable talking to. Help them make pairs or groups of four or so and give each pair or group a piece of paper, pencil and crayons. Tell the class about Sam (could be a boy or a girl) who is the same age as they are. Ask them to imagine Sam has a secret he or she wants to tell the class about, but is a bit nervous. Sam wonders what the other children might think. Their task is to draw a big outline of Sam, and then inside their drawing to draw or write all the things that the rest of the children in the class could do to help Sam feel comfortable enough to tell the secret to the whole class. Outside the outline, draw or write all the things other children in the class could do that would make Sam feel uncomfortable, and not want to say the secret.

Take feedback from the class on all the things inside the outline drawings. Ask how each one would make the children feel. Make a list of these feelings, too. Ask what else might make Sam feel it was safe to tell the secret. When the lists of actions, conditions, promises and feelings are exhausted, ask the children to tell you the things they have drawn or written outside the outline of Sam. Ask for and list the feelings they cause. Is there anything else that would make Sam feel unsafe to say the secret? What might the class need to promise not to do *after* Sam has told them the secret? Should those things be added to the second list, too?

Would Sam *have* to tell the secret if the children did everything in the first list? Of course not – Sam would have a choice. But emphasise that if Sam feels safe and comfortable (or any of the other positive feelings on the list) then he or she could choose what to say without being pressured either way, and could still decide to keep the secret. Suppose what Sam wanted to say wasn't really a secret but he or she was still not sure what the class would think or say. Would the things in the first list help? What about the things in the second list? Is everyone in the class prepared to put up their hand to say they will keep to the first list and not do the things on the second?

In this scenario the children have generated the promises they need. The lists can be mounted on the wall. They can be added to or amended as time goes on. If your guidance is needed, particularly with the very young, you will guide. But the children's own ideas about constraints provide the basis from which they can learn how effective the promises are as they put them into practice. Make sure the class knows these promises are to help everyone in this class feel safe and comfortable enough to say what's in their head or on their mind but are not intended to try to force them to say anything they don't want to. The draw and write technique is described more generally, and fully, in Chapter 4.

Towards the top end of junior school, with children aged 9–11 years, one useful activity we have found for generating such promises is to use paper squares as bricks to build a solid foundation of helpful behaviours. Invite individuals or small groups to generate promises, one to a square. Make sure each 'promise' is on a separate paper square and Blu-Tacked up to make a wall of promises – this means they can be moved up and down if one needs to be given a higher focus: 'Let's all try really hard to work on this one' or 'What could we do better to meet this one?' Celebrate when a promise is so well kept that it doesn't need to be displayed any more. Remove it, and keep it in an envelope in case it's needed again later. Be ready to revisit any promise that causes difficulty, checking it's understood and that everyone values it and promises to keep it.

Return to the list of promises whenever you need to, and ask the class how well they are working. If and when promises are broken, use the opportunity to ask what should be done to make sure people keep their promises, and what might happen when they don't. Emphasise that you want promises kept, but not promise-breakers made to feel bad! Perhaps they will suggest saying sorry if they laugh or interrupt, or saying or doing something nice to try to make up for saying or doing something unhelpful, thoughtless or hurtful.

Classroom climate – foundation activity

For older children, the process is very similar though perhaps with more sophisticated contributions. If they are ready, you could suggest that they work in pairs to generate promises (or whatever helpful name seems more appropriate), using the same stimulus of secrets, sensitive ideas or stories, points of view or feelings, and the behaviours and conditions that make the class feel safe enough to express them when nervous of laughter, derision or dissent. Ask the pairs to write them on squares of paper, one to a slip. Then, invite the pairs to think of their slips as bricks, and tell them the class will build a wall of promises brick by brick. Get each pair to add one, explaining their thinking, and ask the class to amend it if necessary until they agree to be bound by it. By ages 9 to 11 years, they may be familiar with the term 'put-downs' and may suggest that 'put-ups' may go some way to heal hurt feelings. Go with their ideas as much as possible.

Can the children take some responsibility for ensuring the promises are kept and for pointing out when they are not? Explore the mechanics of this with them – it may vary from age to age. Personal investment in promise-keeping reinforces the idea of children being responsible for their own behaviour and not always relying on you or another adult to act as the authority figure. Avoid simply appointing a 'police officer' from among the class, as this may serve to remove responsibility for promise-keeping from everyone else.

It is hard to overstate the importance of a positive, safe, trusting climate within the class. It can set just the right tone for PSHE education, though its constructive influence is not limited to one subject – all subjects can benefit from this positive climate.

Active methodology

Incomplete sentences

One strategy for introducing a topic or starting a class discussion is to start with an incomplete sentence such as 'It is risky if you ...' or 'It is always safe to ...', and ask the children to complete it individually or in groups before sharing ideas with the whole class. If you choose a sentence where content is likely to be sensitive, and writing is appropriate, slips could be used and then collected in to ensure anonymity. But in any case class discussion to explore the ideas generated can helpfully highlight harmonious or conflicting views. It can be useful to invite those brave enough to explain what their response means or why they hold a particular opinion. This can be very powerful in getting children to think for themselves, to challenge each other constructively and perhaps to re-assess their standpoints.

Working alone

A short period of individual work can ensure that everyone has a contribution to make when group or class interaction follows. Tasks may be varied, but may include reflection, drawing and listing. For example, an instruction such as 'Draw (or write) one thing you are allowed to do, and one thing you are not' could lead on to a shared group or class discussion about disapproval, fairness, health, safety, freedom, limits, rules and laws. There may be differences in what is permitted or encouraged at home and school, or between one home and another. Judge carefully when you think the children are mature enough to discuss such differences, or whether it is more appropriate simply to accept them.

Overall, there is less of a role for individual reading and writing exercises in primary school PSHE education, although these may have their place, particularly as pupils become more competent in these skills. As IT skills increase, individual research and feedback can confer status and avoid you always appearing to act as information giver. Surveys among family members may also be effective at plumbing adults' opinions. For example, the results for a class-home survey 'How many hours' sleep do you think I should have?' can spark a discussion about how much is needed, the range of bedtimes, and bedtime routines like teeth cleaning and story time. 'Can you tell me something you know now that you wish you had known when you were my age and that you think all young people should know?' can elicit wise words from parents, carers and other grown-up relatives. Written responses will enable you to edit and select.

Working in groups

When children are old enough to be given a task to complete by themselves in a small group, there can be tangible advantages. For a child to speak in a small group, as long as the groups are ordered in such a way that everyone feels comfortable, may not be so daunting as speaking in front of the whole class. Ground can be covered quite fast when many young brains can pool ideas and several discussions can occur at once, often followed with enthusiastic feedback to the whole class.

Group organisation

A well-established classroom climate can assist smooth working among any combination of pupils, but you may want to engineer groupings yourself, to ensure that all the 'talkers', creative thinkers and shy children are judiciously shared between the groups; that social contact spreads more widely than friendship groups; that there is a good gender mix; that any pairs with an antipathy are kept apart, and so on. These criteria might depend on the subject matter and the task. In some situations, shyer children may work better together, in others they may gain more from being with more self-confident children. Sometimes the usual daily class seating arrangement may be a good basis for group tasks but varying the combinations can ring helpful changes. Sometimes random groups will work well, though the class may need to be prepared before issuing demanding instructions like 'Get into groups of three or four' or 'Get into groups with three others you haven't worked with before'. Beware of hurtful exclusions if you try self-selection. Where random groups seem like a good idea, a better method may be to line the class up according to height, birth date, alphabetically by given name or surname, and then to count off one by one – group 1, group 2, and so on – until everyone has been assigned to one of the perhaps five or six groups.

Otherwise, it will often be quicker and more satisfactory to select the groups yourself, on the basis of personalities you know, particularly if the children are very young. It can be a time-saving one-off task to make re-usable, named and laminated cards displaying several group symbols (e.g. animals, colours, objects, numbers). With some thought you can predetermine four different groupings in this way. Each child keeps their personalised card safe, and when asked to get into groups of animals, all the cats make a group, and the dogs, the elephants, etc. Numbers will produce a different set of groups, each digit having been selected by you beforehand and put carefully on the cards as you make them, to ensure the membership you choose.

Figure 6.1 Sample, named card with four categories for group formation

Group tasks might include pooling ideas or suggestions (sometimes called a brainstorm), a discussion on a particular subject, generation of a storyline, the production of a short presentation, the drawing of a storyboard or frieze to illustrate a situation – the list is long. Feedback to the class is important, giving everyone the chance to hear or see the contributions of others. Ask for one thing from each group to start with, to ensure no group is left out. The group task may be a precursor to a later task, for example: thinking of 'worrying situations' to be pooled and discussed as a class. However, sometimes the group task will be more substantial and self-contained. Feedback may then be rather different.

Mind the shop

One way to share children's ideas is simply to display them, perhaps on the wall. This is fine if they don't need any explanation. If they do, a longer method is to allow each group some time in turn to present their efforts to the class. One way to shorten this is to invite the class to walk round, looking at the work of the other groups, but leaving one person from each group behind to 'mind the shop'. The task for this minder is to answer questions the 'shoppers' might put, to interpret the group's work or explain their thinking. Leave a little time for the minders to look round, too, with a substitute minder if required.

Vivid stimulus

At the lower end of the age range, try introducing a topic with a vivid stimulus, such as a scenario forming the opening of a story, and give opportunities to the children to say how they feel about it and its characters, and what they think might/could/should happen next. You can help the class to generate extensions to the storyline by using words like 'Supposing …', with the children invited to say what it is they are asking their peers to 'suppose', before joining in to explore its ramifications.

Example (adapted from King, 2001)

> Gina was talking to her friend Josie as they walked out into the playground at the beginning of playtime.
>
> 'I like your bag. I want one like that.'
>
> 'Well you can't have mine, my Mum gave it to me.'
>
> 'I don't want yours, anyway. My Dad can get me a blue one if I ask him.'

Gina paused and then asked, 'What's in it?'

'My story book and an apple and my purse with £2.50 inside.'

Gina's eyes opened a bit wider. She knew they weren't supposed to bring money to school.

'Don't tell Miss Weston, or you'll be in trouble! What are you going to spend it on?'

'Sweets. At the sweet shop down the road.'

'Can I come?'

'OK, as long as you don't tell. If we go now when they're not looking, we can be back before playtime's over.'

Gina's eyes opened wider still and her eyebrows almost disappeared under her fringe …

What will Gina do? What would happen if she …? The children's imagination can make Gina strong or weak, daring or cautious, good or naughty, and help them explore the different scenarios that could ensue. Will Josie be susceptible to reason or is her mind made up? Is she trying to impress Gina? Does she just want a friend? (How do people pick friends?) What did Gina and Josie do? What happened next? Where were they when playtime ended? Did Miss Weston find out? What did she say? What did she do? And so on. There is no need to seek or emphasise a 'right' outcome to the story; instead, chair a discussion to consider the consequences so that the children shape what happens next, and perhaps a range of possible scenarios, each with a different ending. Allowing difference of view, emphasis or detail is part of supporting individual children to think they are trusted to think and act sensibly without always being told what to do, though your judgement will always be there, when needed, to decide precisely when to 'chair' and when to intervene. The lessons the children think Gina and Josie might learn as a result of the unfolding story might be turned into advice for bag-owners, friend-seekers or playground-players. But the story can be adapted as you go, or before you start. And the names and genders can be changed to anything else you like. What else might be in Josie's bag? Avoid introducing anything else that is dubious or forbidden into Josie's bag if very young children choose to omit them. Instead, let their own ideas determine what they explore. Further up the school, they may tentatively find such things in the fictitious bag as matches, other forbidden things, or things which aren't theirs. Help them explore their ideas.

There can be safety and security for children when dealing with issues at arm's length (a story, imaginary people, the ability to try out real ideas with characters other than themselves). The value of inviting children to imagine they are observors or advisors may not feel quite so safe: What would you be thinking? How might you feel? If you were to say anything to (name) what would it be? This device for inviting the children, or an individual child, to get closer to the action *reduces* the feelings of safety built into dealing with fiction – however real the situation itself. It needs careful thought and equally careful handling. We explore these steps more fully in the next section, where we look at the power of using story.

Using children's literature

How can the use of story assist us in teaching PSHE effectively? One way of making sense of PSHE education is not directly through topics or issues but by exploring 'moments' in our lives where these issues or topics become relevant. For example instead of 'Today we are going to talk about bullying', we could begin with a situation: 'Imagine someone you knew came to you and said, "Can you help me? They are bullying me!"' We could begin by asking pupils, 'In pairs, what would be the first question we might ask them?' We are already building a story.

In this country we have available to us one of the largest and most imaginative collections of children's literature in the world. Authors have created stories that both are engaging and provide us with the opportunity to take our classes into a wealth of wonderful and complex situations. Many primary schools build much of their PSHE education through the planned use of story.

Story offers one of the most powerful and emotionally safe routes into many of the various highly sensitive issues contained within PSHE education. For this reason we have devoted a major section of this chapter on pedagogy to the use of story.

We start by considering the use of someone else's story. However, there are many other ways story can be used: by inviting children either to construct their own stories or to complete unfinished stories. Stories can be written, told or acted out by children or perhaps puppets.

As a result of the sensitive nature of many of the issues explored within PSHE education it can sometimes be a challenge to find a route into the work. The use of story can help to slightly 'distance' an issue from the child. Rather than starting out by imagining ourselves in a difficult situation or dilemma, known as being 'associated in', we can use story to place other people in a similar situation or dilemma, known as 'working disassociated'.

> **Personal activity**
>
> Imagine looking up at someone of about your age standing at the top of a really high building looking down.
> Now imagine you are standing at the top of a really high building and you are the person looking down. Does it feel different?

This is more than just a 'clever idea'. Our brains react differently when considering someone else in a situation, or imagining ourselves in that same situation and 'seeing it through our own eyes'. This is even truer if we have had direct personal experience of a similar situation that we might recall.

One way of thinking about this is through emotional 'zones'. If we tell a story about a stranger this is in an emotionally cool zone. It doesn't mean we can't feel for them; it is just that it is slightly removed from us. Now imagine this person was a member of our class. This moves us a little closer. Now imagine it was our friend or best friend. Now we are closer still. Finally, and only if we consider it safe to do so, we can imagine it is us in this situation or facing this dilemma. It is happening to us right here, right now. This is the hot zone.

We can use our imagination, perhaps imagining ourselves there as bystanders to events but invisible and safe. Perhaps only one person in the story can see us and they ask us for our advice. As teachers we can literally 'play' with story using it in creative ways to help our pupils consider and deepen their understanding about complicated issues by exploring moments in the lives of the story's characters.

Human beings throughout history and in all cultures have liked listening to stories and, with the invention of writing and then printing, reading stories either to others or for ourselves. Children and adults who will admit to it love the opening 'Once upon a time' and the use of story to pass on our history; to share experiences and wisdom from our collective past is part of the oral tradition of story-telling.

When we hear the opening of a good story, one that we really connect with, many of us make pictures in our heads perhaps half seen or fully realised. We may hear the characters speaking; we may experience gentle or powerful emotions. Great authors help us imagine their story in our heads. It is a joint undertaking between the story-teller and the audience and each one of us creates our own internal version of the story, drawing on our prior experiences.

Perhaps we find ourselves anticipating the next part of the story or imagining the end. Perhaps we are disappointed with the direction of the story and want to construct a different plot or ending of our own. For children of all ages sharing in listening to a story is in itself a bonding activity. We collectively share something powerful, which is why people will often talk about a story long after it has finished.

A heard or read story is different from a film or television story. Here the images are all provided for us, we don't have to create the location or imagine the characters. Their feelings are expressed directly to us. We do not create the story in our own heads; we are presented with a location, characters and their reactions.

It is because the power of a good story can take an audience inside their heads to a situation, dilemma or choice, and draw on their own experience, that it offers such a powerful resource for teaching virtually all aspects of PSHE education.

Stories can be drawn from existing literature and can be complete stories or we can make them up ourselves. They can be very short:

> Jenny was sobbing. 'I can't believe she told everyone? How could she be so cruel? I trusted her and she totally let me down!'
>
> Sally sat down beside her. 'Tell me what has happened.'
>
> Jenny looked up, her eyes full of tears, 'Well,' she said. 'You know last night? Well I ...'

Or the shortest story Hemingway wrote:

> For sale, baby shoes, never worn.

These few words have a sort of 'gravity'; they pull us in through our imagination and encourage or perhaps even force us to be curious to know more.

Picture books

Perhaps picture books lie somewhere between film and text-based story. For children with limited experience they provide their imaginations with vivid images of key moments in the story and help children fill in the rest with their imaginations.

We have a truly amazing variety of picture books in virtually every classroom and these offer one of the richest resources for teaching PSHE that is available to us. In fact PSHE education programmes in many schools are based around the progressive use of children's storybooks. Many of these picture books are illustrated by some of the most talented artists in literature and their images are often both expressive and highly detailed, offering extra levels of communication in the same way as a great actor enriches the author's initial script. Many stories are also quite short, offering their message in only a few pages.

We would urge you not to consider picture books as only appropriate for use with younger children. With humour a picture book can be used to stimulate deep discussion with children of all ages and many can be used with adults. For example, in some instances a picture storybook used to raise important subject matter with younger children could be used with older age groups. Inviting them to consider how the teacher might make use of the book in this way may act as a stimulus to identifying significant issues for themselves.

Selecting stories

In the UK we have one of the richest collections of children's literature and a wealth of great stories many of which, with imagination, can take young people on a journey that is relevant to the learning that PSHE education seeks.

First and foremost a story must be a good one, one that you know will draw children in and hold their attention. Avoid books that have been deliberately written for teachers to use in the classroom to 'explore issues' or provide a 'moral'. Children see through these very quickly and few of these are really engaging. A story passes one of the easiest tests when your class ask you to read it again, and probably again and again.

The story should involve characters that find themselves in situations that are relevant to children. There is no need for characters to be human. It is the situation, the dilemmas, the feelings and the choices the characters make and the strategies that they use to overcome problems that are important. With imagination one story can be used to explore more than one issue. Look carefully at the strategies the characters use. Ask yourself if your children could learn from this strategy. For example, a mouse that overcomes a difficulty by making friends with other animals and working together could be replicated by our children, whereas a fictional child who steals a magic wand to solve their problems couldn't.

Ideally the characters in the story should learn something or change as a result of the decisions they make or the strategies that they use.

> **Personal activity**
>
> Choose a children's story with which you are familiar. Think about the concepts and skills that we need to develop through PSHE education. Which of these might this story help to introduce or explore? Good examples include *Elmer and the Lost Teddy* by David McKee (2008) or *Don't Do That!* by Tony Ross (2010).

Deconstructing a story

Let us now consider how to deconstruct a story. It is important to respect any author's work and not ruin it for children. For this reason we suggest reading the complete story or extract again after making use of it, to 'put the story back together'. You may want to use only an extract of a longer story. If you do, it is helpful to set the extract into context by providing a synopsis of the story up to the point of the extract.

Think of a story as being like a DVD. Just as with a DVD it can be played, paused, wound forward or rewound along its timeline. You can even 'select a scene'. At difficult moments or choices pupils can be asked to imagine what might happen next, pretend to be 'invisible observers' and consider what advice they might offer, or make predictions about the consequences of the characters' choices. Endings can be imagined and if appropriate new endings constructed.

These next sections are offered only as illustrations. Many questions would be inappropriate for some children's age and readiness so they need to be selected critically or the language adapted. It is also important not to deconstruct a story to the point where you have torn it to pieces. Instead be clear about your learning objective and select questions that focus on that learning objective. You might only use a few key questions with any particular story.

You can offer these questions to a class or a small group and ask for their responses, or you can use questions more formally by sitting the children in a circle and perhaps collecting their contributions onto paper in the middle of the circle. (If you do this it is fine if more than one child offers the same contribution.)

Imagine you have stopped the story at an interesting moment. You can explore the present through questions such as:

- How do you think the characters are feeling right now? (You could spend some time collecting up these words and talking about them. Do some mean the same thing? Are some feelings good to have or feel

nice inside? Are some not so good or make us feel not so good inside? Can some feeling words be added to the class Circle of Feelings?)
- How do we know what they are feeling? How does author or artist help us to know?
- Could they be having more than one or even lots of different feelings at the same time?
- Do you think what they are feeling and thinking is different from what they are saying and doing? Can you explain why that might be?
- What do you think their feelings might be pushing or encouraging them to say or do next?
- Might they have other feelings encouraging them to say or do something different?
- Could some feelings be encouraging them to do something (for example, feeling curious)? Could some be holding them back from doing something (for example, feeling scared)? Which feeling do you think they will follow?
- Which part of them is in charge right now? Their thinking self (what they think it's best to do) or their feeling self (what they feel they want to do) or perhaps even their 'ought to' self (what they think an adult would tell them to do)?
- If someone who really cared for them was watching them now, what would they be feeling? Is it different? Why? What might they want, or be hoping, that the character will do or decide?
- If someone in authority (perhaps a teacher, a midday assistant or even a police officer) was watching, what would they be thinking?

As you read the story you can help the class explore how the characters' feelings are changing, why they are changing, who is helping them to change and how they are helping.

Now we can take a step into the story:

- Imagine you were inside the story but invisible and in a really safe place. If you were there watching and listening what would you be feeling? What would you want to say and do? Is there someone you would feel you ought to tell?

And a second step:

- Imagine that suddenly one of the characters can see you, but the rest of the story is on 'pause'. The character asks your advice. What would you tell them to say or do? They think for a minute and then ask you 'Why?' Could you convince them? What more would you like/need to know to really convince them?

If we could go from when this decision is being made, or this incident in the story is happening, into the future (the next page, the next hour, day, week, month, year, ten years):

- What might we see? What might the characters be saying? How are people feeling now? How do we know? Let's turn over the page and find out if you are right!

With many stories what happens next is obvious, and children, particularly young children, love the fact that they can accurately predict the next page. Many great authors know this and can catch children by surprise by taking the story in an unexpected direction. This 'what might happen next' skill we are helping children to develop – prediction – is an essential skill and 'habit' vital for their personal safety and also in managing their relationships with others. One of the most important questions we can ask them to ponder is 'What if …?'

We can explore the future through questions such as:

- What do you think will happen next (or perhaps when we turn the page)? Is that good or not so good?
- Is anyone 'at risk', could someone get hurt? Their body? Their feelings?
- Could anyone not actually in this present situation still end up getting hurt later? Who? Why? How? In what way?
- What seems to be going really well?
- What do you think might happen tomorrow, next week, in the future if this decision is made?
- Who else might become involved in the future?
- What might others feel and say now, soon, in the future? Is that good or not so good? Are things getting better or worse? If they are getting better will they stay better?
- Can you think of better/healthier/safer ways this story could develop?
- If you can think of a better/healthier/safer way, what has to be said or done differently? Who has to do it? What might push them forward? What might hold them back? What might help?

We can explore the past through questions such as:

- If we could turn the clock back what do you think might have happened before this situation or this moment in the story?
- Could there have been a critical moment when someone could have said or done something different that could have stopped this situation from happening?
- Would it have been easier to have said or done something then rather than now?

Only if we feel it is completely safe and appropriate should we then take our pupils into the situation. These questions have to be used carefully. If children haven't experienced any events or situations covered in the story they will be using their imagination, but if they have had personal experience children will be recalling memories and that is quite different. This is why it is so important that teachers of PSHE education really know their children.

What if (this character) was you? (Early questions in the list may be suitable for all primary ages; later questions may be appropriate for older primary school children.)

- Could you ever imagine this happening to you?
- Where might you be? Who might you be with?
- What would you be feeling? Saying? Doing?
- Can you have more than one feeling in a situation like this?
- Might your feelings conflict with one another? Could they be encouraging you to do different things or even opposite things?
- What would be the risks for you now, tomorrow, soon? How do you feel about this?
- Do you think you know enough to make a good/healthy/safe choice? One you would be happy to live with tomorrow, next week, in the future? If not, what would you like to know?
- Could you have made decisions earlier that would have stopped you getting into this sort of situation? What would they have been?
- Suppose things didn't go according to what you intended and you realise you have made a bad choice. Who could you talk to about it?
- Imagine you could see into the future and change it. If you could see yourselves in this situation what would you say and do differently now?
- Imagine you could split yourself into two and take an 'invisible you' with you. What advice would you give yourself?
- Imagine you could take anyone you want with you invisibly – someone that you know would be really good in a situation like this. Who would it be? You don't have to say – but you know who it is. Your best friend? A member of your family? A character you admire from a book/film/soap? (It is your imagination so they don't have to be real!) A favourite musician or singer or sports person? (Perhaps even your pet!) What is it about that person that gives you confidence in them? What are they like? How do they see things? What can they do? What advice would they give you to say and do?
- Could you be held responsible/accountable for anything? Who might hold you responsible/accountable? What might be the consequences of that responsibility?

But what about the actual teaching?

Up until now we have been helping our pupils unpack the story and really think about it. But suppose it is pretty obvious that a little more actual factual knowledge might be useful. The story has helped us reach a point where new learning is relevant, so, 'Let's stop the story at this point and let's add something …' With the relevant, knowledge in mind (the Green Cross Code, broken glass is sharp, not all dogs are friendly, when people are cross they don't always think clearly):

- You now know, or perhaps you already knew …
- Imagine you have just discovered … and now you say to yourself, 'I know …'
- Imagine telling yourself, 'I know …'
- Imagine I told you …
- Imagine someone you trusted told you …
- Imagine you read …

In the last three bullets, some of the emphasis is on the credibility of the source of the information. In the first three bullets the language is 'clean', and encouraging thinking that begins 'I know …' can be very powerful. Ethically we should consider using this type of language very carefully.

If you are confident that all young people in a group are making unwise or dangerous choices or if a little knowledge would open up new possibilities it may be appropriate to ask:

- Now you know … How will this change what you are going to say or do if someone asks your advice or you find yourself in a situation like this?

If you are not certain, then a softer:

- Now you know … Does this change what you might say or do?

This is much safer since it allows young people with safe or healthy strategies to retain them.

You can also use stories to explore young people's perceptions about the behaviour of their peers. Children's perceptions can be highly inaccurate yet may act as powerful influences on their thinking and subsequent behaviour. Perhaps you remember a time when you felt 'Everyone my age is doing this except me!' The chances are that almost everyone was thinking the same thing as you. But it may not have been true. It is therefore really important to challenge any incorrect assumptions you discover:

- Do you think this type of situation happens often?
- What do you think most young people would want to do in a situation like this?
- What do you think most young people would actually do in a situation like this? (Is there a difference, and if so, why?)

You could open up the issue more widely:

- Do you think that many of the young people of your age (a little older than you) are making these choices?
- What decision do you believe most young people make?
- How common do you think (this type of behaviour) is among young people who are (specify age)? (Or do you think this sort of thing happens often? Rarely? Never?)
- What makes you think this? (Friends' stories? Overheard conversations? Media?)

Now, if appropriate, offer information or data that may support, clarify or challenge their perceptions:

- Do you think there might be a difference between what people say and what is really happening? Why?
- Consider this information/data from (whichever) source. Are we confident it is a reliable source? Why?
- If you now know ... is the real situation (for example, only (a certain) percentage of young people your age use/do/have ever done/tried ...), how do you feel now? Are you surprised? Reassured? Is this encouraging you to rethink your own choices?
- Knowing that most young people actually choose ... why do you think they make this choice? Are there reasons that you would agree with/support? Are there some you would challenge?

> **Personal activity**
>
> Take a story that you are familiar with and, using or adapting the questions above, create a plan for colleagues showing how this story could be used as part of a PSHE education programme. Think of the age group. Select a sequence of questions – it doesn't have to be many – to create a learning journey for these children. Think about the feelings, vocabulary, strategies and skills your pupils could explore or develop through this story.

Try to locate a copy of *Not Now Bernard* by David McKee (1980). In their book, *Hand in Hand*, Judy Hunter, Sheila Phillips and Noreen Wetton (1998) outlined the questions they used to explore this story:

- Did Bernard's parents listen to him?
- What did Bernard say and do to try to get Mum and Dad to turn around and listen?
- What did the monster say and do?
- What did Bernard's parents keep saying?
- How does the author show in his pictures what people were thinking?
- From the illustrations how do you think the monster feels?
- How do we get someone to listen? (Or 'What advice could you offer Bernard to get his parents to listen to him?)
- How do I, as your teacher, get you to listen?
- How do you get me to listen to you?
- We don't want our classroom to be a 'Not Now Bernard' classroom. Could we have a key word we could use when we wanted to tell each other something and we think the person isn't listening?
- I think Bernard's fears and worries were about … and if his mum and dad had listened to him …

They then draw together the learning by creating a class motto, which will help all the children remember to listen to one another.

As the writers argue: 'Sometimes our fears and worries can feel like monsters. It can help sometimes to share these worries. In our class we want to try to listen to each other and help each other to overcome any worries or fears we might have' (Hunter et al., 1998: 43).

For another great story to explore worries look for *The Huge Bag of Worries* by Virginia Ironside (2004).

Using images

Does there have to be a complete story? A photograph, painting or drawing, especially an illustration, can be a frozen moment in time. Just as with a complete story we can imagine what has led up to this moment, what is happening right now and how we imagine the story continuing. As a teacher you can build up your own image banks either drawn from books or magazines or from online sites. In each case ask yourself: 'Where could I take my children through the use of this image? What issues could we explore together? What feelings could we identify through this image and what feelings might we be feeling inside?'

Creating stories

Up to now we have considered published stories. But what about stories our children can make up for themselves? You can provide children with a starting point. 'Imagine two children a little younger than you, who decide to go and play in their garden shed. Make up a story with a not so good ending.' If children need a prompt, suggest one of the children does something to scare the other, or does something that might cause the other to be hurt.

'Now imagine a different story. This time it is the same two children but the story must have a good ending where no one gets scared or hurt.'

And then: 'What is it that makes the two stories different? Did someone say something different? Did they do something different? Did they ask someone if it was okay to play there?'

Stories do not have to be written down. They can be acted out or children can create puppets to play characters. The class can act as an audience, and the story or performance can be used to explore the story and different actions the characters made and choices they took.

It is easy to take a story intended for younger children and use it with far older children. Simply invite them to explore the story and help you create a lesson plan for younger children. Perhaps: 'I know that this story is for younger children but I need your help. If you were thinking about younger children in our school what sort of things could this story help them to think about?'

The use of children's stories in PSHE education is limited only by your imagination. You may also find this publication helpful as it takes popular children's stories found in many school libraries and class bookshelves and considers how they can be used to support PSHE education.

Seize opportunities

Children's literature is rich, as we have discussed, but a story equally rich with learning potential does not need to come from a book, nor involve great length. If it is simply to stimulate study, it can be made up by you beforehand or in response to a dilemma that arises during some class discussion. Sometimes potent learning situations arise unexpectedly, and children can be invited to name the characters and create the background. A story opening can invite intrepid authors (alone, in pairs or in groups) to continue the story and thereby flesh out characters and explore their thoughts, feelings, actions and the consequences that might ensue. Comparing the storylines from different groups starting at the same point can illustrate the wide open nature of life itself, where the next step is not always what we expect it to be.

behavioural issues.

Because children respond more readily to a fictitious scenario with pretend characters than one which might implicate them, this can feel quite safe even if the scenario is an uncomfortable one such as a brewing row, an accusation or bullying. Only when you judge they are ready might you invite them to take a step closer to personal involvement as observer or player 'for real' as we mentioned earlier.

Using drama (including the use of puppets)

We have now stepped over the line from story into drama (or 'Let's pretend!').

Drama can be used *ad hoc* to extend the exploration process into scenes or situations that come from the children's own imagination. It has nothing to do with the 'performance' or 'learning lines' for the Christmas play. In the way we suggested earlier, ask the class, perhaps in small groups, to write (or, for young ones, tell you about) a story or scene to illustrate a point, and choose from the range of responses. Perhaps they think of a scene where two people are having an earnest discussion, maybe even a disagreement. This could be explored using puppets or role-play. Someone suggests Lisa and Toni are the characters, and outlines the way the conversation is going. 'OK Narinda, pretend you're Lisa in the story. What can you make her say to Toni that you think would help? Who'd like to be Toni? OK, Sara. Be ready to answer Lisa; just say what you think Toni would have said. Narinda, how do you think Lisa would be feeling …?' etc. Temporarily 'freezing' a scene can make a space for discussion, a chosen situation being explored as presented or re-run from a variety of perspectives. Say, 'Let's look at that again, but this time …' with pupils suggesting changes once they understand what might be called for, and how it might help. Scenes that refuse to resolve in a single, satisfactory way will sometimes help prepare children for situations where more than one direction may be OK, or where none may be safe. (Adapted from King, 2001.)

It is important to keep in mind that if one child takes on a role, you ensure the others in the class do not confuse character and player, but instead recognise that the player is exploring the feelings and opinions of someone else. This will be more straightforward if the role is somewhat caricatured (a finger wagging parent saying 'Stop that at once!') but harder for some class members if, say, a male classmate 'plays' a fictitious boy his own age with quite different opinions or making different choices.

It is also essential to 'de-role' the players after using these techniques; by, for instance inviting them to tell the class their name, and something else which makes them different from the character they were playing, and then to ensure that nobody is left worried or upset as a result of scene just played.

Using other structured tasks

Puzzles

Avoid the sort of puzzles that challenge children to find words or messages from an array of letters. Avoid, too, any temptation to invite children to colour pictures of safe or dangerous behaviour. They may be effective at occupying children's attention, but it is unlikely they will learn much, if anything, of use about the subject matter. Beware otherwise high quality resources where such distractions can still to be found.

Quizzes

Quizzes that the children set to challenge their classmates and plumb their knowledge can be fun. However, while they can be a useful way to consolidate learning they are not very effective for introducing it. If you want to use a quiz, you may want to restrict material to sources of known quality and relevance, or draw from information that has emerged or been presented in previous sessions. In contrast, a quiz used to find out how much children know or remember is not a quiz, it's a test. Try not to confuse your need to record how much they know with the fun they may have setting relevant questions for another group or team. When children set quizzes they tend to choose the language and knowledge level that is likely to match the rest of the class. This can itself be revealing.

An inbuilt disadvantage of quizzes can be the simple 'right or wrong' nature of most facts. The children's more valuable learning may lie beyond the facts, in their relevance and application, and be far more significant than mere recall. Avoid 'true or false' quizzes of any kind as at best they present minimal educational value, and can be an effective way to learn *false* information, which is nonetheless memorable.

Television and video

Try not to assume that professionally produced resources necessarily contain high quality material. Sitting children down to receive 'expert input' from such media may feel attractive, but the only way to discover the value of a resource is to view it and carefully assess its place, if any, in your work. Pre-record TV programmes and view DVDs carefully before deciding whether to use them. There is more on selecting materials in Chapter 7.

Showing a short, carefully chosen section of a programme or DVD can often retain interest better than playing a whole programme. The visual impact of watching a screen can be great, but short attention spans may make a long input unwise. Pausing, repeating, omitting and re-ordering are all possible and can help you maximise the visual input as a stimulus to discussion, in a similar way to use of story or drama in class. Ask pupils to reflect upon what they have seen and to explore its purpose and value. This can help them to take more from it than simply to observe. Perhaps not every child will have seen it in the same way, or noticed what others did. These differences may be helpful and can be elicited with gentle questions using 'Do you think' and 'Did you find' to invite points of view rather than 'right' answers. Use closed questions to draw attention to any important facts. More open-ended questions give children much more freedom:

- What did you find interesting or challenging about the programme/video? Why was that?
- If you had been (in that scene) what would you have done differently?
- What other things could you do or say (in that situation)?
- Is there anything you'd like to say to (named character)?

In many ways, when fiction is used to focus on a particular issue, situation or character, DVDs, videos and TV programmes can be treated in exactly the same way as story and drama. When they involve non-fiction, you need to be clear that the length, content, relevance and treatment of the subject are in accordance with your view of the children's readiness and their needs. We consider selection of commercial resources more fully in Chapter 7.

Using visitors to help you

Though visitors or outside agencies can have value, great care is needed to integrate their contribution fully into your programme. For example, visitors are still being asked to deliver drugs education in schools where teachers believe that an 'expert' is required who has greater credibility and confidence than they, often principally to provide information about dangers (though this is less common in primary schools). The value of pure information-giving such as this is limited and as soon as the need for class exploration and discussion are recognised, you may well be a better 'expert' than any visitor. See Chapter 7 where we deal with the use of visitors more fully.

Processing

It can be very useful to children to reflect upon a lesson they have just been involved in, and to think about what use or relevance it has for them individually. Perhaps it conjured thoughts about something they might do differently, or helped them make more sense of something that has already happened to them. Maybe it confirms something they believed, or reinforces a decision they once made, or challenges those things. Perhaps it only starts to make real sense to them when they hear what *others* have made of it. A skilled teacher may probe and prompt in order to bring about particular insight, but beware giving the message that only one view or impression should be taken from any input or experience, still less that this should necessarily accord with your own. Ask what the *children* made of their lesson. Listen to, and record, the responses they provide and encourage the others in the class to listen, too.

Any attempt to help pupils identify and explore the value of what they have been doing in a lesson might be called processing (sometimes known as reviewing or debriefing). It will often be during this follow-up interchange, *which should be a part of every PSHE education lesson*, that the most significant learning will take place.

Chapter summary

In this chapter we have shown how the approach to teaching PSHE education is different in many respects from the teaching of more academic subjects. We have discussed how to act as facilitator, and how to ensure both an active class and interactivity between children who value the contributions of their peers to their learning. We have looked at how children's own experiences can provide rich material for exploration and how story-telling can widen understanding beyond current experience to encompass a wide range of characters and situations.

> **Further reading**
>
> Gateshill, P. (2010) 'Effective teaching and learning in PSHE education', presentation from PSHE Association Conference 2010.
> *A short but pithy presentation, which includes a comprehensive checklist of characteristics of effective teaching and learning in PSHE and a list of active classroom teaching methods. (A copy of this presentation may be obtained from the PSHE Association on request.)*
> Hunter, J., Phillips, S. and Wetton, N. (1998) *Hand in Hand: Emotional Development Through Literature*. Wheathampstead: Saffire Press.
> *A very clear and helpful step-by-step approach to using literature as a developmental tool with young children.*
> Wetton, N. and Collins, M. (2003) *Pictures of Health*. Dunstable: Belair Publications.
> *This 72-page book is teeming with illustration and classroom activities, split into topics such as 'Friends and Friendship', 'Managing Change', 'Personal Safety and Risks'.*

References

Boddington, N. and Wetton, N. (2006) *Health for Life 11–14*. Cheltenham: Nelson Thornes.

Hunter, J., Phillips, S. and Wetton, N. (1998) *Hand in Hand: Emotional Development Through Literature*. Wheathampstead: Saffire Press.

Ironside, V. (2004) *The Huge Bag of Worries*. London: Hodder Children's Books.

King, A. (2001) *Primary School Drugs Education Handbook* (2nd edn). London: Folens.

McKee, D. (1980) *Not Now Bernard*. London: Andersen Press.

McKee, D. (2008) *Elmer and the Lost Teddy*. London: Andersen Press.

Ross, T. (2010) *Don't Do That!* London: Andersen Press.

CHAPTER 7

UNDERSTANDING HOW TO SELECT PSHE EDUCATION TEACHING MATERIAL AND RESOURCES

Aim

There are literally hundreds of commercially produced resources available for PSHE education. Sadly many, while beautifully produced, are very poor in providing or encouraging effective practice in teaching and learning. This chapter aims to clarify how readers may judge teaching materials in terms of suitability and quality.

Learning objectives

After reading and reflecting on this chapter you will:

- be familiar with a comprehensive set of criteria to apply to every potential resource for PSHE education
- be aware both of the possibilities offered by bringing visitors into the classroom and of some key professional considerations.

Getting started

> 💭 **Consider**
>
> Take a look at some of the PSHE education resources available in your school. Are they of good quality? How do you know? What are the elements you would look for in a high quality resource for PSHE education?

Introduction

Before we consider commercial resources it is worth pausing. One of the most powerful resources for PSHE education will always be the children in the class. By exciting their curiosity and by helping them to explore their existing experiences, expectations, values, beliefs, understanding and skills the whole class can benefit from the contributions they make in response to good classroom questioning and dialogue. Chapter 4 describes some ways to tap into the resource they represent.

Powerful learning can be undertaken with little more than large sheets of paper, pens and a well-structured dialogue that encourages children to reflect, question and discuss. A well-chosen photograph, artefact or even a single sentence written on the board can act as a powerful stimulus for learning. However, there will be times when we need external resources to enrich or provide structure to our learning and to take children beyond their existing experience.

Choosing resources for PSHE education can be a daunting task. They range across paper, DVD, online material and often people in the form of 'theatre in education' or 'visiting speakers'.

Resources tend to come in two broad categories: those that offer teachers an entire programme of study and those that focus on a single issue or topic. Some will have been field trialled in classrooms while others will not. Some will be based on sound educational theory while others will not. Some are based on research gathered from young people to ensure that the authors really understand how children and young people are gradually making sense of an issue, and some are not. Some will be free while others can cost a significant amount of money.

If colleagues are unfamiliar with teaching a particular topic within PSHE education, especially a sensitive topic, it can feel reassuring to use a published resource. However, this needs caution, as no author will understand as well as you do the needs of your pupils or the context within which they live.

Visitors to classrooms bring different qualities. While there are experts in the knowledge or 'facts' associated with many of the sensitive issues that teachers of PSHE will address with their pupils, this expertise does not necessarily translate into an expertise in teaching and learning – visitors skilled in their own field do not automatically have the experience and understanding to explore the values or develop the skills children will need to first process and then make use of new knowledge.

There is a saying in PSHE: 'A programme should be led by the needs of young people, not the sequence or structure of a resource'. Put simply: Establish your children's learning needs and hence your learning objectives and outcomes; only then look through your resources for materials that will help you to meet them. Not the other way round.

In the real world, effective, comprehensive resources will often give you teaching ideas that you might not have thought of yourself, so there is a balance to be struck. You need to know what your children will need and how to judge the quality and relevance of teaching resources before investing what could be many hundreds of pounds in purchasing new ones.

The majority of teachers will naturally want to adapt any resource to meet either their children's particular needs or their own personal teaching 'style'. In the hands of a good teacher, many resources end up more as a stimulus for the actual lessons that are taught than a 'script' that they follow.

Practical criteria

If a school is going to invest what is likely to be a few hundred pounds on a programme it is important to get it right.

Before we consider the educational criteria there are some really practical and obvious considerations. The first is: Does the resource require pupils to have individual textbooks? This will greatly increase the price if you need a number of sets for every class. The key question to pose is whether these really add any value. For example, if they contain precise, current factual information might this quickly date?

Even more problematic are resources that require pupil workbooks that can only be used once. While they are useful for pupils to have a record of their work they can be expensive and it's important to ask what real value these add to the learning. If the resource is accessible online do you have sufficient access to computers? Will all children be able to interact equally with the material?

Resources that offer worksheets also need careful scrutiny. Inadequate or unsatisfactory PSHE education frequently consists of 'death by worksheets' – an unhelpful preponderance of non-interactive written work on individual sheets. Worksheets should not be wholly dismissed as a teaching tool, however. There is a world of difference between one that offers only closed questions requiring responses limited to answers that have already been determined by the author, and one that asks open-ended questions that demand independent enquiry, locating and evaluating sources of information, presenting and evidencing findings, and valuing children's differing opinions and experiences.

The critical question when looking at worksheets, whether paper or electronic, is to see each as an individual resource within a wider programme and apply the criteria we have outlined below.

If it is an electronic or online resource will you own it or do you need a licence? If so, how much will it cost and when will it need renewal (probably annually)? How robust is the resource physically – will it stand up to the environment of the class- or staffroom or does it look as though it might quickly fall apart?

Finally, check to see when the resource was published. The factual content of many resources can swiftly date.

Educational criteria

Now consider the educational criteria that should be applied to any potential PSHE education resource. Some will be 'deal breakers'; for example if the values promoted by the resource are not congruent with the school's values you will probably wish to reject it, while others such as failure to offer ideas or material for assessment could be overcome but will require you to do more work.

The overarching principles

- *Are the underpinning values and beliefs stated and are they consistent with those of our school?* Some resources are produced by organisations that promote, either overtly or more subtly through the material offered, a set of values or beliefs. Are these values congruent with

your school's overarching values? Are the values promoted by the resource congruent with relevant school policies?
- *Is it inclusive?* Will all your pupils be able to interact with it? Will some be left out/left behind?
- *Is there guidance on how to identify pupils' existing levels of knowledge and understanding and how to incorporate these into planning?* Does the resource enable you to 'start where your children are' or does it predetermine (i.e 'guess') their prior learning? Does it offer techniques that will enable you to uncover your pupils' existing knowledge, understanding, values or beliefs? (For example, 'brainstorm' or 'first thoughts' activities or draw and write activities.)
- *Do activities cover a range of teaching and learning styles?* Does the resource provide a rich variety of teaching styles or is it restricted to a few? This can be less critical in a single-issue resource that may provide a few lessons but is essential in a larger, more comprehensive programme.
- *Is there guidance on evaluating activities?* This is not the same as assessment (which we address fully in Chapter 13). Does the resource provide opportunities and techniques to enable young people to feed back how useful they found the learning offered by the resource? Will it help you determine whether pupils have achieved the stated learning outcomes?
- *Are the materials free from stereotypes?* Look at images and case studies in particular. Are they stereotyped? Ask yourself, 'Will my pupils be able to see themselves in this resource?' or would they say, 'These people are nothing like me, my friends or my family'. Does the material offer images that focus on the 'extremes of behaviour'? For example are all images of young people who are portrayed as bullies scruffy in appearance or obviously looking aggressive? While it may be rare for a child to be dared to play on railway lines, or to try smoking, might it not be more relevant to explore being dared to do something more likely and yet potentially just as damaging? (Perhaps stealing from a local shop, going to the park without telling a parent or carer, or just staying out in the street past the time their parents said to come in.)
- *Do the materials take account of religious, cultural and physical diversity and special educational needs?* While overtly addressing this full range in each individual lesson might be difficult, what about the overall resource? Each learning experience should enable every young person to 'recognise themselves' in the learning and be able to create their own personal meaning.
- *Has the material been developed in consultation with pupils and teachers and has its effectiveness been evaluated?* It is important to separate the

trivial from the significant. Strong resources are based on research into how children of the target age are making sense of their world, and they provide flexible learning that provides an initial direction and structure that teachers can 'fine tune' for their pupils. There is a world of difference between a research-evidenced resource that has been evaluated in the classroom and one that can only claim 'children really enjoyed these lessons'. 'Enjoying lessons' is great, but it doesn't mean any meaningful learning took place.
- *Does the material include guidance on the knowledge and skills needed by the teacher to ensure effective delivery and to help build teacher confidence?*

All criteria such as these need to be used flexibly and to encourage reflection. Some may be less applicable than others for individual resources. Looking more specifically, it is worth considering the following.

Teaching and learning

- Does the material outline processes for establishing a positive and supportive learning environment, e.g. developing ground rules?
- Is active learning promoted?
- Are discussion and reflection encouraged?
- Do the activities cover the development of knowledge, skills and attitudes? Do they encourage children to share how they feel?
- Is the content differentiated and can it be adapted for use with particular groups of pupils?
- Is guidance given on assessing learning outcomes?

Content

- Does the content covered meet your pupils' needs?
- Is the content factually accurate, balanced, objective and up to date?
- Are learning outcomes clearly stated?
- Are learning outcomes sufficiently challenging?
- Is the content appropriate to the needs of pupils in terms of language, images, attitude, maturity and understanding, and is prior knowledge required?
- Does it include positive images of a range of people and will the imagery and language appeal to pupils?

- Do the activities encourage pupils to think about their attitudes and values and take account of a range of perspectives?
- Do the activities encourage pupils to reflect on their learning and apply it to situations in their own lives?
- Does the content encourage children to obey, or does it help develop their own sense of responsibility to make wise choices?

Curriculum issues

- Does it contribute to broad and balanced PSHE education provision?
- Does the material say how it covers statutory and non-statutory learning outcomes?
- Does the resource support continuity and progression across all ages? And across curriculum subjects?

Consider

Consider one resource used in a school's PSHE education programme and, using these criteria, critically review either the whole resource or even just one lesson. Where does it meet the criteria, where does it not? How would you adapt it to make it more suitable for children of the age you plan to teach?

Using visitors in the classroom

Now consider a different type of resource, the 'visitor to the classroom', and how they can support and enrich PSHE education. Visitors can sometimes make a powerful contribution to any PSHE education programme. As part of a well-planned developmental programme they can add real value to pupils' learning. Any visit should enrich a planned PSHE education programme and never be treated as a 'one off'. (There is one exception, discussed at the end of this chapter.)

A visitor to your classroom should never be left unattended by you. This is no reflection on them, but is simply for mutual professional safety. The teacher is responsible for the work a visitor does in the classroom. Always check with your school senior leadership team the necessity for any visitor to have DBS (Disclosure and Barring Service) checks undertaken before working with your class.

Why use 'visitors' at all?

Teachers cannot be expected to have a complete and current knowledge of every topic covered by a comprehensive PSHE education programme, and therefore the use of visitors is an important adjunct to many schools' programmes.

With any piece of learning the first question is always: 'What am I trying to achieve?' (What are my learning objectives, the learning outcomes I expect to see demonstrated by my students, and how will I assess these?) This is followed by: 'Is inviting a visitor the best way to organise this learning?' Then ask: 'Can this visitor provide something worthwhile that I cannot?'

It is important to think about a visitor as a classroom resource and not as a substitute teacher. Some professional organisations provide comprehensive training for personnel expected to work with school children while others will have little or no training or experience. For this reason we have used the term 'visitor' instead of 'speaker'.

What can a visitor bring to the classroom?

- If they are competent in their own field, they can bring expertise in a particular, relevant issue or topic that a teacher may not have (nor should be expected to have).
- They can act as an expert witness, recounting events in their lives from a personal or professional perspective. In this way they can help make learning 'real', especially for younger children. Examples include a mother with a new baby, an older person reflecting on how the community has changed, someone sharing their working practice, the person who acts as the school crossing patrol, a local councillor or the mayor discussing their work. Visitors to the classroom may also be older pupils or pupils who have recently left the school and can talk about their new experiences, perhaps in having moved up to junior or secondary school.
- They have a 'novelty' value and we know the brain finds it easier to recall novelty. Can you recall a visitor coming into your own classroom to provide an input to a lesson or a 'talk'? Now try to recall the lesson before and after it. The chances are that you can't.
- In addition to meeting shared learning objectives they can establish a 'first contact' to a support agency. For example, it can be really hard for a young person to approach any source of support 'cold'. Establishing a relationship in a classroom session can help to overcome this. (For example, establishing a relationship with a school nurse or a police officer.)

Bringing a visitor into the classroom should be an active rather than passive learning experience. The skills of selecting and interacting with a visitor are transferable, while the actual information they impart may swiftly date or be forgotten.

Try to recall visitors from your own primary classroom when you were a child. Perhaps you can recall them and have an impression of what type of person they were. The chances are also quite strong that you can't remember much, if any, of what they actually said, perhaps just one or two key points.

> **Consider**
>
> Find out how visitors are used in the PSHE education programme in a school with which you are familiar.
>
> Why have they been chosen?
>
> What is it that they bring to the learning?
>
> How is their input evaluated?
>
> How is this learning assessed?

Why is it so important to consider these sessions carefully?

As the session facilitator, regardless of who is working with your class, you, the teacher, are responsible for managing the learning.

Young people are always learning at a variety of levels. For example, a visitor will not only be providing their input, they will be transmitting and modelling messages about who they are and also the values of whoever they represent officially or by association. When you invite a visitor to work with young people you get the whole package, not just the content of their input.

Some essential considerations

- Who is or are the people you are inviting into your lesson?
- What skills, needs, expectations, experiences or knowledge do they bring? And how do you know?

These are absolutely essential to consider. Never confuse a leaflet, a fantastic website or the written testimonials of other teachers or head teachers (unless you can contact them in person) with the expertise the actual visitor needs to work with the children in your class.

If a visitor brings a body of knowledge, does it come with a personal message or set of attached values? Do you know what these are, and are they in harmony with your school policies? It is important not to confuse 'passionate and well intentioned' with 'appropriate and skilled'.

> **Consider**
>
> Many issues within PSHE education generate strong views in different parts of society. Many of these issues are the focus of organisations that hold a particular position, often with great conviction, and the organisations are keen to promote this position in schools.
>
> In the context of your school or community what issues do you think might need careful consideration when planning for balance?
>
> Do you have a responsibility to consider the legitimacy of any organisation's position prior to any invitation to work with your pupils?
>
> Does the fact that you have invited a speaker imply to your pupils that you (or your school) have sympathy with their position on an issue?

Is the visitor happy to act as a 'resource' with you managing the learning, or do they expect to 'run the whole session'? If they do expect to take the lead role, are you confident they have the teaching and classroom management skills to achieve your shared learning objectives and outcomes with this particular age group, in your community, with young people they have never met before?

If they have been endorsed or recommended by another organisation ask yourself what confidence you can have in that organisation to assess the visitor's ability to work with your young people. Does that organisation have the expertise to really make a valid assessment?

In an ideal world we should try to watch any visitor work in a similar learning environment before confirming their visit to our session, but more realistically we could ask what other local schools or settings they have worked in, and talk to professional colleagues in that school or setting.

A visitor to your classroom or setting should never be left unattended by you. This is no reflection on them, but is simply for mutual professional safety.

There may be times when you know the visitor is an expert in their field, sympathetic and friendly to children, but hasn't the skills to work interactively with children. The follow-up work that you do can extend and crystallise the learning the visitor promoted. You can ask what they remember being told, how useful they think it will be, whether they still have questions in their minds about it. You can help widen and deepen their understanding. This is another reason why you need to be present when a visitor is working with your class.

Negotiation

If you think there might be any professional role conflict (for example, a member of an organisation or agency has a policy or protocol for confidentiality that differs from that of the school), this needs sorting out before any session takes place and ground rules to be renegotiated, if necessary with the young people attending the session.

- Does this visit fit into and build on your scheme of work?
- Is the input relevant?
- Does it build on, extend or enrich previous work?
- Does it offer a stimulus for future work and if so, do you (or your team) have the skills and knowledge to capitalise on it?

What do you plan to do after the visit? Following any input it is very possible that issues have been opened but left unexplored.

If young people raise questions or express anxieties after the visit, perhaps days or even weeks later, do you have a means to answer their questions or address their concerns?

Confidentiality and school policies

- Might any young person be upset by this input?
- What if a young person becomes upset or reveals something disturbing about their own or another's personal experience?

PSHE education, perhaps more than any other area of the curriculum, should work in the young person's immediate reality and help them explore how they feel about it. For this reason you need to be sensitive to their prior experiences and be ready for them to share their present experiences and feelings. It is wise to have a protocol in place to support any young person who becomes distressed (for example, a colleague or member of the school's senior management team who is aware the lesson is taking place can offer support or escalate to the named person for safeguarding if required.)

No matter what policies the visitor (or any organisation they might represent) has with regard to confidentiality, your school's or local authority's policies will always take priority. It is essential that 'Safeguarding' protocols and policies are clearly shared with any visitor to the classroom, including the boundaries about what can and cannot be kept confidential, and that these protocols and policies are fully adhered to.

During prior planning with a visitor it is important to alert them to and discuss any vulnerable children or reasons for concern. For example, there may be a child whose family members have experienced a road accident and may be distressed in a lesson on road safety, or a child with a specific learning difficulty or behavioural issue such as Tourette's syndrome.

Involving children

For a visitor experience to be at its most valuable, children need to be fully involved from an early stage. Using some of the following questions, consider how children could be involved:

- How has this visitor been selected? Who selected them? What were the criteria:
  - for deciding a visitor was needed?
  - for deciding who should visit?
- What do or will the children know about the visitor prior to their session? Who do they work for? What do they do? What is their role? What might they look like?
- How big will the audience be? If large, what opportunity will there be to ask questions or break into smaller discussion groups?
- Were young people involved in the selection? Practically this might only be realistic if the visitor has been before, and the children are old enough to be involved, but offering a range of possibilities, considering the pros and cons of each, is often possible if the actual visit is some time ahead.
- If you have selected the visitor, have you explained to the children your criteria for their selection? ('We decided to invite a local firefighter – someone who knows the houses where you live.') Why do you feel you can trust them as a source of information or advice? What gives you confidence they are a reliable source of support?
- Do children already have a relationship with, knowledge of, or experience with this visitor? (For example, the school's site manager, school cook, school nurse, school crossing patrol, local mother or father.)
- How will the visitor be invited? By letter? By email? By telephone?

- Who will make the arrangements? Will they need a map? Where will you arrange for them to be met and by whom?
- How will the visitor be briefed and by whom?
- Will the visitor be provided with questions in advance? How will you balance the input of their information with children's questions?
- If questions are to be provided, how will they be generated?
- If there are lots of questions, how will the young people prioritise them?
- Who will 'chair' the session?
- Who will escort the visitor off the premises? Who will thank the visitor and how?
- Will the visitor receive any feedback? Will they be informed about what young people feel they learnt?
- What did the children find interesting or surprising? What has the visit made them think about for the first time, think more about or think differently about the issue or role? What did they enjoy?
- Will there be an opportunity for follow-up questions? Will the young people be able to forward recordings of their subsequent work, for example emailing photographs of displays?

Sometimes it will be better if a visitor interacts with one or more small groups of children. In the real world this may not be possible and you may be compelled to have them work with larger groups or the whole class. Again this needs careful consideration.

Consider the difference between:

- a class of mixed ability and life experience, well prepared, and arranged in groups of six of similar ability, experiencing a combination of expert input and question-and-answer session, with a carefully briefed selected visitor building on the children's previous PSHE education learning;

and

- the same class of mixed ability and life experience being addressed by a speaker talking from a script about the dangers of a particular behaviour. This may be better than nothing – but not necessarily! The time and effort involved in the follow-up that will be needed to ensure the children gained usefully from this would have been better spent setting up the first scenario.

Where possible, visitors need to work interactively with small audiences where young people not only can receive the benefit of their input, but also can practise the skills of gathering information from someone they haven't met before and begin to form a relationship with them and, if appropriate, their organisation.

Turn the experience 'upside down'

The best 'visitor sessions' are always a collaboration between you, the visitor and the children. For example, consider turning the session upside down and making the visitor the learner, though this will need time to set up.

Ask the children to create questions that they have about the visitor's subject matter, perhaps supplemented by your own questions. These become lines of enquiry that the class investigates. The children are now ready to present their findings to the 'expert visitor' who assesses each presentation with regard to its depth, breadth and accuracy and then adds anything they feel has been missed.

For example, children are asked to investigate how to keep safe in different situations, perhaps near roads, railways, water, parks or other relevant locations. Now they might create posters to show all their key messages, perhaps aimed at helping a younger class. Now picture them presenting their posters and explaining them to a visiting expert, perhaps a police officer, a nurse or a road safety officer, and asking for feedback on how to get the message across.

You can extend this idea. What if the results of the children's investigations could be presented to a local decision maker? Could they present information gathered about road safety near their school to a local councillor?

> ### Exception to the no 'one off' rule
>
> The only exception to the no 'one off' rule is a response to a local, sudden and unexpected issue – perhaps as a result of an incident. Pragmatically you might realise that an immediate local danger will not be covered in your programme for some time and that young people need to quickly have their attention drawn to this particular issue or threat.
>
> Any 'one off', however, can only raise awareness and perhaps offer, or – better – remind, children of some quick strategies. If children need to act on these, they will be still drawing on the range of decision making, problem solving and communication skills they have developed through their previous PSHE education programme. A 'one off' can't possibly teach such skills but can connect them to an immediate threat or issue. It is highly likely that an emergency response such as this will still need follow-up work.

Chapter summary

This chapter set out the things to be considered when choosing teaching material and resources for PSHE education in your classroom. In particular, it warned about materials that, despite their appearance, might contain unsuitable content or represent dubious quality. We offered a set of criteria to enable you to identify good teaching material confidently. The second half of the chapter considered the use of visitors to the classroom to help enrich and extend learning.

Further reading

LASER Alliance. Available at: www.lasersafety.org.uk (accessed 17 October 2013).
LASER stands for Learning About Safety by Experiencing Risk. The LASER Alliance has been set up by RoSPA to support the professional development of safety education practitioners who work in schools or develop resources for schools. They have developed a 'Resource profiler' which members use to quality-assure safety education materials. Take a look at the website and check if they have members near your school.

PSHE Association (2013) *Criteria for Resources – Good Practice Principles*. Available at: www.pshe-association.org.uk/content.aspx?CategoryID=1048 (accessed 7 January 2014).

PART 2

8	Understanding safety and risk education	145
9	Understanding sex and relationships education	164
10	Understanding how to address bullying behaviour in PSHE education	189
11	Understanding medicine and drug education	208
12	Understanding personal finance education	235

In this part we show how the advice we have given in the previous chapters can be put *into practice* in some important aspects of PSHE education. We do not mean to suggest that PSHE education should be broken down into separate topics – far from it. But we do know that students and newly qualified teachers ask for support in these aspects in particular. Just because we have not included a chapter about healthy eating or exercise, for example, does not mean that these are not relevant to primary schools, their pupils or parents, but you will probably find it easier to apply the advice we have given to these subjects than to the subjects we write about here.

CHAPTER 8

UNDERSTANDING SAFETY AND RISK EDUCATION

Aim

To introduce effective approaches to teaching safety and risk education.

Learning objectives

By reading and reflecting on the content of this chapter you will:

- know how to start where children are in safety and risk education
- understand the role of safety education and risk education in helping children to keep themselves safe
- be able to plan and implement effective lessons in safety and risk education within a whole school approach to teaching safely and teaching safety
- to be able to create opportunities for your pupils to take decisions which will help them to enjoy challenging activities while being safe.

Getting started

Take a group of children on a learning walk around the school building or grounds. Older children could use a digital camera to photograph what they see, or you could record the children's discussions at points throughout the walk. Ask the children to look out for examples of safety messages or features. These could include notices, safety glass, fire doors and crash mats, soft play surfaces, fences and gates. All of these have been built into the children's environment to help them to be safe at school. How do they help the children to be safe? Are the fences there to keep out wolves and monsters, or to keep the children in? What might happen if these features were no longer there? Make a list of their responses and use them to develop a class safety charter or in an assembly to show other children how these features make their school a safe place to learn.

Later in this chapter we will show you how children can make good and bad decisions based on their perceptions of the safety of their environment. We will also show you how this simple activity can help children to become risk competent individuals, prepared for the hazards and adventures they will face in everyday life.

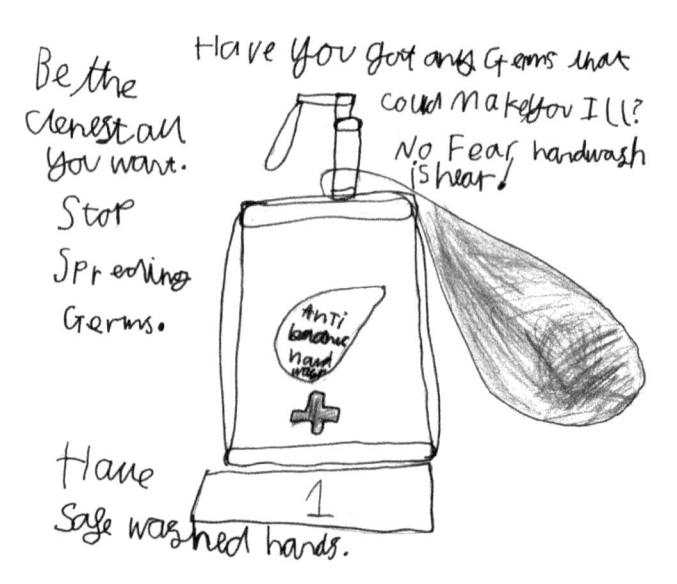

Figure 8.1 During a learning walk about keeping safe at school the children noticed lots of signs in the kitchen about hygiene. This poster is one ten-year-old child's response

Source: Ten-year-old pupil at Brindishe Green Primary School, Lewisham

Introduction

Safety education is so much a part of good practice in primary education that it is difficult to imagine a school which does not include safety education at some point. Safety education may form part of a lesson in a specific area of the curriculum such as how to use tools safely in Design and Technology, or might be part of everyday rules such as 'Walk, don't run in the corridors'. Children will take part in fire practice and might wear high visibility tabards when taking the 'walking bus' to get to school. (Walking bus refers to a group of adults (usually parent volunteers) who 'collect' children at a specific time every day on a predetermined route to school, so the children are accompanied to school in a safe way.) More formally they may take part in a range of activities to help them to be safer pedestrians or cyclists. All of these activities contribute to safety education.

Children may also be taught about personal safety and how to keep themselves safe from bullying or other threats to their mental and emotional wellbeing, such as internet safety. The mental and emotional aspects of 'staying safe' are addressed in more depth in Chapter 3. We address the need for safeguarding in Appendix 1. This chapter focuses on the role of safety education in the prevention of accidents – or unintentional injury. (The latter term is used by those organisations which want to reinforce the idea that most, if not all, accidents are preventable.) Effective safety and risk education should encourage children's natural risk taking behaviour, while also encouraging adults to manage risks without abolishing them, so that children can develop the knowledge, attitudes and skills they need to keep themselves safe.

It may seem curious that, despite the importance and wide range of topics which could be included in safety education, a recent survey of adopting safe practices in schools (RoSPA, 2010) found that safety education in schools is of variable quality and is often poorly planned and co-ordinated across a school. Another survey of PSHE practice by Formby et al. (2010) found that safety education is often delivered by external contributors such as police community support officers or fire and rescue or ambulance crews.

While these visitors have great expertise in (and passion for) specific aspects of safety, they may not have a teaching qualification or an understanding of how children learn. This means their approach and their resources may not always integrate well with the rest of your scheme of work or reflect your understanding of good practice. As a result you should always plan alongside expert visitors so that they can get their messages across in the most effective ways and you can integrate what they bring with the rest of your planned programme.

Safety education can be seen as a 'safe' subject among primary school teachers, when compared with drug or sex and relationships education. Courses abound in the so-called 'sensitive issues' in PSHE education, perhaps because these subjects have a high profile in the national media, and can be a cause of great concern for parents. By contrast, courses for teachers in safety education are few and far between and parents welcome your efforts to help their children develop the understanding and skills they need to keep themselves safe.

Preventing unintentional injury

Safety education is just one part of injury prevention, the overall purpose of which is to prevent one of the leading causes of death and injury among children of school age. Even a relatively minor injury can lead to days off school (and sometimes days off work for parents) while serious injury can be life changing, not just for the victim but for their family and friends. No teacher wants to be the one who has to break the news of the death of a child to their class, whatever the cause, but if that cause was preventable it is even more tragic.

What is the scale of the problem?

Recently the Royal Society for the Prevention of Accidents has looked at accidents compared with other preventable causes of death, and estimated the number of years of life lost (YLL) as a result. Their analysis of ONS (Office for National Statistics) and NHS data shows that accidents were the leading cause of preventable premature death for people of all ages from birth to 60 years in England and Wales for 2010. They have also looked at the causes of injury reported to Accident and Emergency departments among different age groups. Among the under-fives, accidents at home are most common, while most injuries for teenagers and young adults happen during leisure activities and on the road, with an increasing number happening in the workplace from the age of 14 years.

If unintentional injury is the leading preventable cause of death among young people, you may be surprised to realise that injury prevention is a low priority generally among public health practitioners. Rather, their focus is on preventing heart disease, cancer and other illnesses that mainly affect older adults. To some leaders in public health,

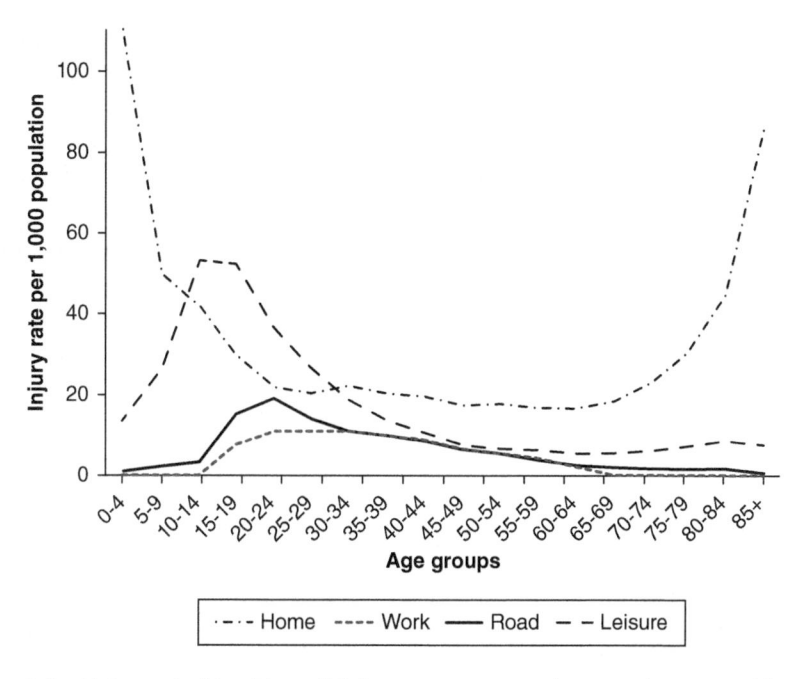

Figure 8.2 Unintended (accidental) injury rates reported to A&E by age and location
Source: RoSPA, 2012a: 11

safety education can even be seen to be counterproductive to their aims to reduce the burden of ill health. If safety education makes children and their parents fearful and risk averse, and children are not allowed to play outdoors, ride their bikes and climb trees, then they can become inactive, exacerbating the risk of obesity and contributing to unhealthy lifestyles in adult life.

Campaigners for adventurous and outdoor play, led by Tim Gill (2009), Steven Moss (2012) and others, have reminded us that play, especially outdoors, is good for children and should be encouraged.

Despite vociferous campaigns, however, safety education can appear to be a 'Cinderella' subject within PSHE, undemanding of a teacher's creativity and attention, easily taken care of by external contributors and overlooked or dismissed as a public health issue.

Teaching safely

Of course, teachers have a moral and legal responsibility to teach in such a way that keeps children safe. Schools, like all workplaces, have a duty of care for their staff and visitors (and in the case of schools, pupils). Governors, local authorities or proprietors must take all reasonable, practicable steps to ensure pupils' safety while on the school premises and when learning outside the classroom, although this responsibility may be delegated to head teachers or health and safety officers. Because safety is so well regulated in our society generally, the provision for health and safety has gained a reputation for being bureaucratic and overly burdensome. We are in danger of having a 'tick box' approach, where health and safety issues are addressed because they have to be, rather than seen as a shared responsibility of one human being for another.

As a result of regulation your school will have a wide range of policies and routine practices which provide you, and the children you teach, with a safe environment in which to work and learn. These policies should be reviewed regularly by senior staff and governors. Perhaps because the responsibilities for teaching about safety, and health and safety policies are split, it could appear that 'teaching safety' and 'teaching safely' have very little to do with one another on a day-to-day basis. However, Ofsted look at both through their inspections of behaviour and safety across all aspects of school. We hope to show you how teaching safely and teaching safety are integral parts of a whole school approach to safety.

Where to begin? What do children know and understand about keeping themselves safe?

One of the common mistakes that adults (including teachers and safety experts) make with regard to safety education is to assume that because children have a lot of accidents, they don't know much about how to keep themselves safe. This is a false premise which can lead to a lot of disappointing evaluation reports, suggesting little or no benefit from safety education. This does not mean that children know everything they need to know to be able to keep themselves safe; neither does it mean there is no role for experts in safety education. It means that we have to start where children are if we are to make a difference.

As long ago as 1985, Noreen Wetton and her colleagues Trefor Williams and Alysoun Moon used draw and write to find out what primary school children know and understand about keeping safe, indoors and outdoors. The specific instructions are reproduced here from *A Way In: Five Key Areas of Health Education* (1989). See Chapter 4 for important information about how to carry out classroom-based research using draw and write.

A draw and write about keeping safe; invitations to participate:

- Draw a picture of yourself keeping yourself safe indoors.
- What are you keeping yourself safe from?
- How are you keeping yourself safe?
- Draw a picture of yourself keeping yourself safe outdoors.
- What are you keeping yourself safe from?
- How are you keeping yourself safe?
- Whose job is it/who is responsible for keeping you safe wherever you are?

(Williams et al., 1989: 19)

One of the most important findings from this research was the number of children who described imaginary or impossible hazards from which they were keeping safe, both indoors and outdoors. Children (especially, but not exclusively, those in Key Stage 1) drew pictures of ghosts, monsters, skeletons and aliens as well as characters from well-known television programmes. Outdoors, children were keeping safe from giant insects and fierce jungle animals such as lions, tigers, snakes and other reptiles that are not commonly found roaming wild in Nottingham or Newcastle-upon-Tyne where the research was carried out. Just because these hazards are imaginary they should not be dismissed as 'funny', or worse, 'wrong'. It is simply an example of children making sense of what they don't know by reference to what they do know, and evidence for the constructivists' view of learning (see Chapter 2).

More importantly, when the children were asked how they were keepings safe from these hazards, they wrote about crying, hiding or running away. Members of the emergency services who heard about this research said it helped them to understand why young children trapped in house fires are often found under beds or in cupboards, rather than at the windows or doors. To a young child, a hazard can be something to hide away from, where you cannot see it, and it cannot see you. This is a strategy which works well when the hazard is a scary-shaped shadow on the bedroom wall, or a character from a story book who has intruded into the child's everyday world. But when faced with a real hazard, such as a fire, hiding increases the risk of harm. Once you know some children think like this, you can plan your safety education so that you carefully and gently challenge these ideas, as well as offer children more appropriate ways to keep themselves safe, which they can practise.

The research also revealed that children identified objects and appliances they were keeping safe from, such as kitchen gadgets, tools, scissors and other sharp objects. Some objects were harmful because they could be easily broken and get children into trouble with their parents. Interestingly, some children wrote about objects as if they had intentions, for example 'knives to cut you' and 'cars to run you over'. This matches Piaget's observations from his work with young children – and draws attention to the way in which adults unwittingly reinforce a child's non-sense (but not nonsense) view of the world. How often have you said say to a child, 'Be careful with those scissors, they will cut you', rather than the more accurate 'Be careful with those scissors, you will cut yourself'? And how many parents jokingly smack the table when a child has bumped themselves, saying, 'Naughty table, did it hurt you?' Clearly it did not!

Children also drew and wrote about specific people (real and fictitious) as well as the kinds of people who could harm them, such as burglars, muggers, drunks and members of gangs. Sadly they also referred to people who are in authority, but whose job is to keep children safe, such as police officers, teachers and swimming pool attendants. Keeping safe from some of these people means staying indoors, staying with friends, telling people where you are going, and avoiding the people who can harm you. But avoiding police officers could result in children putting themselves at greater risk of harm.

Finally, children identified places indoors and out which were unsafe, such as: stairs, the kitchen, or roads, rivers and railways. Where the places were familiar they often had a set of rules which they could follow to keep themselves safe such as 'Find a safe place to cross the road', all of which reflected the very good safety education they had learned from, whether at home or at school.

The last question, 'Whose responsibility is it to keep you safe, wherever you are?', was also very revealing. Most frequently mentioned were parents and close family members, along with some generic 'grown-ups' but also adults with specific roles such as teachers, police officers (again!) and school crossing patrols. Some children thought more widely than this and mentioned prominent politicians, and a few wrote about God. Very few of the youngest children thought it was their responsibility to keep themselves safe (despite the rather loaded questions asked at the beginning) and at the age of ten years around half of the children still thought it was someone else's job to keep them safe. However, by the age of 11 years, some children thought they alone were responsible for keeping themselves safe, wherever they were.

> ### 💭 Consider
>
> Who helps to keep you safe in your everyday life? Is it just you, or does your list include individuals and organisations with statutory responsibilities for your safety? What about the health and safety officer at your school? If children as young as 11 think it is their sole responsibility to keep themselves safe, wherever they are, will they be more or less likely to ask a trustworthy adult for help if they feel unsafe? How could you encourage children in your class to think of all the people whose job it is to help them to stay safe as they move into independent, adult life?

The original research involved a sample of 926 children aged 4–11 years, but similar findings have been replicated in classrooms all over the UK. The findings were used to plot a spiral of children's changing understanding of keeping safe, which developed in complexity as they matured. The results enabled the researchers to develop a series of 'action planners' which consisted of groups of questions teachers could ask, and children could answer, which would help the children to develop their ideas about keeping themselves (and others) safe according to their age and level of understanding, resulting in a spiral curriculum for keeping safe (see Chapter 2). The research was later updated and the teaching materials revised (Wetton and Williams, 2000).

Planning a spiral curriculum in response to school-based action research like this will be the responsibility of the PSHE co-ordinator in your school, but you should still consider doing a draw and write activity when you are planning some safety education for your class. Remember to share the findings with any external contributor you are planning to invite to the classroom to enrich the children's learning, so they, like you, can start where the children are, not where they are expected to be.

Making safety education relevant to other school priorities

You could adapt the 'invitations to participate' above to fit a particular activity or theme (see Chapter 4 for points to bear in mind when developing your own classroom-based research questions). For example, every year there is a 'Walk to School Week' with a focus on encouraging children to walk to school to improve their health and fitness. I was curious to know what children would say about keeping safe on their way to school and so asked children in two primary schools in Edinburgh to help me just before 'Walk to School Week' in 2009 (McWhirter, 2009). Primary 6 (the equivalent of Year 6 in England and Wales) teachers asked the children (aged 10–11 years) to draw themselves on their way to school, keeping themselves safe, and to write what they are keeping safe from. They were then invited to write how they are keeping themselves safe, and finally, as in the original research, whose responsibility it is to keep them safe on their way to school.

Many of the responses were predictably about keeping safe on the road, either as pedestrians or as passengers in cars driven by their parents or carers. Children wrote about keeping safe by using crossings, looking out for traffic, wearing seat belts and not distracting car drivers. In most of these situations the children had a clear idea about how to keep themselves safe. Some children also wrote about keeping safe from fierce dogs and other people, such as older children and bullies. At one school the children wrote about keeping safe from 'winos' and 'junkies' and drew some scary people outside a local pub, which was on the same side of the road as their school. In this and many of the examples where the children described keeping safe from 'bad dogs', older children or adults, the children kept themselves safe by going another way to school or by crossing the road – and then crossing back again.

While this strategy may have made the children *feel* safer, in fact it meant they were exposed to one of the most dangerous hazards in their environment, the road. Whether their fear was misplaced or not, the children were exposed to heavy traffic twice, when they did not need to cross the road in the first place.

This small-scale classroom-based research reinforced what the teachers had expected and had planned to include in their safety lessons. It also revealed an issue which the teachers had not anticipated, and gave a new direction to their teaching so that they could address the children's concerns. Without the draw and write activity, the teachers could have focused the learning on the narrow aspects of road safety, about which the children already had a great deal of knowledge.

Why safety *and* risk education?

The title of this chapter is 'Understanding safety and risk education', but so far we have focused mainly on safety education. The problem with safety education is that there is specific safety advice which applies to every situation. By focusing on road safety, water safety and home safety (and within road safety: pedestrian safety, cycle safety, in-car safety), we quickly realise there is not enough time in the curriculum for all of it – never mind the rest of PSHE education. Specific campaigning groups produce resources for schools which address their particular safety issue or concern, but most do not help children learn transferable knowledge or acquire skills which they can apply in another situation.

For this reason researchers and practitioners have been trying to identify concepts underpinning PSHE education which could help children to make the link between what they are learning in safety education – and what they are learning in the rest of PSHE education – and their real lives, now and in the future. Risk is one of those unifying concepts, and the risk assessment process (hazard recognition, risk assessment, risk management) is a unifying process which applies in a multitude of scenarios, from crossing the road to accepting a lift from a stranger, or buying a pill at a festival.

Risk is a concept which is much discussed in public, but not always well understood. Risk is often defined as the 'probability of harm', where a hazard is something with the potential to cause harm. When we do a risk assessment we are assessing two factors – what could happen (severity of consequences) and how likely it is that the consequence will happen (probability). Risk is the product of these two factors:

risk = severity × probability

This technical definition of risk is highly biased towards negative outcomes – and with good reasons if we are thinking about industrial accidents or protection of the public at large events. The aim is to identify the risks which are tolerable and those which are intolerable. If the intolerable risks cannot be managed or reduced, then the activity must be avoided.

However, in education (and indeed in wider society) we too often tend to overlook the positive aspects of risk taking – the benefits to children and young people if they can face up to and overcome a challenge. Most good teachers and schools offer children challenging activities, while managing the potential risks so that, in the words of one safety charity, RoSPA, the activity becomes 'as safe as necessary, not as safe as possible' (RoSPA, 2012b).

According to Ofsted, to be outstanding, teachers and schools should go one step further, and engage children in the process of risk assessment, making the process more explicit and transparent to all.

When evaluating the behaviour and safety of pupils at the school, Ofsted inspectors are asked to consider:

- the extent to which pupils' attitudes to learning help or hinder their progress in lessons
- pupils' attitudes to school, conduct and behaviour during and outside of lessons, and their attitudes to other pupils, teachers and other staff
- the school's analysis of, and response to, pupils' behaviour over time, for example incident logs and records of rewards and sanctions
- rates, patterns of, and reasons for permanent and fixed-period exclusions[1]
- pupils' respect for courtesy and good manners towards each other and adults, and their understanding of how such behaviour contributes to school life, relationships, adult life and work
- types, rates and patterns of bullying and the effectiveness of the school's actions to prevent and tackle all forms of bullying and harassment. This includes cyber-bullying and prejudice-based bullying related to special educational need, sexual orientation, sex, race, religion and belief, gender reassignment or disability
- the school's success in keeping pupils safe, whether within school or during external activities through, for instance, *effective risk assessments*, e-safety arrangements, and action taken following any serious safeguarding incident
- the effectiveness of the school's actions to prevent and tackle discriminatory and derogatory language – this includes homophobic and racist language, and language that is derogatory about disabled people
- *the extent to which pupils are able to understand and respond to risk*, for example risks associated with extremism[2]
- the school's response to any extremist behaviour shown by pupils
- overall and persistent absence and attendance rates for different groups
- punctuality over time in arriving at school and at lessons
- the impact of the school's strategies to improve behaviour and attendance[3]
- the number of pupils taken off roll in the last year as a result of factors related to behaviour, safety and attendance
- the views of parents, staff and governors.

(Taken from the framework for inspecting schools in England under section 5 of the Education Act 2005 (Ofsted, 2013) emphasis added.)

---

[1] This includes patterns of permanent and fixed-period exclusions for different groups of pupils; the impact on behaviour of fixed-period exclusion and the impact of the school's work to follow up and support excluded pupils; the use and impact of internal exclusion; and the typical behaviour of any pupils who are not in school during inspection.

[2] This also includes risks associated with e-safety, substance misuse, knives and gangs, relationships (including sexual relationships), water, fire, roads and railways.

[3] This includes the use of rewards and sanctions, the effectiveness of any additional on-site provision to support behaviour, work with parents and absence 'follow-up'.

Think about a spiral curriculum for the development of risk competence (see Chapter 2). At the top of the spiral is the head teacher or manager who needs the skills, knowledge and understanding to take responsibility for their own safety and that of their pupils and employees. Just below this on the spiral is the experienced teacher or employee who should know and understand their part in the safety culture of an organisation, where it is their responsibility to act on or report hazards in the workplace so that they and their pupils and colleagues are safe to go about their daily work. Just below this is the new worker, or pupil on work experience, who find themselves in an unfamiliar environment with a new and unfamiliar task. Unless risk education has been included in the school curriculum, this young person could be accustomed to a safety culture where everything is made as safe as necessary, but has never shared any responsibility for their own safety.

The process described above is known as 'backward mapping'. It often helps to clarify the overall outcomes we are working towards, even when we are planning to teach the youngest children in school, so that we can plan to introduce the most appropriate language and to provide opportunities for children to practise the skills they will need on their journey to adulthood.

A fully developed spiral of risk competence has been included in a resource about road safety for healthy schools. It shows how knowledge of children's understanding of risk, from the age of 4 years to 18-plus can help to plan a spiral curriculum in road safety. This spiral focuses on the knowledge and skills children need to become safe road users as pedestrians, cyclists and ultimately drivers.

Consider

Redraw the spiral from Figure 8.3, retaining just the information on the right-hand side – and replacing the information on the left about road safety with water safety. How might you describe the steps to becoming someone who is safe in, on or by water to match the children's understanding of risk at different key stages? What are the implications for your class? What language, knowledge, understanding, attitudes and skills might your pupils need which are appropriate for their age and stage of development?

This spiral is based on children's responses to various small-and large-scale research projects carried out by McWhirter in Hampshire, Wiltshire

Become a safe road user

Becoming a safe road user	Becoming risk aware	Key Stage
Through experience, develop and adopt safer driving practices. Recognise how changing road and weather conditions affect the risk of accidents happening. Be aware of and respond to the needs of other road users and passengers.	Can promote safe behaviour in others by example.	Higher education student, young worker, young driver
And		
Be aware of the range of road hazards which increase the risk of road accidents. Recognise and, where appropriate, use existing measures to control risks such as seat belts, speed limits and traffic calming measures.	Can identify a range of hazards to self and others in unfamiliar situations based on advice, training and prior experience. Can assess risk to self and others and take action to manage risks.	Key Stage 5, young worker, pre-driver
And		
Be aware of the needs of a range of road users including pedestrians, cyclists and horse riders. Recognise, use and explain the role of control measures intended to reduce the chance of serious injury such as pedestrian crossings, cycle helmets, street lighting. Become familiar with the Highway Code.	Can identify some hazards in unfamiliar situations based on advice, training and prior experience.	Key Stage 4
And		
Identify and use safely a variety of safe routes to school and leisure facilities in your neighbourhood on foot, by bike and using public transport. Be able to explain what is meant by a safe route.	Can identify hazards, assess risks, make recommendations intended to manage risk to self and others in familiar situations.	Key Stage 3
And		
Understand and explain simple road safety advice such as 'Stop, look and listen'. Apply the rules in a controlled setting in your neighbourhood.	Can identify hazards and explain how to manage the risk to self and others in familiar situations. Can take action to manage risk to self in familiar situations.	Key Stage 2
And		
Follow rules to keep safe by the roadside such as 'Hold hands with an adult', 'Wear a seat belt'.	Can describe ways of keeping oneself safe in familiar settings.	Foundation and Key Stage 1

Figure 8.3 Becoming a safe road user
Source: RoSPA, 2008: 4

and Essex in the last ten years (see McWhirter and South (2004) for more information). Once again, it is important to start where the children in your class actually are, rather than where samples of children from other parts of the country once were. For young children you can use (or adapt) the draw and write about keeping safe above. For children aged nine years and over, you could try the following draw and write technique:

SAFETY AND RISK EDUCATION   159

- Invite the children to begin by drawing someone their own age, doing something risky.
- Next, ask them to write what is happening in the picture.
- Then, ask them to write what makes it risky.
- Finally ask them to draw themselves in the picture. What are they saying or doing to help?

As with all draw and write techniques aimed at establishing the starting point for your teaching, ask the children to work independently to begin with and don't give any prior explanation about what you mean by risk.

You can carry out a simple analysis of the findings by categorising the responses the children give. Among the highest-scoring categories will be extreme height (cliff tops, bungee jumping and parachuting) and misbehaviour (everything from naughtiness and disobedience to law-breaking and physical violence).

Yr 3   Boy

Tight rope Walking
Bee because you could
Sull.He is feeling scared
and worried.

Uh, OH You shouldnt
do that it is very
very dangerous

Figure 8.4 Boys of all ages often associate risk with extreme danger

Source: RoSPA, 2012a: 11

Year 6 boy

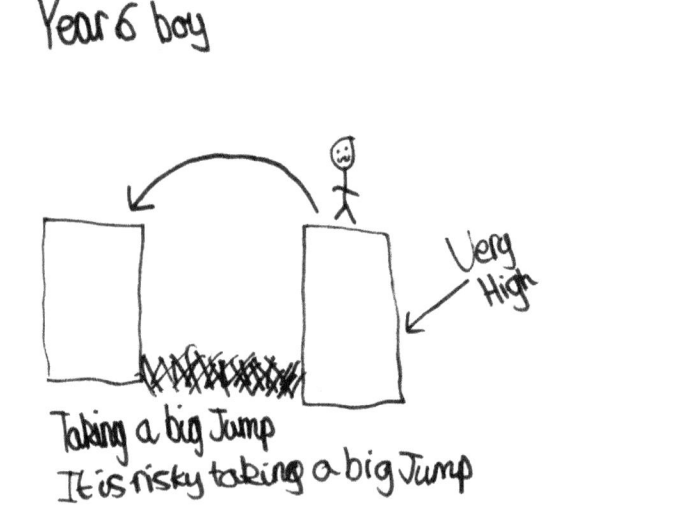

Taking a big Jump — Very High

It is risky taking a big Jump

nervous

Still nervous but excited

there Silly and not making the right choices

Figure 8.5 But not all see the risk of being in a high place negatively

Source: Moulsham Junior School, Essex

You will also find more daily forms of risk taking such as crossing the road, as well as smoking, drinking alcohol and hazards more often associated with adult life. In many of the examples the children will describe the most severe (and often least likely) consequence. If so this will confirm the findings of previous research which suggests that children interpret 'risky' as 'dangerous', where there is little uncertainty about the outcome and very little benefit.

Risk education in practice

What practical steps can you take to help children reflect on their understanding of risk? Think back to the learning walk, suggested at the beginning of this chapter. Could you extend this to a walk beyond the school gates, or other environments you might be visiting as part of their learning in another curriculum area? This could be a useful 'induction' for pupils at the start of a residential visit or perhaps a day trip to a zoo or farm. What has been done to keep the animals safe from the children, as well as the children safe from the animals?

You could use photographs of playgrounds and adventure activity centres you will be visiting to discuss the hazards they might find there and what the children could do if they were there to keep themselves (and others) safe. What might happen if the weather changed – would there be anything else they might have to do?

When you are planning a school visit, you could involve the class (or different groups within the class over a year) to help you with the routine risk assessments you should be doing. Prior to the visit itself the children could make a presentation to remind their classmates of any rules there are about keeping safe when out and about – and make sure that any which apply specifically to the particular visit are introduced so that everyone is aware of what their role is.

Each of these activities uses the language of risk – hazard, might, could, would, risk, benefit – in realistic and relevant settings. Words such as 'dangerous' and 'safe' should be used sparingly, when the situation is genuinely dangerous (where serious consequences are very likely) or absolutely safe (very rare!).

You could invite representatives from local emergency services to meet the children and explain what they do to keep themselves safe when they are at work, and how their work helps to keep the public safe. The children could also think about ways they could help the emergency services to do their job better.

If your school provides Forest School experiences for children you are very well placed to show parents (and Ofsted!) that it is possible for pupils to enjoy the benefits of challenging activities while helping children learn how to keep themselves safe. The Forest Schools movement encourages schools to enable young children to spend regular periods of time each week outdoors, in almost all weathers. The outdoor spaces can be large or small but are natural and wild, far from the neatly kept and 'safe' play areas we usually see in schools (Knight, 2011).

If you are fortunate enough to have a safety centre near to your school look into what they can offer for Year 6 pupils as they prepare to move to the 'big school'. These centres create realistic scenarios where children can discuss and practise effective strategies to keep themselves safe.

And finally, think twice before photocopying that 'spot the hazard' colouring-in sheet and handing it out to everyone in the class, assuming it will help them to learn how to keep themselves safe. The worst examples exaggerate the risks, and offer no practical solutions. The best will keep children occupied during wet playtimes.

> **Chapter summary**
>
> As a teacher you are responsible for the safety of children in your care, in the classroom, in the school grounds and when they are learning outside the classroom. As they mature, children are developmentally more and more capable of sharing that responsibility. Safety and risk education enables you: to find out what children are capable of; to offer realistic and relevant ways for them to develop the attitudes, knowledge, skills and understanding they will need to stay safe; and to plan opportunities for children to benefit from a wide range of challenging activities.

Further reading

Barton, B. (2007) *Safety, Risk and Adventure in Outdoor Activities*. London: Sage.
This explores the safety versus adventure debate and provides practical advice about planning outdoor and adventurous activities.

Knight, S. (2011) *Forest School for All*. London: Sage.
This includes case studies which emphasise the role of Forest Schools in personal and social development for children of all ages and a variety of needs.

RoSPA (Royal Society for the Prevention of Accidents) (2013) *Planning and Leading School Visits and Adventurous Activities*. Birmingham: RoSPA. Available at: www.rospa.com/schoolandcollegesafety/teachingsafely/info/school-visits-guide.pdf (accessed 17 October 2013).
This offers sensible and comprehensive advice for those planning school visits.

References

Formby, E., Coldwell, M., Stiell, B., Demack, S., Stevens, A., Shipton, C., Wolstenholme, C. and Willis, B. (2010) *PSHE Education: A Mapping Study of the Prevalent Models of Delivery and Their Effectiveness*. Department for Education Research Report DFE-RR080. Available at: www.gov.uk/government/uploads/system/uploads/attachment_data/file/170096/DFE-RR080.pdf (accessed 9 May 2013).

Gill, T. (2009) 'Now for free-range childhood', in *The Guardian*, 2 April. Available at: www.guardian.co.uk/commentisfree/2009/apr/02/children-safety (accessed 17 October 2013).

Knight, S. (2011) *Forest School for All*. London: Sage.

McWhirter, J. (2009) 'Walking to school', *Safety Education*, Summer: 6–7. www.rospa.com/schoolandcollegesafety/teachingsafety/safetyeducationjournal/info/SE_Summer2009.pdf (accessed 17 October 2013).

McWhirter, J.M. and South, N. (2004) *Young People and Risk*. Report for Government Office East.

Moss, S. (2012) *Natural Childhood*. National Trust. Available at: www.nationaltrust.org.uk/document-1355766991839/ (accessed 17 October 2013).

Ofsted (2013) 'The framework for school inspection', as amended April 2013. Available at: www.ofsted.gov.uk/resources/framework-for-school-inspection (accessed 17 October 2013).

RoSPA (Royal Society for the Prevention of Accidents) (2008) *Road Safety: A Guide for Healthy Schools*. Birmingham: RoSPA.

RoSPA (Royal Society for the Prevention of Accidents) (2010) *Learning to Adopt Safe Practices: A Survey for the Child Safety Education Coalition*. Available at: www.rospa.com/schoolandcollegesafety/teachingsafety/info/safe-practices-survey-report.pdf (accessed 9 May 2013).

RoSPA (Royal Society for the Prevention of Accidents) (2012a) *The Big Book of Accident Prevention*. Birmingham: RoSPA.

RoSPA (Royal Society for the Prevention of Accidents) (2012b) *Managing Safety in Schools and Colleges*. Available at: www.rospa.com/schoolandcollegesafety/info/managing-safety-schools-colleges.pdf (accessed 17 October 2013).

Wetton, N. and Williams, T. (2000) *Health for Life* (2 vols). Cheltenham: Nelson Thornes.

Williams, T., Wetton, N. and Moon, A. (1989) *A Way In: Five Key Areas of Health Education*. London: HEA.

CHAPTER 9

UNDERSTANDING SEX AND RELATIONSHIPS EDUCATION

Aim

To ensure you understand the concept of sex and relationships education (SRE) and what this concept means in the context of primary school education.

Learning objectives

By the time you have finished this chapter you will:

- have a clear understanding of sex and relationships education in primary education
- be able to assess what is and is not appropriate sex and relationships education in a primary school curriculum
- have a clear understanding of practical ways into exploring sex and relationships education with primary school pupils
- be able to choose appropriate (and avoid inappropriate) resources to use in your classroom.

Getting started

This chapter explores what is perhaps one of the most controversial aspects of personal, social and health education in primary education, that of sex and relationships education. The end of the chapter details two commonly used themes used by schools to provide a context for sex and relationships education.

> **Consider**
> Primary schools take children from the edge of babyhood, some reluctantly leaving babyhood behind, and pass them to secondary schools where they quickly reach the brink of adulthood. There is no period when children go through as much change as they do between reception infants and their final term of primary school.

Please ensure that the class teacher is aware that you want to undertake this activity before starting. If this is not the age group you are teaching, ask to borrow someone else's class for a while, but make sure the class teacher knows what you are planning to ask the children to do. Before starting, refer to Chapter 4 (starting where children are) to understand how to address sensitive issues in the classroom.

> **Teaching activity**
> (Please check with class teacher first!)
> Ask some children aged 10 and/or 11 years to:
>
> - Draw either (choose a girl's name, not from the class) or (choose a boy's name, not from the class) going out in the evening, dressed up and looking grown-up. Write how you can tell from the picture that (girl's name) or (boy's name) is growing up.
> - Think about how (girl's name) or (boy's name) is feeling about going out, looking grown-up. Write what (girl's name) or (boy's name) is feeling and draw a thought bubble around what you have written about how (girl's name) or (boy's name) feels about going out, looking grown-up.
> - Write what (girl's name) or (boy's name) is taking with them which shows that they are growing up.
>
> (Adapted from McWhirter, 1993)

Take a close look at each child's written statements, but also, in this case, at the drawing. Has the child chosen to draw someone the same gender as themselves? What kind of clothing have they shown? Are there identifiable 'labels'? What kinds of feelings do the children describe in their thought bubble – are they mainly positive, confident feelings, or are they worried, anxious feelings, or mixed? Finally what objects do they take which show the drawn person is growing up – money, house or car keys, tampons, condoms, drugs including cigarettes?

Ask yourself, what does this reveal about the children's understanding of 'growing up'? Is there a match between the outer signs and the inner feelings? Or, as is often the case with this age group, are the outward signs positive and confident, while the inner thoughts are more concerned and worried? How much about growing up is about consumerism and how much about taking responsibility? Remember, if the children draw and write about cigarettes or condoms it does not mean they are smokers or sexually active. It means they associate these objects (or just the words) with people who are 'growing up'.

Their responses will reflect what they have talked about, overheard and seen at home, the content of the SRE they have received at school so far, and, importantly, the classroom climate – whether they feel safe to write about more personal aspects of physical development and about feelings (not at this stage their own feelings, but those they can project on to someone else, see Chapter 4).

This first of three invitations should help you to build up a picture of the children's understanding and therefore of their entitlement to sex and relationships education. Completing this draw and write will give you much more information around which to build an SRE plan for your class. If you teach younger children, you can use backward mapping to decide the steps needed to ensure children approach SRE with confidence. We describe this more fully later in this chapter.

The second stage of this investigation invites the children to draw a picture of either the boy or girl character in or just getting out of the shower (giving this choice is important: it allows children to draw someone behind a curtain or with a towel around them if they feel uncomfortable drawing a naked person). How can we tell they are growing up and changing?

The final invitation is simply a page with thought bubbles on it. We then ask the children to write how they feel about growing up and changing (McWhirter, 1993).

Introduction

On hearing the words 'sex and relationships education' or more narrowly just 'sex education' many people focus not unreasonably on the word 'sex', which in turn leads to thoughts of sexual intercourse and reproduction. It is therefore not surprising that many people instantly question the appropriateness of this work in primary schools. Unlike most other living things, reproduction is often not the first reason human beings engage in sexual activity. The vast majority of sexual behaviour is a shared intimacy between people because they enjoy it, and between couples it can create more love. It is not a coincidence that many people use the term 'making love' to describe sexual activity.

We need to step back a little and see a much larger picture. The first step may be to switch around the words. If instead we start with 'relationships', then helping children to constructively form, maintain and perhaps gently (or sometimes suddenly) end a wide variety of different relationships seems perfectly reasonable. They will have many different relationships throughout their lives. They will have acquaintances – those people they know perhaps on a casual basis – friends, close friends, best friends, distant and close family relations, classmates. One day they will have work colleagues, and perhaps a person, or maybe more than one, with whom they share a sexual relationship.

They may have physical contact of some sort with all of these people, from handshakes, to holding hands, to hugging, cuddling and kissing. Learning to judge what is appropriate and feels right to us and what is appropriate and feels right to others is a skill partly learnt over time and partly inside us. We know from a very young age when someone we are uncomfortable with comes too close, and how it makes us feel.

Long before they are emotionally or socially ready, children emerging from puberty are physically capable of becoming parents, and ignorance is no protection against pregnancy or sexually transmitted infections. There is a mistaken view that sex and relationships education is 'teaching children how to have sex'. No life form on our planet needs to be taught how to reproduce and that includes human beings. SRE is better thought of as the learning that helps us to understand the changes that happen at puberty, the new feelings that come with these changes and how to manage them in order keep ourselves and others we care about healthy and safe.

Because the majority of us share – with all other life-forms – a drive to reproduce, we know that this drive lies in some of the oldest parts of our physiology. These parts need managing by the newer, more cognitive areas of our brain that can understand this drive and assess consequences. Developing this management requires learning.

To further complicate matters, sexual activity can be defined in a variety of ways and sexual behaviour between human beings comes with an almost endless variety and creativity.

Before we go on we need to clarify some terms:

- *Sex* refers to our biological status, male or female, in a reproductive sense (or in rare cases intersex – a combination of both).
- *Gender* refers to a person's sense of identity as masculine or feminine, and their *gender identity* to how they perceive themselves.
- *Sexual orientation* or *sexuality* is a separate part of gender and refers to the sexual attraction they may feel. This also appears as a 'spectrum of behaviours'. Same-sex relationships (*homo* – meaning 'same' in Greek) are described as being gay or lesbian.
- *Transgender* refers to someone who lives in the opposite gender role to their outward physical characteristics. Some may choose surgical procedures to change their physical appearance.

The child's perspective

Young children will notice pregnant women, perhaps their own mother or carer pregnant with a sibling. We are living at a time when children are surrounded by sexual imagery. Consider many adverts, for example perfume adverts. It is virtually impossible to convey visually what is basically a smell that will, we hope, make us seem attractive. Advertisers therefore need to convey not the product but the desired effect. News stories concerning celebrities' ever-changing relationships are presented in great detail in the media. Issues of sexuality are explored in our evening soap operas and in family television.

There used to be a commonly held belief that 'everything "adult" goes over children's heads', basically assuming that if children do not understand something they will simply ignore it. Nothing could be further from the truth. Children's brains have evolved to learn. They have evolved to move from total dependence to relative independence in a very few years. In the first few years of their lives they learn to interpret and speak language, in some cases more than one language. They will learn to interpret marks on paper as language and interpret its meaning from what they see. They do this while learning to walk, run and skip.

Children are looking at and listening to much that they are experiencing. What they haven't developed are the skills and behaviours which show others that they are paying attention. As adults, when we listen to one another, we make eye contact, nod, smile or frown to convey that we are in 'rapport' with the person communicating with us. Children simply get on with what they are doing, but they are still watching and listening. 'Little pigs have big ears' might be a better guide! But this does not mean we should not discuss sexual matters with children. We just need to remember that they will make their own sense of what they hear, and may need help to understand. Not speaking, or abruptly ending conversations when they look as though they might get awkward (for you!), would be a backward step.

According to a constructivist viewpoint (see Chapter 2) children make sense of what they do not know and understand by trying to connect it up with the concepts that they already hold. Put simply, 'They make sense of the unknown by linking it to the known'. We do this as adults. If we are asked to describe something to someone we may reply, 'It is like … only instead of … it's …' As a strategy this can work well but sometimes we get a new piece of information that either connects up in the wrong way and we get misunderstanding, or it gives us an 'Ah-ha!' moment and means we have to take apart the whole concept and completely rebuild it in a new and richer way. Adults often find this harder than children!

Creating their own explanations

If we ask children where they imagine babies come from, the descriptions they offer us can be extraordinarily elegant and can make a lot more sense than the biological reality.

Consider this. Adults often have a reluctance to use correct medical terms with young children so they may hear that babies grow in their 'mummy's tummy'. No they don't, mummy's stomach is filled with dilute hydrochloric acid to help with digestion. Mummy's womb is a much better description, but if children see pregnant women who appear overweight as a result, they may believe, instead, their first piece of misinformation.

When you are a young child what is the only way anything gets into your stomach? You have to swallow it. Where is the only place you know solid matter comes out of the human body when you are a child? What do women look like when they are giving birth on television perhaps in one of the many hospital dramas? Could it appear to be extreme constipation?

Children are often able to offer us beautifully complex and completely logical ways a baby is conceived and grows, based on observation and overheard conversation, but it is often completely wrong. If a child says something like 'The stork delivered me' or 'It's magic' then an adult will have told them this. No child will construct this type of explanation; children's explanations are usually far more elegant and far more logical. It may appear to be non-sense, but it is never nonsense.

Many primary schools will provide a block of learning about the conception, development and birth of a baby (usually at the age of 10 or 11 years). By this age many children will be re-learning much that they already have worked out for themselves. These lessons help pull together concepts that may be almost formed or add in those small pieces of critical knowledge that complete what may be slightly fragmented understanding.

Moving into puberty

Before those crucial and interesting lessons in Year 6, children are learning about relationships but they are also physically growing and changing. Of course puberty is a big change as they move from childhood into adulthood, but the simple process of growing taller offers teachers routes into talking about the new opportunities and responsibilities growing up brings with it. For example, what can a child who is growing taller do now that they couldn't do before? Perhaps reach a window catch, the controls of an electric or gas cooker, the front door handle, or a kettle. With each new opportunity comes the need for new knowledge, new strategies, skills and a new responsibility that our pupils must learn. They need to know how to keep themselves safe and perhaps a younger sibling or even a pet. A gradual revisiting of a topic about growing and changing can offer a gentle lead into puberty, a very big change that can lead eventually to the huge responsibility of becoming a parent.

Children begin to enter puberty while still in primary school and some may be well into this phase before moving to secondary school. Boys may experience nocturnal emissions or 'wet dreams', or erections in class, and a growing number of girls will experience menarche, the start of their menstrual cycle, while still in primary school. They have a right to learning that will help them to understand that what is happening to them is a natural part of growing from a child into an adult. Without this understanding these experiences can be embarrassing or even terrifying to some children.

Many children, especially those that have had the opportunity to talk with adults about growing and changing into adults, look forward to becoming adults themselves. It is seldom the purely biological changes that concern children, which is why science lessons are not enough, although it is vitally important to reassure them that what is happening to them, or will happen soon, is a natural process.

What is more likely to worry children is the social issues. For example, in the case of menstruation, 'Will I be first in my class? Will I be last? What if my first period happens during a lesson and I am not prepared? What if the boys notice and laugh?' For boys it might be, 'What if I get an erection in class? What will if feel like if my voice breaks? Will it hurt? What if it never breaks?' For both boys and girls common anxieties include 'getting hairy', suddenly becoming the tallest, shortest, biggest or smallest. Being the first to change or being the last can both be worrying.

If you can't recall this just go and look at a class of children aged 10 and 11 years. Some physically continue to look like children; others are already small (or not so small) adults. It is important to remind ourselves that their emotional maturity may bear no relation to their outward physical maturity. (This is an easy trap for inexperienced teachers to fall into.)

The power of great PSHE education is that it doesn't presume to know what a class is thinking or feeling. Through effective questioning we provide opportunities to allow children to share their thoughts and feelings and through their disclosures of their experiences tell us where they are and what they are ready for. Children never cease to surprise us with their answers, although teachers often find themselves, with hindsight, having their own 'Ah-ha!' moment as they realise that 'Of course children *would* see it like that!'

Building a developmental programme

Sex and relationships education should have been happening long before the age of 10 and 11 years and this is where we start to explore just how complex and rich SRE teaching really is. Although this chapter focuses on SRE within PSHE, there may be supporting work taking place through the school's science programme that will include learning about the physical processes of growing and changing. While in secondary school these lessons may be separated on the timetable, in primary schools it is much easier to incorporate the science with the psychology – the facts with the feelings – when it seems natural to do so.

We encourage the teaching of all PSHE to be organised through a spiral curriculum that revisits topics or themes as their teachers build deeper learning and greater challenges. We now have two themes within which we can locate SRE. Perhaps we could call them 'Growing and changing' and 'Me and my relationships'. These or similar themes will gradually build the learning that will underpin our overt sex education, which will usually take place in Year 5 or 6.

The following activity is aimed at teachers, or student teachers, not at children.

> **Consider**
>
> NB: This is not intended as a classroom activity. It is intended to focus on young people who are over 16 years (the legal age of consent in the UK). We are not suggesting that these topics are appropriate for children in primary schools although some will be emotionally and socially ready for this level of information. This is the 'end point' of our 'spiral curriculum'.
>
> Imagine two young people aged 17 years. They have been 'going steady' for a few months and have decided they are both deeply in love. They have engaged in mutual masturbation and have decided to have sexual intercourse for the first time tonight.
>
> What would these two young people need:
>
> - to know and understand?
> - to feel about themselves?
> - to understand about how others feel – perhaps friends or parents?
>
> And:
>
> - What values would they need to hold about themselves and others?
> - What vocabulary might they need?
> - What skills and strategies would they need?
>
> What responsibilities do they need to understand they have:
>
> - If they are either to go ahead and have a positive and safe experience?
> - Or if one of them changes their mind and says, 'No, wait, I am not ready'?

It would be really easy to focus solely on the biological facts and issues such as knowing about conception and contraception, and indeed it is important that children are able to develop a correct, medical language for parts of their bodies including external genitalia. It is likely they already have a family language for these parts of their bodies and as they grow may acquire a language used by their peers, but correct terms ensures clarity in the classroom and in any future discussion with a medical professional. These are relatively easy to teach and, contrary to many adults' beliefs, children readily accept this learning. But is knowing about contraception the main issue? Knowing where to get contraception is not the same as actually being able to go and get it. Though condoms are openly sold in supermarkets, even adults can find accessing contraception embarrassing.

What if one person says they don't want to use contraception; perhaps they do not like condoms? Now we are into negotiation. What has to be in place for real and successful negotiation to take place? Do we need respect, trust and a sense of fairness? What about good communication skills? What if the negotiation doesn't seem to be going well? It will help if the pair have practised their assertiveness skills. If negotiation is really breaking down they might need to be able to handle confrontation, manage aggression or even to escape.

Perhaps the final nightmare scene described above is a little pessimistic, but it is offered only to illustrate all that needs to be in place for a person be 'sexually well educated'. The reality is that probably 90 per cent (or even 99 per cent) of SRE in primary schools is not exclusively to do with sex. It is all the work that gradually builds those underlying values, skills, language and strategies that enable young people to develop the types of positive, healthy and safe relationships, including sexual relationships, that they may want.

Backward mapping

Now, take one step backwards in the curriculum timeline. Before these young people embarked on learning these key, adult skills, what would they have needed to know, to understand and to be able to do already? In other words, what would already need to be in place for these young adults that showed they were prepared for big steps such as that one in their (or any other) relationship? And are there further steps backwards we can take to show us earlier elements of learning that need to be in place? The more steps backwards we take, the closer we get to where the children are now, and the learning they need to start them on the path towards the competence of conducting sexual relationships. And that's where you start – with that first, next step.

If we need to construct a programme of learning in any sensitive issue, one way of doing it is to imagine a situation where a young person might encounter it. Next deconstruct the learning they need in order to manage that moment. Then backward map the learning that would need to underpin it. In this way the learning cascades back down the years and much of it overlaps. We have also illustrated this method for curriculum planning in safety and risk education in Chapter 8.

> **Consider**
>
> Consider a young person being offered a drug for the first time by their peers. Of course the *knowledge* they need is different from that required before they have sex – but what sort of *skills* would they need in order to manage the situation? How similar are they to those needed for safe first-time sexual experiences?

Imagine an infant classroom where children are playing together and learning to share a toy. They are learning respect and the concept of fairness. When they have to decide who takes the first turn and who comes next they are learning to negotiate. When they listen to and explore the feelings of a character in a story – perhaps learning new vocabulary to identify those feelings in themselves and share those feelings with others – they are developing empathy. When they learn the skills of making their voice heard in group work without shouting others down, or being shouted down by others, they are learning assertiveness. When a teacher demonstrates that even though a child's answer to a question is completely wrong, their contribution to the lesson is really important, they are learning that they and their voice are of genuine value.

In some ways SRE is no different from mathematics education. If we expect young adults to understand the concept of compound interest so that they can manage their first credit card, the concepts and skills they will need are built on the first numeracy lessons they took in the infant school. You cannot understand compound interest without first understanding percentages, which requires understanding multiplication, which requires understanding addition, which requires a concept of number.

You may hear the assertion that 'Sex education should be "age appropriate"'. Please be careful of this. It is not chronological age that is important, it is educational readiness – intellectual and emotional readiness. This is why SRE is best taught by teachers who know their pupils and can gauge that readiness. Sometimes you will need to move work earlier in the curriculum, sometimes later. Sometimes you will have built in enough preparatory work, sometimes you may need to build in a little more or revisit some prior learning. What is important is to retain flexibility. Relevance and appropriateness are both important.

'Layer by layer' not 'lump by lump'

SRE, like all learning in PSHE, is built up gradually 'layer by layer', extending existing concepts, developing skills, vocabulary and strategies, and helping to explore and develop values and beliefs. It is not built up 'lump by lump'. We do not 'do sex education' in a few lessons with a particular age group, in the same way we do not 'do mathematics education'. As part of a developmental PSHE programme we might focus on a topic such as conception but this will have been built on work undertaken in previous years gradually exploring growth and change. People sometimes ask, 'How do we know children are ready to learn about this?' Just as with any other area of the curriculum, it is because a planned programme of learning with rigorous teacher assessment has gradually prepared them for these lessons. Put simply, we get them ready. And we will know if they are not.

Getting the climate right

Before we begin to look specifically at a topic of sex education, rather than the broader relationships education or even broader PSHE programme, we need to step back for a moment once again and ask what sort of classroom climate we need in order to be able to undertake this work safely. It is likely that you will have established some form of 'class rules' or 'promises' (see Chapter 6) for guiding the children on how to behave, and it is important to remind them of these. You may feel you need to add or amend some rules, ideally working this through with the class. Even the very youngest know just what you mean when you ask them to 'be nice to each other'. It is important to remind children about what can and cannot be kept confidential and that we will not ask them personal questions. This is important. It is possible that a child may ask you a personal question either to test you or because they are genuinely interested and do not have the maturity to recognise boundaries. If you have agreed in advance that there are no personal questions then simply and gently restate that ground rule and move the lesson on. It is important not to over-react. Other children who may be vulnerable or even at risk will watch how you respond to questions, and seeing how you respond to one child's question may either encourage or discourage their own approach to you. (See also Chapter 6, pedagogy.)

Managing the questions all teachers dread

Something all teachers, regardless of experience, wonder is: What questions might pupils raise and how will I respond? All teachers imagine questions they dread coming up during sex education lessons. It is important to ask yourself 'what if ...' and consider how you might respond. Ask yourself, 'What questions would cause me concern either because I would be uncertain how to answer or because such a question would cause me to be concerned for the pupil's welfare?' Because we live in such a sexualised society it is not possible to predict the questions you may be asked.

You have to make a judgement about questions. Always ask yourself if the question is 'appropriate for this child'. It may simply be something a child has overheard and genuinely is curious about. A simple answer may be adequate. Or if the question is relevant to everyone, a fuller answer may be just what's needed. However, it may be about something you feel sure the class is not ready to examine, and all you need to do is gloss over it and move on. But it may be an indicator of a child at risk. When it comes to child protection there is a simple rule for teachers – 'If in doubt, shout' – in terms of telling an appropriate colleague. Every school has a member of staff responsible for safeguarding children (see Appendix 1, Safeguarding). Often in primary school this is the head teacher. If you have genuine concerns about the language or detail in a child's question, talk to the responsible person. Sometimes it is hard to pin down exactly what is wrong so always trust your instincts. If a child's comments or questions make you feel uneasy in any way never hesitate to share your concern, no matter how trivial or ridiculous it seems, with a senior colleague or the person designated with responsibility for child protection. It is important to remember that senior colleagues may already have other information about a child and your additional concern could be the final trigger for action.

However, it is important to recognise that there is no need to answer children's questions immediately. If you have a question from a child that you are uncertain how to answer, simply respond with something like 'That is a really good question. It is going to take me a little time to think about a really good answer. Let me talk to you later.' There is also no need to create an answer on your own. As a member of a school staff it is appropriate to ask a senior colleague how the school would wish you to respond to a question you find challenging or difficult. There is no hurry and it is always better to give yourself space, and if necessary talk to colleagues, rather than give an immediate and perhaps inappropriate answer.

Many schools provide a 'question box' that allows children to anonymously ask questions they may feel embarrassed to ask in front of their peers. It is important to recognise that this approach may disadvantage children with poor writing skills, although agreeing that this is one of those occasions when spelling doesn't matter can help.

The importance of school policy

So what might a planned programme of SRE contain? Before we look at that we again need to take a step back. The majority of primary schools will have an SRE policy. It is essential that all teachers are aware of the content of this policy. Unlike many other policies, this one will often specify the details of the programme of study as well as the values that the programme seeks to promote. It may include details on the place of marriage and the promotion of sexual activity taking place within a stable relationship. School policy should also make reference to cultural diversity and the differing values held by families whose children attend the school. If the school is a faith school, it will reflect the values of the faith it espouses. Regardless of your individual point of view or personal values or beliefs it is essential that as a professional teacher you work within your school's agreed policy. Some policies will state, 'Children's questions will be answered as and when they arise'. In a minority of schools this is a substitute for having a planned programme. This is very challenging for a teacher because without an understanding of children's prior learning it is difficult to construct a spontaneous, meaningful and appropriate answer. Curious children are seldom satisfied with one question. It is always appropriate to give yourself some space to either think of a suitable answer or consult with colleagues and then decide whether to respond to the individual on their own, or the class as a whole.

> **Personal activity**
>
> Ask to see a school's sex and relationships education policy.
>
> - What does it contain?
> - How does it help you to understand what will and perhaps will not be taught to children in this school?
> - Does it offer support with sensitive issues such as confidentiality? Child protection? Teachers' training and support needs?

Some policies specify which topics will be taught to different year groups and may even specify in which term. This can present a problem because, just as in any other subject, different children may progress through their PSHE programme at different speeds, and increasingly schools are recognising the need to remain flexible.

A partnership with families

Many parents and carers feel strongly that they need to know when any specific work may be covered so this they are prepared for any questions their children may have following this lesson or series of lessons. Effective SRE is a partnership between schools and families or carers, and clear communication is essential if this is to happen.

In contrast to the fears expressed in the media and by some vocal groups, the British Market Research Bureau tracking survey (BMRB International, 2003) shows strong support for sex and relationships education: 88 per cent of young people and 86 per cent of parents saw SRE as helping young people to be more responsible about sex. Three quarters of young people and two thirds of parents were not of the opinion that sex education encourages young people to have sex too early.

Most parents feel they ought to have a role as sex and relationships educators. Nine out of ten parents surveyed in one region of England felt they should discuss sex with their children, but only half reported actually doing so (Ingham and Carrera, 1998 – survey of 750 parents in Wessex). In another survey with 500 parents in Bristol, 77 per cent said children should be getting information about sex and relationships from their parents (NHS Bristol, 2009). Ironically, another survey found that over half of parents say they find it embarrassing to talk about sex with their child (Naik, 2008) and value support from their children's school.

Under current legislation a parent may withdraw their child from any and every aspect of sex education not covered in the statutory national curriculum. This presents a problem because we have already explored just how wide the definition of sex and relationships education could be. In reality the lessons children are withdrawn from are seldom more than the narrow work on the process of conception and contraception. There is, however, a further difficulty. It is important that their teacher treats any child who is withdrawn from these lessons with great sensitivity. Many parents who choose to withdraw their children may forget that their children will be curious and usually discuss the content of the lessons they have missed with their peers in the hours or days that follow.

We live in one of the most culturally diverse communities in the world, and a school's policy should reflect that diversity. Different cultures will view sexual activity in different ways and it is important that children experience a programme that both respects their own cultures, values and beliefs and also encourages them to respect the diversity of cultures and beliefs of their peers and the wider community. One of the most comprehensive online sources of support for teachers in sex and relationships education is the Sex Education Forum's website, which provides expert guidance and resources for teachers (see Further reading at the end of this chapter).

Sexuality

As we said earlier, human sexuality is both rich and complex. The issue of discussing gender and particularly homosexuality is often contentious, especially in primary schools. This begs the question, why? In the real world many children are very aware of same-sex relationships. They see same-sex relationships on television, they may have gay or bisexual relations within their families, or classmates with same-sex parents or carers. One of the most important qualities we need to develop in a diverse society is that of understanding, tolerance and respect for others' lifestyles.

Depending on your choice of statistics, 7 per cent of the adult population are gay or bisexual, and probably nearer to 11 per cent. This means it is safe to assume that at least one member, and perhaps more, of any class of 30 pupils is likely to be or become gay or bisexual. While this may not manifest until secondary school or even later, many gay and bisexual individuals will recall knowing that they felt differently from their peers from a very young age; building attitudes of general tolerance for difference is important throughout all age groups.

Teaching about sexuality demonstrates the value of a planned programme of PSHE. If, as part of such a programme, questions such as 'Who are our special people? How do they show us they care for us? How do we show them we care for them?' have been explored, it is easy to refer back and to build on this. Should pupils raise the issue of homosexuality or bisexuality, or if your school policy includes this as part of the programme, it is easy simply to say, 'Do you remember when we discussed how people love and care for one another? Well, some men fall in love with another man and some women fall in love with another woman. Some men and women feel they can fall in love with both men and women.' Referring back to, and building on, prior learning is almost always easier than trying to teach sensitive issues outside of a planned programme. And in a climate where there is political pressure for legal, same-sex marriages, it would seem like a strange omission indeed if the subject were never to be raised in primary school classrooms.

Into practice

In this section we show what learning a spiral programme might contain.

The first section details a developmental theme of 'relationships', which could be covered during a half-term of work. The second section sets out possible content of a theme of 'growing and changing'. As part of a planned PSHE programme this theme might be covered during a half-term of work revisited in each year. The example of an SRE programme of study on the following page has been drawn and adapted from Essex Local Authority's PSHE programme planning toolkit and produced by Nicola Speechley-Watson when she was their local Authority Adviser.

Teaching the process of conception and reproduction

In our view, it is inappropriate to ask a student teacher or newly qualified teacher to teach the biological aspects of puberty, sexual intercourse and reproduction. It is always best to shadow a more experienced colleague before teaching this for the first time. However, as teacher-educators we are aware that student teachers and NQTs may be given this task. Think carefully and seek advice from your mentor, tutor and PSHE co-ordinator if this happens to you.

Table 9.1 Example of an SRE programme

Age of primary school children	Theme	Theme
	Relationships	Growing and Changing
Year 1, ages 5 to 6	<ul><li>that there are physical attributes and feelings that they all share</li><li>that we are alike in many ways but that each of us is unique and special</li><li>to view difference and diversity positively</li><li>about how it might feel to be left out</li><li>that we have a right not to be afraid or hurt</li><li>that difference is not an excuse for bullying</li><li>about the value of being a friend and having friends</li><li>about what friends do with and for each other</li><li>skills for getting on with each other: co-operating as part of a group</li><li>about ways that we can show care and support for others</li><li>how to recognise how other people are feeling, and act accordingly</li></ul>	<ul><li>that humans produce babies who grow into children and then into adults</li><li>about some of the things that children can do for themselves that babies cannot</li><li>about what animals and babies need to grow</li><li>to identify some of the people who have helped them to grow and what these people did to help them grow</li><li>that we all have memories about being younger; these memories are special to us and our families</li><li>how it feels to do something for the first time</li><li>to celebrate their achievements</li><li>that there are lots of things to learn as they grow up</li><li>that they will need effort, practice and help to learn the skills they need</li></ul>

(Continued)

Table 9.1 (Continued)

Age of primary school children	Theme: Relationships	Theme: Growing and Changing
Year 2, ages 6 to 7	<ul><li>about networks of special people</li><li>that other people's networks may be different from their own</li><li>that there are different types of family</li><li>to reflect on how their family is special and how family members care for each other</li><li>about their networks of friends</li><li>the skills of making friends</li><li>that people do not have to like/do everything that their friends like/do to be friends</li><li>how it might feel to quarrel with a friend and ways to manage these feelings</li><li>strategies for staying friends/repairing friendships (e.g. not being bossy/unkind, helping each other, sharing and taking turns, saying sorry, recognising how other people are feeling)</li><li>to recognise and be able to empathise with how others are feeling</li><li>how to help others to feel valued and appreciated</li></ul>	<ul><li>that as they get older they can do more things for themselves</li><li>to be positive about their achievements and capabilities</li><li>that as they are growing to greater independence they will need a greater range of skills; what some of these skills are</li><li>who can help them to develop their skills and what their own responsibilities are</li><li>about ways that they can take greater responsibility for looking after themselves and keeping themselves safe as they get bigger and older</li><li>about the process of growing from young to old</li><li>about some of the changes that take place from babyhood to adulthood</li><li>about how people's needs change at each stage of growth</li><li>to identify how their needs have changed as they have grown</li></ul>

Age of primary school children	Theme		Theme	
	Relationships		Growing and Changing	
Year 3, ages 7 to 8	<ul><li>about extended relationship networks beyond the immediate family</li><li>about how networks grow and change with time</li><li>to manage feelings surrounding new people joining their networks</li><li>about what it means to 'care for' people/pets in our networks</li><li>that some people have disabilities and may need special care</li><li>that some people with disabilities may not or may not always, need help</li><li>about how they might help, when needed</li><li>that some people with disabilities may not or may not always, need help</li><li>to empathise with others</li><li>that we are meeting new people all the time</li><li>how to make friends and make people feel welcome in their networks</li><li>that an important skill in resolving relationship disputes is being able to see things from someone else's point of view</li><li>about the behaviour and attitudes that contribute to maintaining friendships and relationships</li><li>about how each of us has a positive contribution to make to our networks</li><li>about how it feels to belong to a group and the importance of this</li></ul>		<ul><li>to recognise ways in which they have changed over the past year</li><li>to reflect positively on their own growth and change</li><li>that there are two kinds of changes – physical and emotional – and that learning to manage these is an important skill in growing up healthily and happily</li><li>about how they grow year by year</li><li>that with this physical growth comes development in their capabilities</li><li>about new responsibilities that come as they grow and grow up</li><li>how their responsibilities have changed as they have grown</li><li>what responsibilities they now have</li></ul>	

(Continued)

Table 9.1 (Continued)

Age of primary school children	Theme Relationships	Theme Growing and Changing
Year 4, ages 8 to 9	• that someone who bullies makes him/herself feel better by making someone else feel worse • how easy it is for some to slip into bullying behaviour; to recognise possible motivations for doing this and stop • about the danger of stereotyping people as 'bullies' because of their physical characteristics • strategies for dealing with bullying behaviour • a vocabulary of feelings surrounding bullying • that there is no acceptable reason for bullying • to deal positively with their fears and distress surrounding bullying • that when bullying happens and they see it or are involved, they are faced with a responsibility to intervene or get help • what it means to 'put yourself in someone else's shoes' and how this can help them to make the decision to act • strategies for recognising and minimising the risks of bullying • to recognise critical moments • strategies to protect themselves from being bullied physically or mentally: e.g. walk tall, have confidence, communication skills, assertiveness	• about the stages in life from pregnancy to old age • about changes in growth at each stage • to recognise and challenge stereotyping on the basis of age • that memories are an important part of people's lives • how they can show respect for things that are special to others • about how people change and become grown up • about stages at which people learn to be responsible for different things, for example to manage money • to reflect upon what they want to be when they are grown up and how they hope to see themselves

Age of primary school children	Theme	Theme
	Relationships	Growing and Changing
Year 5, ages 9 to 10	• rules for getting on with others; that different relationships might have different rules • rules and laws which help communities to keep good relationships and the way these are set up • skills for getting to know new people • what is meant by 'stereotyping' and 'discrimination' • about why it is important to examine and challenge stereotypical attitudes • how discrimination and bullying can escalate • about how to resolve conflict effectively • about the prerequisites for conflict resolution and problem solving techniques: how to stay focused on the 'problem' rather than attacking the person • to use language assertively when resolving conflict • about the steps of conflict resolution: how they are feeling; why they are feeling this way and what they need; what action they would like to see	• about the main physical and emotional changes at puberty for both boys and girls • why changes at puberty occur at different rates • skills and strategies for managing changes at puberty • to deal positively with questions they have about puberty • about sources of reliable and accurate information for puberty issues • that there is a range of places to get help and support for puberty issues • the skills to access this range of support • about the kinds of things that grown-ups are responsible for and the kinds of things that children are responsible for • about ways in which they can become more responsible as they grow up

(Continued)

Table 9.1 (Continued)

Age of primary school children	Theme Relationships	Theme Growing and Changing
Year 6, ages 10 to 11	• about the personal skills of leadership • about the qualities of an effective leader • to value the different aspects of their personality and the personalities of others • strategies for resisting persuasion from special friends or from a larger friendship group • a vocabulary of feelings to deal with being left out of a group and strategies for dealing with these feelings • the importance of 'image' and being part of the 'group'; the influence of the media and especially advertising • about the impact of group image and the pressure to conform which this can cause • about their preferred styles of conflict resolution • about the skills needed for active listening and effective communication • to put these skills into practice • to put their conflict management skills into practice • about ways of building strong relationships with people within networks • about tensions which may arise within networks, and positive ways of resolving these tensions	• about ways that people may change in appearance, personality and relationships as they grow and grow up, and ways that they may stay the same • a vocabulary of feelings associated with change • to assess the risks in trying to grow up too soon • about letting the growing-up process take its course and what this means • about the responsibilities of parenthood and the problems for girls and boys of becoming very young parents • to deepen their understanding of what it means to be responsible and to take on responsibilities

At this point you are probably asking yourself: but how do we actually teach the biological aspects of puberty, sexual intercourse and reproduction? In some respects this is the easy part. As part of a school policy the majority of schools will have identified the specific resources they will use to support this learning. It usually consists of a combination of video material backed up through classroom discussion. Some teachers will work with their local school nurses who 'team teach' this more focused aspect of SRE. Many schools will provide opportunities for parents and carers to view teaching material in order that they can be prepared to reinforce and discuss the classroom learning in their homes.

Historically there has been an on-going debate about whether the specific lessons on aspects of puberty should be taught in mixed- or single-sex classes. The best model is to teach in mixed-sex classes because it is essential that boys and girls understand the changes each is or will be experiencing. It can be helpful, however, to offer single-sex opportunities to ensure that both boys and girls have the opportunity to ask any questions that a mixed-sex session might inhibit. Once again it is a question of knowing your class.

Chapter summary

This chapter explored the fears and myths surrounding sex and relationships education for younger children, replacing them with a sound understanding of the need for SRE from an early age. It considered relevance, appropriateness and the need for sensitivity and flexibility, arguing that if we are to expect competence in all relationships, including sexual ones, we cannot afford to leave children uneducated until puberty. It offers clear guidance about suitable content.

Further reading

Blake, S. (2002) *Sex and Relationships Education: A Step-by-Step Guide for Teachers*. London: David Fulton.
   A sound, practical approach to this important topic.
Blake, S. and Katrak, Z. (2002) *Faith, Values and Sex & Relationships Education: Addressing the Issues*. London: NCB.
   The authors tackle this sensitive issue with confidence and clarity.
Sex Education Forum, www.sexeducationforum.org.uk.

References

BMRB International (2003) *Evaluation of the Teenage Pregnancy Strategy. Tracking Survey*, Report of results of nine waves of research. London: BMRB International.

Ingham, R. and Carrera, C. (1998) 'Liaison between parents and schools on sex education policies', *Sex Education Matters*, 15: 11.

McWhirter, J.M. (1993) 'A teenager's view of puberty', *Health Education*, May: 9–11.

Naik, A. (2008) *Everyday Conversations, Every Day*. London: Parents Centre/Department for Children, Schools and Families.

NHS Bristol (2009) 'Parent attitudes to teenage sexual health pregnancy and sex and relationships education: telephone interviews', MSS Research (Project number MR4689).

Speechly-Watson, N. (n.d.) Planning tool for PSHE&C. Essex Local Authority.

CHAPTER 10

UNDERSTANDING HOW TO ADDRESS BULLYING BEHAVIOUR IN PSHE EDUCATION

Aim

To ensure that you understand bullying and the role PSHE education plays in minimising and addressing bullying as part of a whole school approach.

Learning objectives

By the time you finish this chapter you will:

- have a personal understanding of the term 'bullying'
- have strategies for building work on bullying into your teaching of PSHE education.

Key ideas underpinning this chapter

- Bullying behaviour can have a significant impact on a pupil's ability to learn and achieve.
- The experience of bullying can have long lasting, far reaching, damaging effects on a pupil's wellbeing.
- PSHE education has a role to play in minimising bullying behaviour within a school.
- To label a child as 'bully' or 'victim' can be unhelpful.

'It isn't that frightened children won't learn, frightened children can't learn!'

Bill Rice (unpublished comment)

Getting started

> **Teaching activity**
>
> Ask the children to help you complete this sentence:
>   If someone was being bullied at this school they could tell …
>
> And answer this question:
>   If they tell this person, *what would happen next*?

Introduction

This chapter explores the issue of bullying. It considers the role PSHE education can play in minimising the likelihood of bullying behaviours and addressing the needs of perpetrators and targets if it does occur. It explores how PSHE education can equip pupils with the skills and 'inner resources' they need to manage situations where they or someone else is experiencing bullying. It also reinforces the importance of encouraging them, if they either cannot manage or feel it is unsafe to try, to get appropriate help.

The majority of schools will have an 'anti-bullying policy' that defines the accumulation of activities and protocols the school has devised to minimise and if necessary address incidents of bullying. Communication requires both a 'listening school community' but also a school community that has learnt 'how to tell'. A planned programme of PSHE education as part of this whole school approach – which may include peer support programmes such as peer mediation and playground leader schemes, and activities promoting positive relationships in the classroom and school – can help to develop both.

Defining terms

> **Personal activity**
>
> Before we start, spend a moment clarifying how you would define 'bullying'. What does the term 'bullying' mean to you? How would you define it for yourself?

It can be interesting trying this activity with some friends or colleagues. While your answers may all have elements in common it is likely that there will be some difference. This is often what happens when we turn a verb into a noun.

Many people have spent a great deal of time trying to define exactly what is and is not bullying. For some it must involve a persistent behaviour, for others it can be a 'one off' action. For some it must be an abuse of power or an attempt to exert power over someone less powerful. For others it is an inevitable part of belonging in a group where a 'pecking order' needs to be established. So where can we turn for a clear definition?

We could begin with the Oxford English Dictionary that defines a bully as 'a person who uses strength or influence to harm or intimidate those who are weaker', and bullying as 'the use (of) superior strength or influence to intimidate (someone), typically to force them to do something'.

In 2013 England's Department for Education stated:

> Bullying is behaviour by an individual or group, repeated over time, that intentionally hurts another individual or group either physically or emotionally. Bullying can take many forms (for instance, cyberbullying via text messages or the internet), and is often motivated by prejudice against particular groups, for example on grounds of race, religion, gender, sexual orientation, or because a child is adopted or has caring responsibilities. It might be motivated by actual differences between children, or perceived differences. Stopping violence and ensuring immediate physical safety is obviously a school's first

priority but emotional bullying can be more damaging than physical; teachers and schools have to make their own judgements about each specific case. (Department of Education, 2013)

If we look to academia, the following is taken from Wolke et al. (2001: 673–4):

> As defined by Olweus (1999 et al., p. 10), 'a student is being bullied or victimised when he or she is exposed repeatedly and over time to negative action on the part of one or more other students'. The negative behaviour has to be intentional, to cause harm to the victim (Farrington, 1993; Smith & Thompson, 1991). It can be physical (hitting, kicking, pinching, taking money or belongings etc.), verbal (name-calling, cruel teasing, taunting, threatening etc.) or, as recently described, psychological (social exclusion, isolation, malicious gossip etc.) (Björkqvist, Lagerspetz & Kaukiainen, 1992; Crick & Grotpeter, 1995; Wolke & Stanford, 1999). Bullying must be a repeated action and occur regularly over time. Thus, occasional negative behaviours or conflict are not viewed as victimization. For behaviour to qualify as bullying, there should also be a real or perceived imbalance in strength (asymmetric power relationship) that can be characterized by physical or mental behaviours. Therefore, it is not bullying when there is conflict between two persons of the same physical or mental strength (Smith et al., 1999).

Whether or not the action is repeated, regularly or otherwise, picking on someone in a way that damages them physically or psychologically is clearly unacceptable, and it is important to make this clear to children – both as warning and as reassurance.

As we have seen from Chapter 2, learning is a physical process; the person that is each of us is a product of the incredibly complex neural activity and responses to stimuli taking place within our brains. The interactions we have with the physical world around us, and the relationships we form as we interact with others as we grow and develop, literally physically shapes the structure of our brains and hence 'us'. Although research is in its early stages, neuroscience appears to indicate that experiencing persistent bullying can have profound and long lasting effects on a child's developing brain, leaving them vulnerable to poor mental health and relationship and lifestyle difficulties in later life. If we consider persistent bullying as leading to 'brain damage', addressing the issue takes on an even greater urgency.

At one time or another many of us might reflect that the way we behaved towards one another may have been perceived as bullying. This is different from the actions of a persistent bully.

In 1978 Olweus identified three different types of persistent bully:

- *Aggressive bullies* who are often physically strong, impulsive and lacking in empathy for others. They can be popular, especially with younger children, but less so as children get older and think more critically about their peers.
- *Passive bullies* who tend to be insecure, lack self-esteem and will often join in bullying instigated by the aggressive bully.
- *Bully-victims* who are a small percentage of bullies who have been bullied themselves. They tend to be unpopular with their peers and are more likely to suffer anxiety and depression.

Wolke (cited in Cassidy, 1999) identified a fourth category:

- *Pure bullies*, described as 'healthy individuals who enjoy school and use bullying to obtain dominance'.

There are different types of victim or target for bullying:

- *Passive victims* (Olweus, 2006) who do not provoke bullies. These pupils are often quiet and withdrawn, and have low self-esteem. This can make them vulnerable to bullying, which in turn enhances these characteristics. Young children may respond by crying, withdrawing from situations, and anger.
- *Vicarious victims* (Besag, 1989) are the peers of the victim who have either witnessed or heard about bullying and who in turn become anxious that they may become targets.
- *False victims* (Besag, 1989) who complain about fictitious bullying in order to attract attention and sympathy from their teacher.
- *Provocative victims* (Olweus, 2006) who deliberately behave in ways that irritate their peers. These children may have learning disabilities that contribute to this behaviour.

It can be helpful to use the terms 'perpetrator' and 'target' rather than 'bully' and 'victim', as the terms 'bully' and 'victim' can become unhelpful, enduring labels.

Helpful definitions and characteristics of perpetrators and targets of bullying can be found on the Kansas Safe School Resource Center website (see Further reading at the end of this chapter).

For teachers of very young children, there is something of a paradox. Young children may not (yet) be perpetrators or targets. Indeed, in some cases the stimulus that eventually provokes such behaviour patterns may not yet have occurred. So there may seem little to look out for. Yet, for other children, they may be beginning to learn that they can derive pleasure, advantage, relief, dominance, etc. from unfair and unreasonable, even forceful and violent, behaviour towards others. And yet others may be starting the cycle of feeling weak, miserable or unworthy. These signs are all vital to look out for. It throws into sharp relief the need to foster fairness, equality, respect and tolerance in all the children in every class, and to ensure that systems are in place for suitable management and support for when bullying does occur, right from the start of schooling.

The 'third group'

We have considered the perpetrator of bullying and the target of the behaviour but there is a third group. These are the 'bystanders' or 'witnesses' who may:

- *be afraid to associate with the victim* for fear of either lowering their own status or of retribution from the bully and becoming victims themselves
- *fear reporting bullying incidents* because they do not want to be called a 'snitch', a 'tattler', or 'informer'
- *experience feelings of guilt and helplessness* for not standing up to the bully on behalf of their classmate
- *be drawn into bullying behaviour* by group pressure
- *feel unsafe*, unable to take action, or a loss of control. (See Kansas Safe School Resource Center in Further reading)

Some may choose to take sides, perhaps joining in the bullying either willingly or out of a need to collude with the perpetrators to avoid becoming a target themselves. Some may try to support the target, while others may just look the other way and hope they will be ignored. Some may be fearful of telling a teacher in case they incur the wrath of the perpetrator.

It is important for teachers to focus on how we prepare pupils to behave if they find themselves witnessing bullying. The perpetrators have a clear agenda and the victim is hardly likely to be at their 'problem solving and self-esteem best'. It may be the witnesses who are best able to react constructively to bullying behaviour.

One of the fastest ways to stop bullying is when the victim's peer group clearly and assertively tell the perpetrators that what they are doing is unacceptable and must stop. This does not mean putting themselves at risk; simply that the power of the peer group in support of the target isolates the perpetrator or perpetrators and can act to stop the behaviour. Consequently, the erstwhile perpetrator may then need support to understand that he or she is OK, but that their *behaviour* was at fault and must stop.

Shifting the perspective

There is clearly an imperative to address bullying behaviour, so what can teachers of PSHE do to address this?

One way of thinking about bullying is to focus on the feelings of the person who believes, rightly or wrongly, that they are being bullied. We might find it complex to define these precisely, but most of us are only too aware of what it may feel like when we think of it happening to us.

Today we must add the issue of cyber-bullying. In the past, children who experienced bullying at school or on the way home could have the sanctuary of their home. With cyber-bullying the behaviour can come directly into their bedrooms, even at night. The use of ICT means that some children can experience bullying virtually all day. Social networking also opens up the potential number of people who can, either in reality or in the perception of the target, collude in the bullying. It is now possible to feel that literally thousands of people are talking cruelly about you and perhaps laughing at or about you.

In primary schools, friendships do break up, arguments or rows happen and are often quickly forgotten, and children may say, 'She is bullying me!' when they mean they have had a 'falling out'. Neither is the teacher who refuses a request, or insists that a child obeys a reasonable instruction, being a bully.

Be careful of the term 'telling tales'. A simple message that 'We don't tell tales' can inhibit hearing about children who genuinely need our help. Children need to understand the difference between having a grumble or a moan and sharing their feelings, or inappropriately divulging someone else's personal information or conversation, and a situation where they need to get skilled help either for themselves or for someone else.

Regardless of whether a child is technically being bullied, their feeling of being bullied can impede their ability to access the curriculum fully and to engage in learning. Not only that: for a child to feel they are being bullied is pretty horrid and for both these reasons they need your support.

Schools address bullying through a number of different routes. For PSHE teachers, the following are separate and distinct issues:

- What is the learning that we need to provide that will reduce the possibility of bullying behaviour occurring within (and beyond) the school community?
- What is the learning that we need to provide to help a pupil who feels they are being bullied to either confront it for themselves or to seek and get help to stop it?
- What is the learning that we need to provide so that, if a bystander feels one of their peers is being bullied, they can either stop it or seek help on their behalf?

Consider first the prevention of bullying behaviour. We need to start with the behaviours pupils see being modelled around them every day in their school lives. While we cannot take responsibility for the behaviours they experience outside of school (although our responsibility to protect their welfare extends into their life beyond school) we can ensure the human interactions they witness and experience throughout their school life are respectful and value everyone equally.

This is wider than the 'curriculum subject' of PSHE education, and demonstrates how the personal and social development of pupils is part of the on-going life of the school and needs to be managed with the same care and consistency as the taught curriculum. This is a good illustration of the connection between the taught PSHE education programme and the concept of the 'healthy school' that we explored in Chapter 3. If the behaviours a child experiences in the day-to-day culture of the school are inconsistent with the learning and values expressed and taught through the PSHE education programme, we are really wasting our time.

The theme of developing and managing relationships in all their forms is a recurring theme within a PSHE education programme. This next section looks more narrowly at bullying as part of that wider theme.

Into practice: exploring children's existing understanding

So how do you start? Returning to the first rule of PSHE education, we started this chapter by asking you to think about what the word 'bullying' means to you, and now you, too, need to start from where your children are. You need to explore how your pupils are making sense of the word 'bullying' and whether they are associating the word with the behaviours we have been describing in this chapter. The simplest way is through a draw and write activity, a process described in more detail in Chapter 4.

This activity is aimed at teachers, or students on teaching practice.

> ### Teaching activity
>
> Tell the class that you want them to work on their own. Say: 'We are going to do some drawing and writing. For this piece of work we are having a "spelling holiday". If you can't spell something just do your best – there's no need to put your hand up to ask.'
>
> 'John and Jane (or choose names that are appropriate for your class) have both been bullying other children. Choose either John or Jane and draw a picture of when they are bullying someone. Under your drawing write all the things you think they do when they bully other people. If you had to describe John or Jane to other people what words would you use to describe them?'
>
> You could extend this. 'Billy and Susan (or choose names that are appropriate for your class) are both being bullied. Choose either Billy or Susan and draw a picture of when they are being bullied. Under your drawing write all the things that you think happen to them when they are being bullied. If you had to describe Billy or Susan to other people what words would you use to describe them?'
>
> You could extend this even further by asking the class to put thought bubbles over their heads and ask the children to suggest all the things they think John, Jane, Billy and Susan are feeling when this is happening.
>
> A further extension could involve asking them for the words that describe bullying itself.

This is a draw and write activity designed to elicit each child's current understanding and meaning of the word 'bullying', and the vocabulary and feelings associated with it. Responses will vary, particularly where there is any personal experience! See Chapter 4 for advice about raising sensitive issues in open ended ways in the classroom.

The data you get back will be illuminating. You may find that for younger children bullies mainly 'hit'. As children get older you might find name-calling being added. With children older still, they begin to grasp that bullying can be doing anything that will either hurt a person physically, or hurt their feelings. Still later they may show you that they understand that bullying can mean doing something but also not doing something, for example leaving someone out of games or encouraging others to ignore them. You might notice differences between the sexes emerging with older pupils.

What is important to grasp is that unless you start where children are, teachers may use words such as 'bullying' with no real understanding of what is being communicated by the word. Remember communication is what is received, not what is sent. If we say to a whole school assembly that we don't tolerate bullying in our school, every child may be hearing something slightly different. If a child has a narrow understanding of bullying, for example being pinched, poked or hit, and is actually repeatedly being called names or left out of games, they may not grasp that you are talking about what is happening to them.

Following on from this investigation we could take the data back to the class and perhaps create a wall display under the headings:

We think bullying is …

We think people who are being bullied feel …

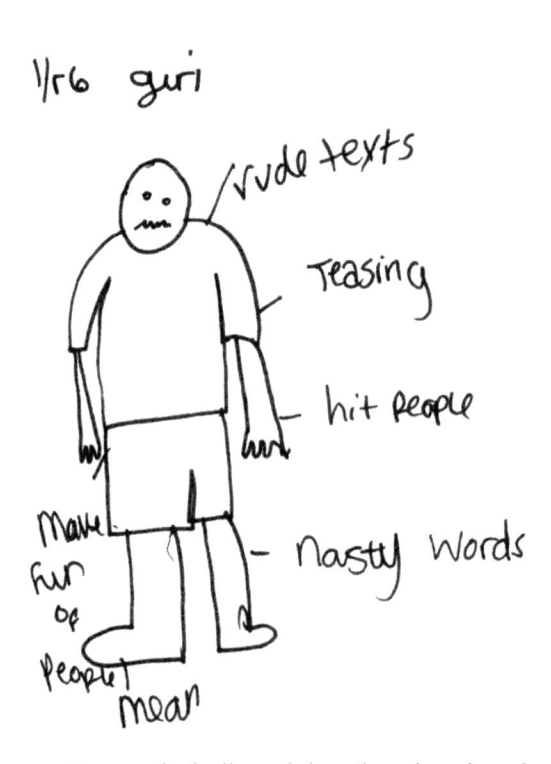

Figure 10.1 Draw a picture of a bully and describe what they do

Source: Ten-year-old girl, Moulsham Junior School, Essex

Figure 10.2 Draw a picture of a bully and describe what they do
Source: Ten-year-old boy, Moulsham Junior School, Essex

We can extend this by asking children to think about all the things people do that might make others *feel* like they are being bullied. Could these also be bullying? What if it isn't meant to hurt the other child? In this way you can gently tease out and deepen your class's understanding of behaviours that could constitute bullying which, even if they don't, may still be unpleasant, unfair and need to be outlawed and to stop. Helping children both to gradually develop and enrich their own concepts through questioning and reflection, and to explore and construct their own meanings, is more effective than giving them a list of behaviours. But do also suggest something they might have missed and ask them if they think this could also be bullying.

The next step is to explore what, if this was happening to anyone in our class, we could say and do to stop it. Ask the children if it would be easy or whether they might feel a bit anxious about doing this. Might it be easier if they all agreed to act together when someone needed help with bullying? If they thought they couldn't stop it, or felt a little scared of who they could tell, what would they say (what words could they use)?

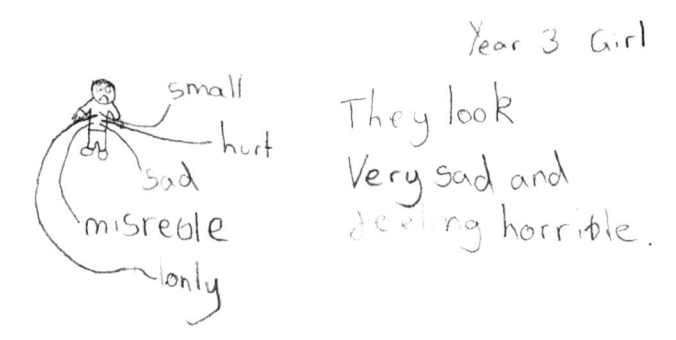

Figure 10.3 Draw a picture of someone who is being bullied. How would you describe them?

Source: Eight-year-old girl, Moulsham Junior School, Essex

When might be the best time to say it and how could they make sure this person really listened? You could also help the class explore what could happen if they didn't do something. We are now into a very practical example of teaching rights and responsibilities in a way that is grounded in the children's real lives.

You can extend this a little further by asking the class how confident they feel about helping others. How could a teacher help them? When should they ask one to help? Is there anything they would like to practise?

This sort of illuminative classroom research can help us identify what is in place in our children's understanding, what is almost there, what is missing and what might be misunderstood. This sort of quality data helps us in planning our teaching. If we really 'pin down' which behaviours are acceptable and which are not, what rights we have, what responsibilities we need to exercise and when we may need help, we are almost at the point when we have agreed our own class policy on bullying. Combining class policies can make an excellent basis for writing or reviewing a whole school policy on bullying.

The reality is that no single piece of work will stop bullying: it has to be part of a programme that builds the skills to manage positive relationships, ideally set in a wider 'healthy school culture'. Bullying may not go away entirely but the way you and the other staff in your school work together can outlaw it while supporting all the children. The way children (and teachers!) look after one another in each class in the school can set a tone that models both caring and equality, as well as rights and responsibilities. This, and behaviour beyond school, now and in the future may need revisiting within your PSHE education programme as needs arise. Let's consider this wider learning.

Planning learning to prevent bullying

> 💭 **Consider**
> Imagine a young person in a primary classroom who is being bullied, or feels they are. What learning do PSHE education teachers need to provide in order to help them to manage what is happening to them?

You might have come up with something like:

- They need to know that what is happening to them is called 'bullying' – as we have established, they may not otherwise know.
- They need to know that it is wrong – not just the way life is for them.
- They need to know it can be stopped.
- They need to believe it can be stopped – this is not the same!
- They need the skills, language and strategies either to make it stop themselves if they can, or to get help if they can't.
- If they go to someone to get help, they need to believe they will be listened to and valued – that this person will help them. They need to know that the bullying will stop – and not, as many children fear, get ten times worse!
- They need to believe that the majority of their peers also know bullying is wrong, that it should be stopped and that they will be supportive.

This list – and perhaps you have thought of other points – is similar for different situations. In the case of the child who witnesses bullying, most points in the above list still apply but you might have added and amended:

- They need to value one another and recognise that everyone has a right to be and feel safe.
- They need to be able to feel empathy – they need to recognise and appreciate how the target is feeling (this is not simply knowing a word for the feeling: it is experiencing an echo of that feeling in themselves).
- They need to understand and accept that they have a responsibility to act, either to intervene or to get help.
- They need the strategies, skills and language to intervene or get help.
- They need to feel confident they won't become the next target for bullying.
- They need to know they have the support of the majority of their peers.

> 💭 **Consider**
>
> Take out the word 'bullying' and substitute 'abuse'. Now read the lists again. Are they still coherent? Does this indicate to you that the preparatory and developmental work on bullying is applicable to a much wider arena? The understanding and skills vital in coping with and managing bullying are transferable.

In Chapter 9 where we address sex and relationships education, we have outlined an entire strand of a PSHE education programme spanning all ages up to and including 11 years old. Within this strand (taken from the Planning Tool for PSHE&C Essex County Council, Speechly-Watson, n.d.) work on bullying prevention might include learning:

- that someone who bullies makes him/herself feel better by making someone else feel worse
- how easy it may be for some children to slip into bullying behaviour, to recognise possible motivation for doing this and stop themselves
- about the danger of stereotyping people as 'bullies' because of their physical characteristics
- strategies for dealing with bullying behaviour
- a vocabulary of feelings surrounding bullying
- that there is no acceptable reason for bullying
- to deal positively with their fears and distress surrounding bullying
- that when bullying happens and you see it or are involved you are faced with a responsibility to intervene or get help
- what it means to 'put yourself in someone else's shoes' and how this can help you to make the decision to act
- strategies for recognising and minimising the risks of bullying
- to recognise critical moments
- strategies to protect yourselves from being bullied physically or mentally, e.g. walk tall, have confidence, communication skills, assertiveness.

Some of these issues can be addressed quickly through a single PSHE education lesson while others, such as the gradual development of empathy – being able to 'put ourselves into someone else's shoes' – or understanding how to be assertive, will require a planned, developmental programme and may need to be revisited in more than one school year.

So how might we develop a concept such as empathy? One approach would be to return to the use of story described in Chapter 6, the pedagogy of PSHE education. There are many story books that offer routes into the issue of bullying directly or into the issues that underpin bullying.

Be cautious, though, of books specifically designed to help children to think about their feelings. We believe children can benefit more from well written and engaging fiction that clearly describes the feelings of its story's characters, and the situations that give rise to those feelings, rather than the direct-but-dull books with a moral, edifying message.

Look at books like *Something Else* by Kathryn Cave (1998) about a creature who is different from all the other creatures and is left out of all their games.

You could try *Rosie and the Pavement bears* by Susie Jenkins-Pearce (1992) about a girl who is being bullied and so steps on cracks in the pavement, and as many children know, stepping on the cracks in the pavement means that the bears will come and get you. Rosie is so desperate for help she hopes the bears will come and instead of eating her, support her. A great question could be: 'If one of us was being bullied how could we be like Rosie's bears?' What is interesting is that the story's readers never know if the bears really come or if Rosie imagines them, and that this alone gives her the strength to stand up against the bullies.

These next questions need exploring with great care. As the story unfolds you could ask, 'What do you think the character is feeling right now?', 'How do you know?' If you feel it is safe you can then extend this with, 'Have you ever felt like that?', 'Is it a good feeling or a not so good feeling?', 'How do people show others they are having this feeling? Take it in turns to show the person beside you how we look when we are having this feeling.'

Try to locate the book *Six Dinner Sid* by Inga Moore (1990). On the surface, this is a story about a cat that lives with six different families in the same street. He does this in order to have six dinners every day. One day Sid gets a cold and goes to the vet six times and gets six doses of medicine. Because residents in the road don't talk to one another Sid's life is at risk. When they all find out they decide to give Sid just one dinner a day. So Sid moves to the next street, where he still tries to get his six dinners but in this street everyone talks to one another so they quickly learn about Sid's habits, and they aren't fooled by him.

Now, explore whether your classroom is more like the first street or the second. What would we all need to say and do to be more like the second street where everyone talks to one another and everyone is safe?

Although a little longer than the stories above, all of which can be read from cover to cover in about ten minutes, possibly one of the best books on bullying is *The Angel of Nitshill Road* by Anne Fine (2007), about a new girl in a school who gradually teaches all the children strategies for managing their relationships.

See also Chapter 6 where we consider the use of story in more detail. Please note that we have not recommended role play for bullying prevention. This needs to be managed carefully to avoid the situation where some children rehearse bullying, while others rehearse being a victim.

But how do I support a pupil who is experiencing bullying?

Will PSHE education, well taught and set in the context of a positive and healthy school culture, be sure to prevent all bullying? The honest answer is no. Despite everything we do in the curriculum and the school's ethos, incidents may still happen. However, the work you do in PSHE education can significantly reduce bullying, can make it easier to address it fully and effectively when it does occur, and can reduce the chance of damage to those involved.

As this book is about PSHE education rather than pastoral care we have focused on the role of the PSHE education programme rather than on intervention. Schools will have their own strategies for managing incidents of bullying, and teachers should work within them.

One strategy for managing bullying that has met both with success in schools and some controversy nationally uses the 'peer support model' that was developed by Barbara Maines and George Robinson. It was first outlined in *Educational Psychology in Practice* (1991). The controversy was caused by its earlier title, the 'No Blame Approach', which many found hard to accept. If we assume that the objective of any intervention is, a) to stop the bullying and, more importantly, b) to stop it from recurring, then in many cases this method has proved highly effective.

The Support Group Approach (previously known as the 'No Blame Approach') emphasised the construction of a solution achieved through a participative, non-punitive approach which involved the pupils resolving the problem. Robinson and Maines (2008: 28–32) focus on the feelings and status of the pupils involved using seven steps:

- *Step 1: Interview the bullied pupil.* Talk with the pupil about his/her feelings. Do not question the child directly about the incident, but do try to establish who is involved.
- *Step 2: Arrange a meeting for all the pupils who are involved.* Set up a meeting for all of the pupils who are directly or indirectly involved. Include pupils who joined in but did not directly bully the other child.
- *Step 3: Explain the problem.* Tell the pupils how the bullied child is feeling. You may want to use a drawing or a poem or piece of writing

written by the pupil to illustrate this. Do not discuss the details of the incident, or allocate blame to any of the bullying pupils.
- *Step 4: Share the responsibility.* State clearly that you know the group are responsible and can do something about it. Focus on resolving the problem rather than blaming the pupil.
- *Step 5: Identify solutions.* In turn, ask each pupil to suggest a way in which they could help the bullied pupil feel happier in school. Show approval of the suggestions but do not ask the pupils to promise to implement their suggestions or go into details about how they will implement them.
- *Step 6: Let the pupils take action themselves.* End the meeting by giving the responsibility to the group to solve the problem. Arrange a time and place to meet again and find out how successful they have been.
- *Step 7: Meet them again.* After about a week, see each student and ask how things have been going. It is usually better to see them on their own in order to avoid any new group accusations about who helped and who didn't. The important thing is to ascertain that the bullying has stopped and the bullied pupil is feeling better.

An evaluation spanning two years using this approach found immediate success in 80 per cent of cases and delayed success in 14 per cent; in only 6 per cent of cases did the victim report continued bullying (Young, 1998). You may find *Bullying: A Complete Guide to the Support Group Method* (Robinson and Maines, 2008) of interest.

While PSHE education alone may not be able to stop every instance of bullying, the learning that children acquire through a planned programme of relationships education can make an intervention such as the Support Group Approach far more effective. It can also contribute to skilled young people being able to offer and engage with activities such as peer mediation and supporting the pupil voice in school councils.

Chapter summary

In this chapter, we explored the meaning of 'bullying' and some of its causes. We looked at the difference between perpetrators and victims, and the need to separate the child from the behaviour and to support both perpetrators and targets. We explored the vital role of 'bystanders' and the need for anyone who sees, feels or experiences bullying to be able to seek help. We offered advice to PSHE education teachers about suitable bullying-related content, and asserted the importance of an effective and well-understood school policy on bullying.

Further reading

Elliott, M. (2010) *Stop Bullying Pocketbook* (2nd edn). Alresford: Teachers' Pocketbooks.
A wealth of useful information in a handy size book.

Kansas Safe School Resource Center website, www.ksde.org/Default.aspx?tabid=3913.

Robinson, G. and Maines, B. (2008) *Bullying: A Complete Guide to the Support Group Method*. London: Sage.
A full description of an approach that values the importance of banishing bullying while supporting both perpetrators and targets.

Wetton, N. and Boddington, N. (1998) *Schools Without Fear: A Realistic Guide to Tackling Bullying as a Whole School Issue*. London: Forbes.
An excellent book reminding teachers that bullying should not be thought of as unwanted events to be responded to, but addressed proactively to develop a school that rejects bullying behaviour positively.

Young, S. (1998) *Preventing Bullying: A Manual for Schools and Communities*. Washington, DC: US Department of Education.
In this US study of junior high and high school students from small Midwestern towns, 88 per cent of students reported having observed bullying, and 76.8 per cent indicated that they had been a victim of bullying at school. The author's research suggests that comprehensive action involving teachers and other school staff, students, parents, and community members is likely to be more effective than purely classroom-based approaches.

References

Besag, V.E. (1989) *Bullies and Victims in Schools*. Milton Keynes: Open University Press.

Björkqvist, K., Lagerspetz, K.M.J. and Kaukiainen, A. (1992) 'Do girls manipulate and boys fight? Development trends in regard to direct and indirect aggression', *Aggressive Behavior*, 18: 117–27.

Cassidy, S. (1999) 'Beware the "pure bully" who never takes time off', *Times Educational Supplement*, News Section, December 24.

Cave, K. (1998) *Something Else*. New York: Mondo Publishing.

Crick, N.R. and Grotpeter, J.K. (1995) 'Relational aggression, gender, and social-psychological adjustment', *Child Development*, 66: 710–22.

Department of Education (2013) 'Preventing and tackling bullying'. Available at: www.education.gov.uk/schools/pupilsupport/behaviour/bullying/f0076899/preventing-and-tackling-bullying (accessed 17 October 2013).

Farrington, D.P. (1993) 'Understanding and preventing bullying', in M. Tonry (ed.), *Crime and Justice, Vol. 17*. Chicago: University of Chicago, pp. 381–458.

Fine, A. (2007) *The Angel of Nitshill Road*. London: Egmont Books.

Jenkins-Pearce, S. (1992) *Rosie and the Pavement Bears*. London: Red Fox Picture Books.

Maines, B. and Robinson, O. (1991) 'Don't beat the bullies', *Educational Psychology in Practice*, 7: 168–72.

Moore, I. (1990) *Six Dinner Sid*. London: Hodder Children's Books.

Olweus, D. (1978) *Aggression in Schools: Bullies and Whipping Boys*. Washington, DC: Hemisphere.

Olweus, D. (2006) *Olweus' Core Program Against Bullying and Antisocial Behavior: A Teacher Handbook*, Version IV. Bergen, Norway: Olweus Research Centre for Health Promotion (Hemil Centre).

Olweus, D., Limber, S. and Mihalic, S. (1999) *OLWEUS Bullying Prevention Program*. Boulder: University of Colorado, Center for the Study and Prevention of Violence.

Robinson, G. and Maines, B. (2008) *Bullying: A Complete Guide to the Support Group Method*. London: Sage.

Smith, P.K. and Thompson, D.A. (1991) *Practical Approaches to Bullying*. London: David Fulton.

Smith, P.K., Morita, Y., Junger-Tas, J., Olweus, D., Catalano, R. and Slee, P. (1999) *The Nature of School Bullying: A Cross-national Perspective*. London: Routledge.

Speechly-Watson, N. (n.d.) Planning tool for PSHE&C. Chelmsford: Essex Local Authority.

Wolke, D. and Stanford, K. (1999) 'Bullying in school children', in D. Messer and S. Millar (eds), *Developmental Psychology*. London: Arnold, pp. 341–60.

Wolke, D., Woods, S., Stanford, K. and Schulz, H. (2001) 'Bullying and victimization of primary school children in England and Germany: prevalence and school factors', *British Journal of Psychology*, 92 (4): 673–96.

Young, S. (1998) 'The support group approach to bullying in schools', *Educational Psychology in Practice*, 14: 32–9.

CHAPTER 11

UNDERSTANDING MEDICINE AND DRUG EDUCATION

Aim

To introduce the rationale for primary school drug education and provide guidance about what constitutes appropriate drug education at this age.

Learning objectives

This chapter will help you to:

- define 'drugs' to include alcohol, tobacco and all legal drugs and medicines as well as illegal drugs
- introduce the rationale underpinning effective approaches to drug education and how they relate to the ten principles for effective PSHE education
- set responsible primary school drug education in the context of genuine need
- help readers understand why some approaches are more effective than others

- know how to create opportunities for your pupils to practise skills they can use in everyday life which will enable them to live safely and confidently in a drug-using world
- introduce guidance to the content and progression of drug education for children aged 5–11 years, to use alongside content determined from investigation of needs.

Getting started

Personal activity

What comes to mind when you think of 'primary school drug education'?

Perhaps: Help! Panic! Not appropriate for primary children! I don't know enough! Surely I won't have to teach this?

Don't worry. Drug education can seem a complex and rather emotive issue, but its execution is really no harder than other elements of PSHE education as we shall explain.

What are drugs?

In education, the word 'drugs' has been clearly established in schools guidance documents to include alcohol, tobacco and all medicines, as well as illegal drugs. There is a definition below.

Definitions

Drug. This book uses the term to refer to *all* drugs, namely:

- all over-the-counter and prescription medicines
- all legal drugs, including alcohol, tobacco, volatile substances (those giving off a gas or vapour that can be inhaled), ketamine, khat, alkyl nitrites (known as poppers)
- all illegal drugs (those controlled by the Misuse of Drugs Act 1971).

(Continued)

> *(Continued)*
>
> **Drug education.** We define drug education as: the systematic provision of learning opportunities that help children, by the time they leave school, to become competent and confident in understanding and managing any situations that involve, or might involve, drugs, and which they have faced or might face in the future.

The purpose of drug education

The Department for Education and Skills' document *Drugs: Guidance for Schools* (DfES, 2004: 27) says:

> Drug education should enable pupils to develop their knowledge, skills, attitudes and understanding about drugs and appreciate the benefits of a healthy lifestyle, relating this to their own and others' actions.

We discuss the role of the PSHE teacher in drug education later in the chapter.

Why teach drug education to young children at all?

When children are very young, the focus of teaching will be on helping them keep safe. They will need to know they can always ask for help whenever they feel unsafe or unsure. Two key tasks are to teach them when help might be needed, and the skills and confidence required to access this help.

During primary school, it is important for children to learn who can keep them safe, from worries, from the dark, from monsters, from real dangers and from things they don't yet know about or understand. They need to know for sure that when they ask for help from any adult at school they will get it. (If the need is visible, they may not need to ask, of course.) They also need to be able to recognise when they don't feel safe, and when they aren't sure and need to ask. They will also learn that they have a growing responsibility to contribute to the job of keeping themselves safe – as their skills, their knowledge and their confidence allow – and that what they are learning means they will eventually be ready to take over the role entirely. Safety in relation to drugs and medicines takes a natural place among a list of possibilities for discomfort or harm about which they also need to learn about – crossing roads, broken glass, deep water, climbing up to reach high shelves, falling over, fighting and so on.

Even before this, exploring what goes on their body, and what goes in their body (and who puts it there), can help them to know that they need to be able to distinguish between the things that rightfully and safely go on or in their bodies, and things it is not safe for them to put on, or in, them. They need to understand that dirty hands should be washed and not put in their mouth unless clean – because dirt and germs may harm them. This doesn't immediately sound like drug education, but it is. It is only a step from there to exploring what medicines are for, that they don't taste very nice, why there is a name on the bottle or package, and why doctors, nurses, parents and carers are always very careful about how much medicine they give to the people who need it. Too much can be dangerous!

For primary school children, their immediate drug education needs are more about understanding the drugs (probably medicines and maybe alcohol and tobacco) they might meet in the home, than understanding the physical hazards of possessing or using illegal ones. You will need to help them avoid becoming confused by the words 'drug' and 'medicine', which are sometimes used interchangeably, at least in medical contexts. For example, the media have been known to describe a new medicine as 'a wonder drug'.

Important facts for young children to learn include:

- while all medicines are drugs, not all drugs are medicines
- not all discomfort or illness needs medicine – the body is good at healing
- each illness or disease has its own special medicine – it's no good taking tummy medicine if you've got chicken pox!
- there are drugs that cannot be used to treat illness or disease
- medicines can themselves be dangerous if used in the wrong way (or by the wrong person).

A further word about medicines

Medicines are not to be confused with food, sweets or other treats, nor are they intended to taste nice. They can hurt us if we pretend they *are* sweets, and that is the reason they are usually kept out of reach. Each has a specific purpose, varying from medicine to medicine, and is often intended for one person only – the name of whom the doctor has written on the box or bottle, with clear instructions about how to take this medicine responsibly, safely and effectively. Medicines are for people who are unwell. Nobody else but this named person should take that medicine. Doctors, nurses and chemists are the people who tell us when we need to take medicines – helped by parents, carers and teachers.

A brief history of drug education in the UK

Despite centuries of use of alcohol and tobacco, and a long-established understanding about the short-term harms of alcohol at least, recognition of the need for young people to be formally prepared for living and coping in a world of drugs has come only relatively recently. In the UK in the 1960s, the use of cannabis, prescription amphetamines and LSD by some young people came to the notice of the general public through the press. This behaviour among a minority of teenagers accompanied the post-war development of a teenage population with money and a culture to go with it. As a result attention began to be paid to the need for young people to be systematically educated about drugs. However, efforts to undertake this task were confined in the main to a few enlightened secondary schools. In 1971, new legislation, the Misuse of Drugs Act, became law. It has since been revised and amended several times, to reflect changing circumstances. Its arrival further reinforced the need for drug education in schools. When it was undertaken, it was usually conducted as a discrete programme, and was still widely viewed as inappropriate for children in primary schools.

Within PSHE education are many so-called 'sensitive issues' among which drug education figures prominently. Sensitive issues are broadly those where there may be a combination of limited teacher confidence, and perhaps even parental ambivalence about whether the issue is a legitimate element of the curriculum at young ages. In the second half of the 1980s, when it was first suggested that drug education should be an element in every primary school, parents were often frightened that their children may not be ready for 'horrid things like that', and worried that their young children would be introduced to illegal drugs in ways that might even stimulate interest in them. They did not yet understand the benign and helpful role drug education can play at primary school level. Even teachers were cautious, often unsure of the best way to help infant and junior children without stepping over the line into 'education by fear'. Many believed they had insufficient understanding about drugs and the issues raised by their availability and use. This naturally sapped their confidence to tackle drug education.

In 1986 the government set aside funds so that each Local Education Authority could appoint a drug education co-ordinator to help support schools to improve their approach to drug education. Their role included support and training for teachers in both primary and secondary schools. At the time little was known about very young children's needs for drug education, or how it should be tackled with infants. In Chapter 4 we have described the draw and write technique – and we offer some specific examples of how its far-reaching function can be applied in the classroom. This technique, and specifically its application to the subject of drugs, was a key factor in bringing about realisation that primary school children need and can benefit from drug education much earlier than had been believed. Below, we describe the way the technique was used to discover information about what would help us plan drug education for primary school children. The data, which consisted of children's own words and drawings, helped to convince many sceptics that children were already exposed to a world of drugs but had many misunderstandings and fears that were not being addressed. Researchers and practitioners successfully argued that children would be safer if they were able to access drug education appropriate to their needs, but also to their age and stage of development.

Consider

The road and the roadside are dangerous environments for primary school age children. Yet there is little disagreement that parents and schools should teach children how to be safe on or by the road. Supposing we took the same attitude to roads (where many children die every year) as we do to drugs: 'We must not teach them about the hazards associated with roads because they might be tempted to try and cross them'!

We believe preparation for living in a world where there are drugs should start young. The most constructive drug education in primary (or secondary) schools identifies the needs of the children in a class and begins to develop the understanding they need to help them forward and to address any worries or misconceptions they may already have. It also begins to develop (or further develops) the skills and attitudes children will need in order to look after themselves later on, when judgement and decisions about drugs may face them. Parental drug, cigarette or alcohol use may be an issue for some and this too may need some (sensitive) attention for some classes. The emphasis is always health and wellbeing and the importance of their maintenance.

Exploring where to begin

Planning and teaching primary school drug education follows much the same process as for any other element of PSHE education. It would be possible to start at the end and work backwards, setting out what secondary school leavers need to understand, and the skills and attitudes that will keep them safe, and using backward mapping from this endpoint to arrive at the early steps of drug education. This is the process we describe in Chapter 9 to determine and confirm the early content of SRE. We recommend using the draw and write technique to investigate children's current perceptions, and referring to local and national guidance to help you determine content and progression. The starting point should, in any case, be determined by where the young people are, and the content should always be relevant and suitable for the age group or developmental stage, addressing their needs in an appropriate way.

Those working closely with young children in any role will know that social and physical competence are targets towards which they are constantly moving, though they might not think to call this drug

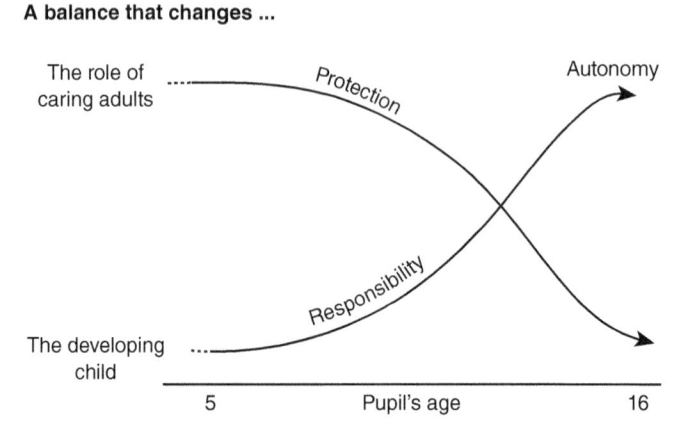

Figure 11.1 The balance of responsibility changes as children grow

education. However, awareness of the world around, and its opportunities and its hazards, are the stuff of daily learning for small children, well capable of getting themselves into difficulty before their competence is very high, and well capable of avoiding problems once they understand how to. They need guidance; they need to understand the ways in which their bodies are vulnerable, and the things that they are vulnerable *to*; and they need to recognise their increasing capacity and developing role in looking after themselves.

Figure 11.1 will be useful; it shows that when a child is very young, the teacher, along with other caring adults, has a key responsibility to protect him or her. The child's responsibility is limited by their capability. When children reach school-leaving age, society expects that they will have developed the capability to behave as autonomous and responsible citizens. At some point (or points!) in between, the child takes over the major responsibility and the teacher's protection role diminishes. The crossing points may not be smooth or without incident, the growing child perhaps wishing to assert identity and flout authority in ways that are not necessarily wise. During such incidents of adolescent self-expression, avoidable accidents may occur. Much resultant learning may also take place. The key element of the diagram, though, is the upward slope of the child's level of responsibility for their own behaviour and their own welfare, as their capability grows. Sometimes this responsibility may extend to the welfare of those around them. Part of the caring adult's role (not shown in Figure 11.1) is to support the upward slope – the development both of the child's *capability* and his or her sense of personal *responsibility*.

At school, the teacher works:

- to ensure children are increasingly well-informed and understand: how health may be preserved and what might threaten it, what 'risk' is, when unknown outcomes may be well worth facing, and what situations involve risks that need skilled management or are best avoided
- to help them develop and practise the skills they will need to cope with life's choices and its pitfalls
- to help them become confident in their own judgement, and their ability in real life situations to put their decisions into practice
- to believe in themselves and their competence, and to understand their limitations
- and above all, to help reinforce their belief that they are worth taking care of.

On the whole, self-confident and well-grounded adults do not put themselves in situations where it is likely they will be damaged – and though some adults are high risk takers and may have accidents as a result of choosing to face risks like hang-gliding, potholing, off-piste skiing or mountain climbing, they nearly always make strenuous efforts to keep themselves as safe as necessary, and they usually understand well the dangers they may face in these activities. Children need to understand the nature of risk – to be able to assess the likelihood of unwanted or damaging outcomes (i.e. the meanings of 'likely' and 'unlikely'), to weigh options and to manage situations where some risk is unavoidable. In Chapter 8, we deal with safety education in greater detail.

> **Personal activity**
>
> Read the bullet list (above) again, thinking first of swimming in the sea or riding a bicycle at night. Then read it a third time thinking about the uses, legitimate or otherwise, of medicines, alcohol and even illegal drugs. The descriptions of the developmental needs of children flow in just the same way for each 'subject'. But the subject of this bullet list is not drug education, nor understanding tides, undercurrents and lifeguards, nor the need for lights, reflective clothing and a helmet. The subject is children and the development of their capacity to cope competently in a world that may not always be safe or kind.

It should now be clear that drug education is not a subject. It is an integral part of PSHE education.

The world of drugs

When you are thinking about an issue like drugs, which can seem emotive, it is very important to make sure you put drug-related problems firmly into perspective. You may be among the many adults that worry about children and the possibility of drug misuse ruining their lives. So, here is a brief list of useful facts to bear in mind:

- The majority of young people never try illegal drugs (Home Office, 2011).
- For those that do (and statistics show it will usually be cannabis, and in their teens) the slope they seem to be on is not actually a very slippery

one. For example, the statistical likelihood of cannabis users progressing to be problem-users of, say, heroin is very small indeed.
- One very hazardous legal activity worryingly attractive to some children is solvent-sniffing (or to give its fuller name, volatile substance abuse). In the VSA report dated 2012 (Ghodse et al., 2012) 124 people under the age of 18 years died from this activity in the UK between 2000 and 2009, including one who was under ten years. More than half of the deaths in 2009 were from butane or aerosol propellants.
- The problems caused by alcohol and cigarettes are both more numerous (by far) and often more serious than those caused by other drugs used or tried for fun (though even this can be harmful, too, and occasionally fatal). Children who try or go on to regular use of alcohol or tobacco are just as likely, and possibly more likely, to be putting their health at risk, either now or in the future, than those who experiment with illegal drugs.
- Laws control the *supply* of alcohol, tobacco and volatile substances such as butane, but not their *possession* or their *use*.
- Health is no respecter of laws. Potential hazards accompanying drug misuse are just as real whatever the legal, social or medicinal status of the drug. No drug is intrinsically 'naughty'.
- Every drug, whatever its legal or medicinal status, is likely to be more hazardous when taken by someone who does not know about its dangers, or who is reckless. Some combinations of drugs, such as alcohol with depressants, are particularly dangerous.

Two further ideas to bear in mind:

- For the small number that become problem drug users later in life, the drugs are almost always not the main problem to start with. Young people who choose to take drugs in a serious and protracted way, perhaps to mask pain, distress or anxiety in their lives, are usually considered vulnerable. A non-exhaustive list of risk factors for drug misuse, and the protective factors that can ameliorate these, is shown at the end of this chapter. Almost always there are serious problems in the lives of these vulnerable young people that should be picked up early through observation and pastoral care systems. Drug education cannot hope to compensate for problems such as parental drug misuse or alcoholism, child abuse or mental ill health.
- The biggest causes of harm to primary school-age children from drugs are parental use/misuse of tobacco/alcohol (Office of the Children's Commissioner, 2012: 2; Royal College of Physicians, 2012: 8).

If you are interested to know more about the nature and causes of problematic drug taking, you are encouraged to seek further information. We recommend consulting the website of DrugScope, a UK charity supporting professionals working in drug and alcohol treatment, drug education and prevention and criminal justice. (See Further reading at the end of this chapter.)

It would not be fair or reasonable for society to put pressure on schools, through their provision of drug education, to solve society's drug-related concerns by magically 'preventing' young people trying any 'naughty' ones. It is not intended that drug education should try to control young people's later decisions, but to develop their confidence, their competence and their will to take care of themselves and their ability to cope with life ahead. But as Figure 11.1 shows, they will need protection until they are responsible and competent enough to manage this by themselves.

Drug education needs to start where young people are. At the age of four or five years, the word 'drug' will probably have limited meaning, while towards the top of junior school at the age of 10 or 11 years, the children are likely to have heard the names of many things they believe to be drugs, and associated paraphernalia, and may be a bit worried about what they have heard, read or seen. The draw and write technique can be used in any classroom and at any age, to find out the children's current starting points – what they know, their incomplete knowledge, what they have heard or believe but which may not be right, their fears or anxieties, and their questions. It is much easier to address the needs of young people after they have told you what they are!

So what about the content of drug education? We have already established the need to develop young people's skills, their self-confidence and their understanding that hazards can be managed in order to avoid upset and hurt. With very young children, it is this emphasis that will help and support them, and they will only occasionally need to hear the word 'drug' as we help them understand how to look after their health and their safety with the help of people they trust.

Meeting the purpose

From the Department for Education and Skills' statement of purpose we quoted at the beginning of the chapter, it is clear that children's knowledge, their skills and their attitudes are crucial. Below we address each of these separately. They can be explored in class using some of the methods we outline in Chapter 7. At the end of *this* chapter, we offer guidance about what may be suitable content for the children you will teach.

Knowledge

In PSHE lessons you can develop children's knowledge, by providing information and exploring its meaning. Its context and relevance can be pinpointed, perhaps with the help of the children themselves, so that they recognise its value. Recognition of increased knowledge can itself boost self-confidence. Knowledge can be tested in a number of ways that show both you and the child how successful you have been at this teaching task and how successful they have been as learners. Children need to know about medicine from quite an early age as we said earlier in the chapter. This knowledge is built upon as time proceeds, and eventually more of the legal, illegal and medicinal drugs will have been explored in ways that are relevant to the age and stage of the children. They will need to know about rules and laws too. And to explore risk and health and responsibility, and more.

Skills

Skills can be explored and practised either in class, or elsewhere, with the invitation to bring the experience back into class to examine it and see how successful or otherwise it was, tweaking the skills where necessary. Children can learn a lot from each other's attempts to put their skills to good use. A skilful child is one who can take pride in what they do and how they manage situations. Children can demonstrate their growth in capability, and you can see it or hear about it. It can be recorded both in your own records and in a form that the child can see and celebrate.

A word of caution here, though. Applying any skill is not solely a matter of knowing what to do, nor even how to do it. A skill is only as useful as the child's decision to use it, and their confidence to apply it in situations that call for it.

To diverge a little further, we have long realised that teaching young people the knowledge that drugs can be hazardous, and where these hazards lie, and giving them the skills to refuse opportunities to try drugs, has not resulted magically in the disappearance of drug experimentation.

Perhaps you recall the sense of excitement and adventure you experienced when young in doing things that were a bit naughty. You are not alone! And the high level of risk with which a few young people feel comfortable means that the very danger of drugs, or of being caught with them, can be an attraction to them. Add to this the fact that it is natural for all young people to feel that they will live forever and that they are invulnerable. We should not be surprised, therefore, that there are times when a child's sense of danger is somewhat dulled, even when they believe the facts they have been given. Children who try drugs for fun invariably believe they will simply 'get away with it'. Not all do.

Sadly, there are some children who are particularly at risk of heavier involvement with drugs, and for whom appropriate knowledge and skills will not be sufficient to banish this risk. We list some of the factors that contribute to this sort of risk, together with some that may protect vulnerable children, at the end of the chapter.

Attitudes

Attitudes are often harder to pin down, but they are critical elements in the picture. It is not easy to guarantee that well-educated children's attitudes will invariably be healthy, as we stated in the last paragraph. Attitudes to drugs, and to drug use and drug users, may seem the key, but attitudes to self-worth, to health, to risk and danger, to adventure, to the future, and to people the child loves and who love them are probably more important. If you take every opportunity you can to develop, to nurture and to reinforce the child's view of themselves as unique, valuable and irreplaceable, you will be rendering them a huge service. With some children it will be an uphill struggle, the more worthwhile for its difficulty – for it is the child who doesn't believe that they are worth looking after who may grow up feeling it is not worth the trouble to look after themselves. Sometimes such children may put themselves in real danger. Or they may already be in danger. This is the at-risk group we mentioned above. They will need the help of services other than you and the school.

It is important to help children explore attitudes. They will learn about each other's attitudes, which will be healthy. They may challenge each other's attitudes, which can be helpful. It will help them recognise the diversity of perspective and viewpoint in the class, when others are in accord with their attitudes and when they are not, and will help prepare them to avoid assumptions and generalisations about what others think. Applying this to drugs, which they will as they progress towards the end of primary school education, they may be less inclined to assume that all secondary children think this or do that. It has been true in the past that before moving to secondary school, 10- and 11-year-olds have reported being nervous that they will be pressured into trying drugs by older children. It is probable they have picked up this nervousness from adults. It is very largely an unfounded adult fear. These children may have already developed a mistaken view of these older children that they are commonly drinking alcohol, smoking cigarettes, trying illegal drugs and, later perhaps, 'having sex'. Secondary school teachers are encouraged to replace false assumptions with locally researched and anonymously given information that shows a more realistic picture about what is 'normal' behaviour in that area and for that age. Your support to primary school children to learn that older children are not homogeneous but are as diverse as they are, and are *not* all smoking, drinking, taking drugs (or having sex), will help prepare them not to jump to conclusions. The unfounded nervousness of the past about older children pressuring them to try drugs when they get to secondary school may not have gone away completely yet, but it is probably much less than it was, now that we understand more clearly the much more common precursors to illicit drug taking. The children who try drugs may be curious, but indications are that those who try them are those who want to, and decide to, rather than being pressured against their will.

Your own attitude is important too; in this instance, your attitude as a teacher to drug education. The government's statement of purpose of drug education we quoted above talks of relating the benefits of a healthy lifestyle to the children's own actions. It will be the children's own responsibility to decide how they use their knowledge and skills, coloured by their attitudes. But perhaps, like us, you hope that they will apply these benefits to their actions and to their lives. You cannot control those lives, and if you could, and you did, you would hardly be preparing them to become the autonomous and responsible adults PSHE education is helping to develop. It is therefore important not to do anything to undermine the children's growing sense of responsibility for themselves. Protect them while they need it, of course, but help them aspire to becoming autonomous, responsible grown-ups. Your own attitude to the drug education you include in PSHE education, and to the outcomes you are invited to work to bring about, is another important part of the jigsaw. Don't forget, your attitude to the children – that they are capable of learning all that they need to in order to become responsible, healthy adults – will communicate itself to them in your teaching.

The draw and write technique for investigating children's starting points

The draw and write developed for drug education (Williams et al., 1989) is a good example of a technique which can be used:

- with your own class to help you plan how to help children to learn about medicines as well as tobacco, alcohol and other substances
- across a whole school or with a larger sample.

Unsurprisingly 'drug education' can be a sensitive issue for teachers, parents and governors, all of whom will have a range of experiences with medicines, alcohol and other mind altering substances. It is also a sensitive issue for children whose parents or older siblings might be misusing alcohol or other drugs. Some children of primary school age may already be experimenting with tobacco, alcohol and solvents and many will have had medication of one sort or another. However, most children and young people will never use illegal drugs, and it is important to bear this in mind. While it is important for you to know what the children know, it is also important not to put ideas into their heads which might confuse or frighten them or 'normalise' drug use.

The researchers handled all these challenges by 'distancing' – a useful technique in PSHE education (see Chapters 4 and 7). This means they asked the children to illustrate a story about fictional characters, about their own age, who find a bag of drugs while on their way home from school. As with other draw and write techniques, no definition of drugs is given, so what the children draw and write about is based on their own interpretation of the word.

The questions (or invitations to participate) gradually focus on the specific issue of drugs, who uses drugs and why, while gradually becoming more personal, without ever suggesting what the word 'drugs' means.

Draw and write about 'A world of drugs' (based on Williams et al., 1989)

Invitation 1: Two children were walking home from school one day when they found a bag with drugs inside it. Draw what you think was in the bag. If you can, write at the side what you have drawn. If you can't write/prefer not to write, whisper to me (or name of helper) what it is that you have drawn, and I (or she/he) will write it for you. Don't worry about spelling. (This may need to be repeated several times.)

Invitation 2: Who do you think lost the bag?

Invitation 3: What do you think that person was going to do with the bag?

Invitation 4: What did the children do with the bag?

Invitation 5: What would you have done if you found the bag?

Invitation 6: Can a drug be good for you/help you? If so, when?

Invitation 7: Can a drug be bad for you/harm you? If so, when?

Along with the invitations to participate are some instructions to help you introduce the activity so that it is as open ended and inclusive as possible, given the constraints of a classroom setting (Table 11.1).

Table 11.1 Instructions for draw and write activity

Spoken instructions	Permitted prompts and reminders	Beware
'Hello. I am going to read you the beginning of a story. Then I am going to ask you to draw and write some of your ideas about the people in the story and what they did.'	'Listen to the story carefully.'	Don't mention the word drugs before it appears in the story.
'Two children were walking home from school one day when they found a bag with drugs inside it.'	If it helps, choose appropriate names for the children in the story.	Ask the children not to comment out loud or ask you or each other any questions. Don't let them share their ideas with others. Don't give any hints or clues as the story unfolds.
Draw what was in the bag. Write what was in the bag. (1) Draw the person who lost the bag. Write about the person who lost the bag. (2) Write what you think that person was going to do with the bag. (3) Write what the children did with the bag. (4) Write what you would have done if you found the bag. (5) Can a drug be good for you/help you? If so, when? (6) Can a drug be bad for you/harm you? If so, when? (7)	Tell the children that there are no wrong answers. All their ideas are right. Remind the children to write, or whisper to you every time they are asked to write (this is because you will only analyse the written answers). To help the children keep their answers organised you could prepare a photocopied sheet with numbered boxes for them to write in. Or ask them to number their written answers. Decide for yourself how many invitations to use.	Remind the children not to comment out loud or ask you or each other any questions. Say you want to collect as many answers as possible.

This draw and write technique is called 'A world of drugs' to reflect that we use all kinds of substances in our society – some of which are medicines, some are legal and some illegal. All are potentially harmful if misused.

Some of the youngest children who took part in the first research study using this technique either misheard or misunderstood the word 'drugs' and wrote about bugs, rugs and even jugs. But some children of a similar age wrote about 'herring' – a white powder in wrappers, or drew fish, reflecting the non-sense they had made of a hard hitting TV health campaign of the period, 'Heroin screws you up'. This confusion seems amusing but is potentially harmful since children making their own sense of this campaign were more, not less, at risk of harm as a result. The confusion also led to the research technique being known by teachers, PSHE co-ordinators and researchers as 'Jugs and Herrings'.

It was clear from the first study with 2,061 children that primary school children knew more about drugs than teachers, researchers and policy makers had guessed (Williams et al., 1989).

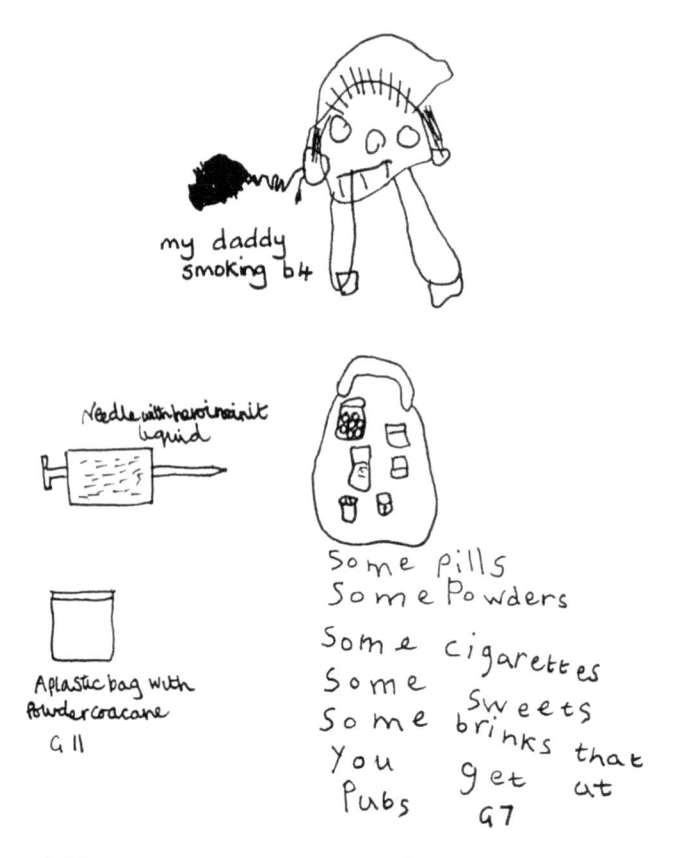

Figure 11.2 Children as young as four display their knowledge

Source: Williams et al., 1989: 71

The youngest children drew and wrote more about medicines and legal substances such as tobacco and alcohol, but by the age of eight years children were drawing and writing with relative accuracy about illegal drugs such as heroin and cocaine. The persons who dropped the bag changed from sick people and health professionals, such as nurses and doctors, to bad people (mostly male) with bad intentions (Figure 11.3).

By the age of 10 and 11 years, far fewer mentioned alcohol and tobacco, perhaps reflecting a different, received interpretation of the word 'drugs'. Some of the children wrote about a downward spiral of consequences of illegal drug use (Figure 11.4).

When asked what they would do with the bag, the children's responses were mainly responsible, including handing them to someone in authority, but some said they would 'keep them', 'eat them', 'hide them' or even 'sell them' (Figure 11.5).

This research has been replicated in small- and medium-scale studies across the UK and internationally (for example, Paxton et al., 1998). The findings were influential in ensuring that drug education, appropriate to the needs, age and stage of the children concerned, became a standard part of PSHE education in primary schools. All schools in England are

Figure 11.3 Eight-year-olds' perceptions of who dropped the bag

Source: Williams et al., 1989: 71, 75

Figure 11.4 An 11-year-old's narrative suggests insight, possibly 'borrowed' from TV drama

Source: Williams et al., 1989: 87

> (2) This young, once pretty girl is the kind of person that dropped the bag of drugs. She is an anti-social dropout – she has a quick temper and as you can see, she is short of money. She uses drugs regularly, and she steals to keep alive. The money she gets from selling the items she uses to get heroin from her dealer who will call Frank. Frank sells drugs at 50 pounds a packet. The effects of drugs are upon her!

years boy

gasp
pick up
and take home
Shock
gasp

Figure 11.5 A 9-year-old shows readiness to take the bag's contents home

Source: Nine-year-old boy, Moulsham Junior School, Essex

now encouraged to have a drug policy which includes medicines, safety and disciplinary matters as well as drug education (DfE/ACPO, 2012). In Wales this is considered a prerequisite for good practice (National Assembly for Wales, 2002). In Scotland, schools are recommended to have a drug policy and doing so is seen as good practice while in Northern Ireland, 'It is a statutory requirement for every grant-aided school to have in place a drugs education policy and to publicise this in their prospectus' (DENI, 2004: 1).

This draw and write has been used to develop local entitlement curricula to meet the needs of different communities and to evaluate the impact of drug education programmes (McWhirter et al., 2000). Using this approach in your classroom will help you to ensure that the drug education you plan will meet the needs of the children in your class and in the community in which they live. To see how to follow up on the findings with classroom activity see Chapter 7, and *Health for Life 4–7* and *Health for Life 8–11* (Wetton and Williams, 2000a, 2000b).

Once children know that it is OK for them to mention 'drugs' in the classroom, there will be less reticence to talking openly about them, and either you or they can raise a related issue without it seeming new, strange or irrelevant. Subsequently, using a formal method of gauging need may seem less applicable. As a consequence there may be very infrequent need for you to introduce drugs by name. Often, names will have been overheard or been read and will be readily mentioned if you ask for news, new things heard about or experienced, or simply give the space for questions or worries to be raised. A new drug word might prompt gentle enquiries from you to see if others in the class have heard of this and whether there may be a local issue of prevalence to address. In the absence of any change in the local area indicating a class need for guidance or vigilance, there is usually no need for a detailed focus on a newly named drug.

The context for information about drugs, health, illness and safety may arise in many different ways. Perhaps a child asks a question. Or you initiate a class discussion about staying safe and what to stay safe from. Or you ask the class to consider what 'healthy' means, or to think of things children might sometimes do that could upset parents, carers or teachers so that you can examine each in turn. Perhaps a child falls over in the playground and comes crying into school with the playground assistant and a grazed knee. What can you help them learn? Perhaps to be more careful in the playground! The graze needs to be washed. Why? Because there are things (dirt, germs) outside the body that can get in (through the graze) and make us unwell. A drug education lesson? Certainly. But we are not compelled to label it 'drug education' in order for it to be useful learning for the children.

Learning such as this (or any other learning) is more likely to stay put if there is a context for it that the children can readily understand. Out of the blue it may have less impact and be less likely to stick. The emphasis on safety, and on health and wellbeing and the children's role in maintaining both, are key elements of drug education within the PSHE curriculum.

A useful trick is to seize opportunities as they arise, as well as planning lessons beforehand. Help the children explore the world they are getting to know, by introducing new concepts, ideas, knowledge, skills, facts and language to augment what is already there. Help them revisit whatever seems either to need reinforcement, or to benefit from a new look as they get a little older and more experienced and are ready to look at something in a slightly different way as a result. Help them develop the vocabulary to talk about the things they explore and to talk about the feelings that go with their learning.

How explicitly should you focus on drugs, and how much on the young people, their skills, their experience, their feelings, their world? We are now straying into areas where there are no answers that apply universally to each age and class of children. Instead, what we offer here are two things. First, use the draw and write exercise we set out earlier to determine the level of understanding they have reached. Second, here is a suggested programme of content for children aged 5–11 years, not necessarily in the order your children will need it. You will want to refer to it as a guide. The content has been taken from the non-statutory programme of study for PSHE education in England. In England the term Key Stage 1 refers to children aged 5–7, and Key Stage 2 refers to children aged 8–11.

Key Stage 1

During Key Stage 1 pupils learn the basic rules and skills for keeping themselves healthy and safe and for behaving well. To develop a healthy, safer lifestyle, pupils should be taught:

- how to make simple choices that improve their health and wellbeing
- how to maintain personal hygiene
- that all household products, including medicines, can be harmful if not used properly
- rules for, and ways of, keeping safe, including basic road safety, and about people who can help them to stay safe
- to agree and follow rules for their group and classroom, and understand how rules help them (e.g. simple safety rules).

To develop confidence and responsibility and make the most of their abilities, pupils should be taught:

- to think about themselves, learn from their experiences and recognise what they are good at.

During Key Stage 1, pupils should be taught the knowledge, skills and understanding through opportunities to:

- take and share responsibility, for example, for their own behaviour, by helping to make classroom rules and following them.

Key Stage 2

During Key Stage 2 pupils learn about themselves as growing and changing individuals with their own experiences and ideas, and as members of their communities. They learn how to make more confident and informed choices about their health and environment, and to take more responsibility, individually and as a group, for their own learning. To develop a healthy, safer lifestyle, pupils should be taught:

- what makes a healthy lifestyle, including the benefits of exercise and healthy eating; what affects mental health; and how to make informed choices
- that bacteria and viruses can affect health and that following simple, safe routines can reduce their spread
- which commonly available substances and drugs are legal and illegal, their effects and risks
- to recognise the different risks in different situations and then decide how to behave responsibly, including sensible road use, and judging what kind of physical contact is acceptable or unacceptable
- that pressure to behave in an unacceptable or risky way can come from a variety of sources, including people they know, and how to ask for help and use basic techniques for resisting pressure to do wrong
- school rules about health and safety, basic emergency aid procedures and where to get help
- why and how rules and laws are made and enforced, why different rules are needed in different situations and how to take part in making and changing rules.

During Key Stage 2, pupils should be taught the knowledge, skills and understanding through opportunities to:

- find information and advice, for example through helplines
- make real choices and decisions, for example about issues affecting their health and wellbeing such as smoking.

School drugs policy

Each school may have a current school drugs policy. Though not a statutory requirement, it is expected. It is possible it will not have this name, as it may be incorporated into another document such as a health and wellbeing policy, or a medicines policy. Whatever form it takes, it will only be genuinely helpful if it has been kept up to date. Guidance for writing a drugs policy has always encouraged schools to set down their approach to drug education within it. There is useful guidance in *Drugs: Guidance for Schools* (DfES, 2004). A good policy is one that guides and supports the school's teachers. However, there may be more of a need to update it to fit with what you plan to do, than to adapt what you do to fit an outdated policy. Updating can reflect changes in thinking, staff responsibilities, sources of help when problems are identified, curriculum statements, teaching materials, recording arrangements, etc. Senior staff will be able to tell you the school's procedures for updating and amending existing policies. We comment further on school policies in Appendix 2.

Risk factors and protective factors

There are many factors that can influence a child's risk level of (later) problematic involvement with drugs. These risk factors, which in combination may make longer-term reliance on drugs more likely, are often determined by conditions beyond the sphere of direct influence of teachers and schools, and for many years beyond the control of the young person, too. Abuses at home or elsewhere, parental misuse of drugs or alcohol, bereavements and other traumatic events, low self-confidence, a poor self-image and mental ill health – any of these (and more) may combine to make the relief and pleasure of some drug taking a solace in a world of sorrow. Skills and knowledge are not enough.

Risk factors

Each of these factors does not necessarily by itself lead to or cause future drug misuse, and where misuse does occur there is usually no simple causal chain. Indeed, in combination they may also indicate heightened risk of other emotional or behavioural problems at school or later in life. Risk factors may be more significant in combination, and are often interrelated. Identified risk factors include:

- chaotic home environments
- parents who misuse drugs or suffer from mental illness
- children with conduct disorders
- lack of parental nurturing
- inappropriate and/or aggressive classroom behaviour
- school failure
- poor coping skills
- low commitment to school
- friendships with 'deviant peers' (those not conforming with expected rules or norms)
- low socio-economic status
- early age of first use
- being labelled as a drug misuser.

Because of the complexity of combinations of these factors, any single intervention addressing a single risk factor is unlikely to be effective. In addition, protective factors may be present, tending to lessen or even outweigh the risk factors.

Protective factors

Some general protective factors have been identified, which include:

- strong family bonds
- experiences of strong parental monitoring with clear family rules
- family involvement in the lives of children
- successful school experiences
- strong bonds with local community activities
- a caring relationship with at least one adult.

However, risk and protective factors do not all carry equal weight, and because drug use and misuse are often determined by many interrelated factors, what is also apparent is that no single organisation or institution can tackle drug misuse by itself. Whereas the risk factors present may, by themselves, be poor at accurately predicting future drug use, to reduce any that are present may also reduce the level of risk. Specific protective factors that schools may try to foster include helping children:

- develop supportive and safe relationships
- attend school regularly
- cope well with academic and social demands at school
- develop good social networks

- develop and rehearse social skills
- have realistic self-knowledge and self-esteem
- acquire a good knowledge of legal and illegal drugs, their effects and their risks
- develop good knowledge of general health and ways of ensuring good mental health
- be able to access help and information
- delay for as long as possible their involvement with legal drugs.

Chapter summary

In this chapter we have defined drugs; considered the rationale for conducting drug education with young children, described what it is and what it aims to achieve; and offered guidance as to suitable teaching content. We have described an activity to discover young children's current level of understanding about drugs and how this can inform starting points for teaching. We have also considered some of the factors that cause children to be considered 'at risk' of future drug misuse.

Further reading

Bradley, B.J. and Greene, A.C. (2013) 'Do health and education agencies in the United States share responsibility for academic achievement and health? A review of 25 years of evidence about the relationship of adolescents' academic achievement and health behaviors', *Journal of Adolescent Health*, 52 (5): 523–32.

DrugScope website: www.drugscope.org.uk.
  DrugScope is the leading UK charity supporting professionals working in drug and alcohol treatment, drug education and prevention and criminal justice. They are also the primary source of independent information on drugs and drug-related issues.

Kellam, S.G., Brown, C.H., Poduska, J.M., Ialongo, N.S., Wang, W., Toyinbo, P., Petras, H., Ford, C., Windham, A. and Wilcox, H.C. (2008) 'Effects of a universal classroom behaviour management programme in first and second grades on young adult behavioural, psychiatric and social outcomes', *Drug and Alcohol Dependence*, 95 (suppl. 1): S5–S28.

Kellam, S.G., MacKenzie, A.C., Brown, C.H., Poduska, J.M., Wang, W., Petras, H. and Wilcox, H.C. (2011) 'The good behavior game and

the future of prevention and treatment', *Addiction Science & Clinical Practice*, 6 (1): 73–84.
From the researchers involved in the trials, a practitioner-friendly account of research on the classroom management technique implemented in the first years of schooling which has led to remarkably strong and persistent impacts on substance use and other problems in later life.

Li, K.-K., Washburn, I., DuBois, D.L., Vuchinich, S., Ji, P., Brechling, V., Day, J., Beets, M.W., Acock, A.C., Berbaum, M., Snyder, F. and Flay, B.R. (2011) 'Effects of the Positive Action programme on problem behaviours in elementary school students: a matched-pair randomised control trial in Chicago', *Psychology and Health*, 26 (2): 187–204.
In Hawaii and then the less-promising schools of Chicago, a primary school programme aiming to improve school climate and pupil character development had substantial and, in Chicago, lasting preventive impacts – another illustration that focusing on drugs is not always the best way to prevent drug problems.

Mentor (2013) *Disengaged from School, Engaged with Drugs and Alcohol? Young People at Risk*, Thinking Prevention briefing paper. London: Mentor UK. Available at: http://mentor-adepis.org/wp-content/uploads/2013/06/30739_Disengagement_8pp_WEB1.pdf (accessed 21 October 2013).
Disengagement from school, including truancy and exclusion, is linked to drug and alcohol use and other risky health behaviours and can start at a young age. The authors argue that this may particularly affect those children from poorer backgrounds and those struggling with basic skills, and that interventions that develop young people's social and emotional capabilities can improve academic achievement and protect against risky behaviour.

Roona, M.R., Streke, A. and Marshall, D. (2003) 'Substances, adolescence (meta-analysis)', in T.P. Gullotta and M. Bloom (eds), *Encyclopedia of Primary Prevention and Health Promotion*. New York: Kluwer Academic/Plenum Publishers, pp. 1073–78.
The most influential finding in drug education research (that interactive teaching methods have the greatest prevention impact) was confirmed by this report, though later questioned by unpublished analyses using better statistical methods – an episode which has left concern and uncertainty in its wake.

Tobler, N.S. (1997) 'School-based adolescent drug prevention: what works and what doesn't, what's next?', in J.U. Gordon (ed.), *A Systems Change Approach to Substance Abuse Prevention*. Lampeter: The Edwin Mellen Press, pp. 21–31.
In a series of renowned meta-analyses, Nancy Tobler integrated research on over 100 school prevention programmes; key message for educators: make it a dialogue, not a lecture.

References

Coggans, N. and McKellar, S. (1994) 'Drug use amongst peers: peer pressure or peer preference?', *Drugs: Education, Prevention, and Policy*, 1 (1): 15–26.

DENI (2004) *Drugs: Guidance for Schools*, Circular 2004/9. Bangor: Department of Education Northern Ireland. Available at: www.deni.gov.uk/2004-13.pdf (accessed 11 November 2013).

DfE/ACPO (2012) *DfE and ACPO Drug Advice for Schools*. Available at: www.gov.uk/government/uploads/system/uploads/attachment_data/file/209993/DfE_and_ACPO_drug_advice_for_schools.pdf (accessed 11 November 2013).

DfES (2004) *Drugs: Guidance for Schools*. London: Department for Education and Skills.

Ghodse, H., Corkery, J., Ahmed, K. and Schifano, F. (2012) *Trends in UK Deaths Associated with Abuse of Volatile Substances, 1971–2009*, VSA Report 24. St George's, University of London: International Centre for Drug Policy. Available at: www.sgul.ac.uk/research/projects/icdp/our-work-programmes/VSA%20annual%20report%20no24.pdf (accessed 17 October 2013).

Home Office (2011) *Drug Misuse Declared: Findings from the 2010/11 British Crime Survey England and Wales*. London: Home Office Statistical Bulletin. Available at: www.gov.uk/government/uploads/system/uploads/attachment_data/file/116333/hosb1211.pdf (accessed 17 October 2013).

McWhirter, J.M., Boddington, N., Perry, D., Clements, I. and Wetton, N. (2000) 'A multi-level approach to community focussed training in drug education: part 2 – teachers as researchers and partners in curriculum development', *Health Education*, 100 (1): 9–22.

National Assembly for Wales (2002) *Substance Misuse: Children and Young People*, Circular No: 17/02. Cardiff: National Assembly for Wales.

Office of the Children's Commissioner (2012) *Silent Voices – Supporting Children and Young People Affected by Parental Alcohol Misuse (Full Report)*. London: Office of the Children's Commissioner.

Paxton, R., Finnigan, S., Haddow, M., Allott, R. and Leonard, R. (1998) 'Drug education in primary schools, putting what we know into practice', *Health Education Journal*, 57 (2): 117–128.

Royal College of Physicians (2012) *Passive Smoking and Children*, Parliamentary Briefing, May. London: Royal College of Physicians. Available at: www.rcplondon.ac.uk/sites/default/files/documents/rcp_parliamentary_briefing_-_passive_smoking_and_children.doc.pdf (accessed 17 October 2013).

Wetton, N. and Williams, T. (2000a) *Health for Life 4–7*. Cheltenham: Nelson Thornes.

Wetton, N. and Williams, T. (2000b) *Health for Life 8–11*. Cheltenham: Nelson Thornes.

Williams, T., Wetton, N. and Moon, A. (1989) *A Way In: Five Key Areas of Health Education*. London: HEA.

CHAPTER 12

UNDERSTANDING PERSONAL FINANCE EDUCATION

Aims

To introduce effective approaches to personal finance education.

Learning objectives

By the time you finish this chapter you will:

- understand the relevance of personal finance education for primary school children
- be able to start where children are in personal finance education
- know how to select resources for teaching about personal finance education
- be able to plan effective lessons in personal finance education
- to be able to create opportunities for children to make real decisions about how to spend and save money and promote their economic wellbeing.

Getting started

Draw round a child in your class on a sheet of lining paper and pin the outline up in the classroom so that everyone can see it. Invite the children to name this fictitious child, who is about their age and has just come to live in their area from another country, with his or her family, to begin a new life and will be coming to their school.

What does this child *need* in order to live comfortably in their new home? Ask the children to write their ideas on Post-it notes and stick them onto the child to 'provide' clothes. Review their suggestions. Are some things 'needs' and other things 'wants'? What is the difference?

Now tell the children that this new child in their class has been given regular pocket money. How much pocket money do they think a child of their age should have every week? Caution – don't ask directly how much each child gets as there will inevitably be some who get more than others. Choose the mode (the most common amount).

The pocket money is for the child to spend on what she or he wants. Ask the children to work in groups to make a list of the kinds of things a child of their age might want.

What would the children in the class do if they had only this amount of pocket money every week but wanted to buy something which costs more? Make a note of their ideas on the white board or using a digital voice recorder.

Introduction

In contrast to some aspects of PSHE education, personal finance education provides you with an ideal opportunity to do some 'real world' activities with the children in your class, no matter what age they are. Money really matters to children, not just the money they have to spend, but also how family finances are managed. There is no doubt that money is an emotional issue for families. It brings pleasure when it is plentiful and misery when there is not enough. In some families (our own included!) discussion about family finances can become a bigger taboo than discussion about sex or drugs. Parents naturally want to protect children from worries about money, especially if the problem is short term. This lack of frankness can mean children recognise the emotion and stress but have no way to explain it, so find their own way to make sense of what is happening around them. In some cases children are well aware of the problem but are powerless to help. Personal finance education makes an important contribution to a child's future economic wellbeing.

> ### 💭 Consider
>
> A teaching assistant supporting a child struggling with maths described how a seemingly everyday classroom activity about budgeting caused a child to break down in tears, who then revealed that his mother cries 'every time she does sums'. Through sensitive questioning the child recalled how Mum does lots of sums every time a letter comes 'from the electric'. He saw 'doing sums' as the cause of his mum's worries, rather than the arrival of the electricity bill. Although Mum was desperately trying to work out how to make ends meet, she was also desperately trying to prevent her child from knowing the extent of their financial problems.
>
> How can you plan to meet the needs of children to be able to manage their own money while recognising the impact that wider economic factors might be having on them and their families?

Developing economic understanding

How children learn about economics – about money, how to acquire, manage and make use of it – has been studied since the 1950s, in different age groups and in different, sometimes changing, cultures. The following summary is based on a review of the development of children's understanding of economics carried out by a leading researcher in this field, Paul Webley (Webley, 2005). It is supplemented by findings from classroom based research, carried out for the development of 'What Money Means' for the Personal Finance Education Group (pfeg) using a draw and write technique with primary school children in Essex and Sunderland (McWhirter et al., 2008, unpublished). The invitations to participate, an analysis framework and some examples of children's responses can be downloaded at: www.pfeg.org/learning-about-money-primary-classroom-support-materials.

It is clear that children's economic thinking develops alongside their cognitive, social and moral development (see Chapter 2). Much of the early research in this area used constructivist approaches which emphasised the 'stages' of children's understanding of economic issues such as the value of individual coins, sources of money, and profit and loss. Their research suggests that children's understanding of economics develops incrementally, based both on past experience and the conflict or challenges that new information and events pose to their existing understanding.

More recently the influence of social context has been explored through comparisons of research with children from different countries and cultures and also based on within-country social class comparisons. In some countries, where children are obliged to contribute financially to the family income, young children have a very clear understanding of what money is, where it comes from and how income is generated.

Whatever their economic situation, however, some researchers say that by the age of 12 years children have the same capacity as an adult to understand economic situations and structures (Webley, 2005). Children who are not economically active simply lack the experience needed to understand how particular institutions operate in the society in which they are living. Even where children do not have to be economically competent to survive, experience of managing money brings benefits. Children whose parents give them pocket money are more able to manage 'credit' than those who have not managed their own money, no matter how small the amount.

Research by Webley (1996) describes children's own economies, which exist largely without benefit of money and are based on bartering, swapping and sharing skills and assets. In fact the structures and systems created by children have much in common with the adult economy which consists of 'labour', 'demand and supply' and 'profit and loss'. These economies are often exploited by companies who market 'collectables' for children which they exchange among themselves and sometimes sell when they have lost interest in them. Children describe an important benefit from these informal economies in terms of developing or cementing friendships. Schools which limit the (financial) value of swaps at school, without banning them outright, could be contributing to children's social as well as economic development.

The 'What Money Means' project found that many children of primary school age no longer go to the shops on a regular basis, especially those who live in rural areas. Goods and services are ordered online and are paid for by typing numbers into a computer. The goods arrive, ready to eat, wear or play with, in the post or in the back of a white van. This means that children have less opportunity to use 'real money' as a concrete object, which may hinder their developing understanding of the financial world.

In the UK, children's understanding of banking changes as they experience how banks operate, although again, parents who bank online may only use ATMs to obtain cash, or use 'cash back' services in large supermarkets, creating more opportunities for confusion about where money comes from. Most five-year-olds think that money is kept physically safe in a bank (and they will get back precisely the coins they deposited) while most of their more sophisticated 11- and 12-year-old friends know 'interest' is added to their savings, but don't know how or why. In the 'What Money Means' project teachers recalled having 'bank books' where amounts paid in and paid out were written in by the clerk at the bank or building society. This record was an encouragement to save as well as a reminder of how much money they had on deposit and how much interest was added. Passive approaches to saving, where parents pay a set amount each month into a savings account which can only be viewed online did not have the same 'feel' as handing over your own birthday or pocket money to the bank for safekeeping.

Children's attitudes to saving relates closely to their ability to defer gratification. By the age of six 'saving' is seen as a good thing, even though six-year-olds do not like saving, and may not be successful savers. However, saving is not the only way children can get more money for what they want – it is just one of a range of alternatives. For example, in the UK, children aged seven to eight years clearly associate money with work.

However, children appear to hold different values about money, compared with adults. Children aged 6–12 years old can weigh up social benefit versus the individual financial benefit, and often place more value on social benefits, behaving more altruistically than adults in a similar situation, for example by sharing their assets or by lending and borrowing. Perhaps this is because they are still more dependent on others, and so recognise they have more to gain from a social contract than adults.

Borrowing has become an accepted way for adults to manage their finances both on a day-to-day basis (for example through pay-day loans) and for the longer term (for example student loans and mortgages). Children learn about the practicality and morality of borrowing at home and in the playground and it makes sense for some attention to be paid to this in PSHE education too. (See the website of the Personal Finance Education Group (known as pfeg) for practical resources, www.pfeg.org.uk.)

Understanding gambling

Children's understanding of economics is often further confounded by their lack of understanding of more complex concepts such as uncertainty and probability. These concepts underpin gambling, which is also practised by children, sometimes with unintended consequences.

Gambling is a relatively loose term when used in everyday language. It is the brother and sister of risk taking, though it doesn't necessarily involve money. You might take a gamble that it won't rain, and leave your umbrella behind. You might take a gamble that the branch won't break when you swing on it. 'Taking a gamble' and 'taking a chance' are pretty much interchangeable terms: gambling is all about risk, probability and consequences, good and bad, which may not always be easy to calculate accurately. Many children of primary school age will 'bet' each other they can or can't achieve something such as swim across a canal or jump from a high place. This form of gambling can have serious physical consequences.

Primary school children will also be familiar with gambling for money through seeing the National Lottery being drawn on the television, or scratch cards on sale in the supermarket or corner shop. At first glance, gambling can look attractive. They may know that children aren't allowed to play these 'games' until they are 18 years old, though they may not understand why. Children may know there's a chance you can win ('You have to be in it, to win it') and they may know that participants often don't. In concrete terms they can see when their numbers don't come up, or the scratch card doesn't reveal the right symbols. They may know all of this, while not being able to understand the odds against winning or where their money goes if they don't win.

Worryingly children may be gambling for money without even knowing it. This can happen within computer games which operate their own currency, enabling children to gain 'coins' or credits for achieving a threshold score. These credits can be used to purchase higher level versions of a free game they have downloaded onto their phone or laptop. Once they have signed up for this they may be encouraged to continue by purchasing credits with real money. Parents who have used a credit card to buy a game may have unwittingly made it possible for the child to make further purchases without putting in the password or PIN. In some cases children have committed their parents to large payments before it is too late to cancel. While there is an element of skill involved in playing these games there is often also an element of chance. A well-known football game which is played online allows you to purchase packs of players, but the names and therefore the skills of the players you are purchasing are not within the customer's control, sometimes leading to great frustration and disappointment. All forms of gambling can be addictive, whether playing cards for matchsticks or gambling chips, or virtual coins in a simulated world on a screen. There are clear overlaps between gaming, gambling and internet safety issues here (Byron, 2008, 2010).

We have already seen that education about personal finance is undoubtedly about much more than acquiring arithmetical skills, although, clearly, these are useful on a day-to-day basis, and experiential learning is vital to enable children to develop their understanding and capability to participate in the economic life of their community.

Education for economic wellbeing requires children and young people to learn how to manage their money on a day-to-day basis and to plan for a future where they can earn their own money through enterprise, as a worker or manager, in the private or public sector. To be effective, education for economic wellbeing will follow the same ten principles as other aspects of PSHE. While the content and the kinds of experiences children may need to learn will vary, teaching and learning strategies will be similar. Selecting resources so that they provide opportunities for experiential learning will provide children with much needed opportunities to manage money in a range of practical ways in the classroom and beyond.

Into practice: developing financial capability

With the youngest children it is important to provide opportunities to exchange, barter and share resources, mirroring the children's natural economy. Setting up a shop in a corner of the classroom where goods can be bought and sold using 'pretend' money can lead on to discussions about how 'cards' work and the functions of cards, often confused by children, including debit and credit cards – and also gift cards and retailers' loyalty cards.

Some schools have set up their own savings banks with pass books into which children save money regularly. Other schools have given some classes control of part of their budget, for example for stationery, or for a class picnic at the end of term. Children become very frugal with the money when they realise it is finite, and teachers report they lose far fewer pencils and scissors if the children are responsible for ordering and paying for more!

Older pupils enjoy applying for, being interviewed and taking on 'jobs' in school for which they can be remunerated with credits they can spend in some form. One teacher promised to pay his class in chocolate bars – and then deducted most of the large bar for national insurance, tax, utility and food bills, leaving just one small square per child at the end of their working week – a harsh but salutary lesson in personal finance. These and other useful ideas can be found on the pfeg website: www.pfeg.org.uk.

> ### Chapter summary
>
> The world of personal finance is complex and the way we navigate it is not just based on cold, rational calculation of monetary cost and benefit. Our emotions and our understanding of relationships plays an equally important role, as you will find when you plan by starting where the children are in this fascinating aspect of PSHE education.

Further reading

All Party Parliamentary Group on Financial Education for Young People (2012) *Financial Education and the Curriculum*. Available at: www.pfeg.org/policy-campaigning/pfeg-and-parliament/appg-primary-and-secondary-schools-strand (accessed 17 October 2012).
The report is the outcome of a six-month enquiry into financial education which drew on evidence from across the education and finance sectors.

Personal Finance Education Group (pfeg): www.pfeg.org.
The pfeg website provides a wide range of resources for personal finance education across the curriculum.

Byron, T. (2008) *Safer Children in a Digital World*. Nottingham: DCSF Publications.
This review looks at the use of video games and social networking and its impact on children. It emphasises the benefits of social media for children as well as highlighting concerns and how parents and responsible organisations can combat these.

Byron, T. (2010) *Do We Have Safer Children in a Digital World?* Nottingham: DCSF Publications.
This review includes how developments in education are helping to transform children's safety on the internet, and makes recommendations for further improvements to promote safer gaming.

References

Byron, T. (2008) *Safer Children in a Digital World*. Nottingham: DCSF Publications.
Byron, T. (2010) *Do We Have Safer Children in a Digital World?* Nottingham: DCSF Publications.
McWhirter, J., Boddington, N. and Hull, T. (2008) unpublished observations. Available at: www.pfeg.org/learning-about-money-primary-classroom-support-materials (accessed 21 October 2013).
Webley, P. (1996) 'Playing the market: the autonomous economic world of children', in P. Lunt and A. Furnham (eds), *The Economic Beliefs and Behaviours of Young Children*. Cheltenham: Edward Elgar, pp. 149–61.
Webley, P. (2005) 'Children's understanding of economics', in M. Barrett and E. Buchanan-Barrow (eds), *Children's Understanding of Society*. Hove: Psychology Press, pp. 43–67.

PART 3

13	Understanding assessment in PSHE education	245
Appendix 1	PSHE education and safeguarding	273
Appendix 2	PSHE education and the school policy framework	275
Appendix 3	'Little Alien' – photocopiable activity plan	277

In this short, final part we discuss the issue of assessment as applied to PSHE education. Having decided to teach it; having planned a programme on the basis of the children's needs that you have worked hard to uncover; and having taught it using materials that help you to help the children reach the learning objectives you have set out – assessing the learning progress of the children (with their help) is the last vital piece in the PSHE education jigsaw. Not that teachers should leave this process until last – but read the next chapter and we will explain.

Finally, our appendices set out the importance of safeguarding children and the role that PSHE education can play, and they offer a reminder that schools have policies and that PSHE education practice needs to take account of whatever policy statements underpin it.

CHAPTER 13

UNDERSTANDING ASSESSMENT IN PSHE EDUCATION

Aim

To establish the value of assessment and introduce strategies for conducting it.

Learning objectives

By reading and reflecting on the content of this chapter you will:

- understand the key principles for assessment *of* learning, assessment *for* learning and assessment *as* learning
- recognise how those principles apply to PSHE education
- be able to assess learning.

Getting started

> **Consider**
>
> Before we start this chapter:
>
> What are your first thoughts about how to assess children's learning in PSHE education?
>
> - Do you think assessment in PSHE education is essential?
> - What might be some of the problems?
> - How might assessment in PSHE education be a positive experience for pupils?
> - How might it be a negative experience?
> - What might we need to consider carefully or to be sensitive about?

Definitions and descriptions that underpin this chapter

The terms used in this chapter need to be very clear, so here we offer short explanations, which are expanded as the chapter progresses.

In all cases you may find that traditional methods of assessment (e.g. pencil and paper tests) do not lend themselves well to PSHE education. This chapter will help you to examine and reflect on some of the alternatives.

Assessment involves gauging what pupils have learnt and what they still need to learn. Assessment focuses on the pupil: 'This is what I have learnt'. In education we often differentiate between assessment *for* learning and assessment *of* learning:

*Assessment **for** learning* – the process of finding out what the child's learning needs are (baseline assessment) or the ongoing assessment that helps teachers and children understand the progress they are making in order to identify and plan next steps in learning (formative assessment).

*Assessment **of** learning* – the process of gathering information that specifies what has been learnt, usually at the end of a sequence of teaching and learning episodes (summative assessment). Learning can be assessed in three ways:

- to measure the progress of an individual against an agreed, external standard – sometimes known as criterion referencing (for example 'Is able to work co-operatively with others')

- to distinguish between individuals (e.g. who has achieved the highest score) – sometimes known as norm referencing
- to show how much progress an individual has made by reference to their original starting point – which can also be called ipsative referencing.

A more recent strategy is gaining currency: *assessment **as** learning* – focuses on the learning process itself and involves the children reflecting on their own learning: what has been learned, how their learning happens, their role in the success of their learning, and how this will help them learn some more. Because PSHE education is so personal the process of critical self-reflection becomes part of the learning process.

Accreditation – is the process of matching a pupil's achievement to an external set of criteria that demonstrates competence against a recognised standard. This usually results in a 'qualification'. External accreditation in PSHE education is usually restricted to Secondary pupils.

Assessment and evaluation

Assessment is an integral part of the learning cycle. It provides an opportunity to reflect on and identify specific learning needs, as well as future needs. These may be presented as a lack of understanding, limited skills or a lack of awareness of differing views. Future learning needs can be identified by the teacher and pupil both independently and together (National Children's Bureau, 2006).

Assessment should not be confused with evaluation (although assessment may form part of an evaluation study). In PSHE it is also important to be clear that assessment is not the same as judgement. That is, PSHE assessments should not make comments judging a child's personality or friendship groups.

Evaluation – considers how effective our lessons, our teaching and our choice of resources or speakers have been in achieving our learning objectives. Evaluation focuses on us and the learning we have provided. 'This lesson was effective in helping these children to learn ...'

We can use assessment data to evaluate the effectiveness of the learning activities we have provided; however, the golden rule is that you cannot evaluate a lesson or programme unless you have first defined the learning objectives. Put simply: you can only claim to have taught effectively when you can state the effects that you were seeking and can show that these were the effects produced. Assessing, perhaps, a sample of pupils' progress using 'working towards', 'working at' and 'working beyond' your intended learning outcomes can help you to reflect on and evaluate the effectiveness of your programme.

We need to mention here one (of the many) key differences between very young and older pupils that needs to be recognised. Significantly more support from the teacher will be needed for early infant pupils than for late junior pupils in assessing learning to date, and particularly in determining what an individual child's next learning priorities are or should be. We presume that until the pupils are both old enough to contribute to this process themselves, and are, to an extent at least, familiar with the process, the teacher will be solely responsible for assessment in whatever form and for whatever purpose.

All forms of assessment described above are appropriate for PSHE although the methods used may be non-traditional. You may wish to know, for example, whether children know the medical names for the parts of the body involved in reproduction (criterion referencing) or to know if a particular child has improved their understanding of the effect of alcohol or tobacco on the body (ipsative referencing). Norm referencing (who has learned most) needs to be used sensitively in PSHE but might be most appropriate to use when assessing the learning in group tasks and activities. At the end of the chapter, we refer to a most useful (downloadable) briefing paper for teachers entitled *Assessment in Drug Education* (DrugScope and Alcohol Concern, 2006), whose advice can be applied across PSHE education.

> **Consider**
>
> Before reading any further, consider what might be the benefits and limitations of using each of the methods of assessing learning in PSHE education that we have described, for the age group you plan to work with. We discuss each method later in the chapter.

Background

Assessment in PSHE education has often been considered contentious. It has been argued that this learning is so personal and so much takes place inside the children that effective assessment of learning is both impossible and inappropriate. On the other hand, in a crowded timetable, would it be reasonable to command curriculum time and require children to attend PSHE lessons if we couldn't provide any evidence that any learning had taken place? In PSHE education there are essential places for effective teacher-, self- and peer-assessment of children's learning and progress, the latter two dependent upon age and aptitude of the children.

Why is assessment important in PSHE education?

Assessment for learning is central to effective teaching and learning in PSHE, setting clear expectations for standards and achievement and helping to ensure progression in understanding and skills. As such it needs to be a planned component of teaching and learning.

Improving learning through assessment is dependent on five key factors (from *Assessment for Learning: Beyond the Black Box*, Assessment Reform Group, 1999: 4–5):

- the provision of effective feedback to pupils
- the active involvement of pupils in their own learning
- adjusting teaching to take account of the results of assessment
- a recognition of the profound influence that assessment has on the motivation and self-esteem of children, both of which are crucial influences on learning
- the need for children to be able to assess themselves and understand how to improve.

Learning objectives and learning outcomes

PSHE education makes use of an 'informal' and 'active' learning pedagogy. This does not mean, however, that the learning has no purpose or is leading to no clear outcome. To clarify:

- Learning objectives are what teachers set out to achieve. *The objective of this lesson is ...* We might ask ourselves, 'What do I intend the child or children to learn? Is this developing a *skill*, exploring, challenging, confirming or clarifying *attitudes, beliefs* or *values*, expanding a *concept* or increasing *knowledge*?'
- Learning outcomes are what the young people will be saying or doing to demonstrate or show evidence that they have met the learning objective. *At the end of this lesson young people will be able to recall/ say/do ...*

What exactly can we assess?

We can help children to assess:

- an increase in knowledge (Before I only knew … Now I also know …)
- an increase in understanding (I always knew … but now I can see how it connects to … and now I can see how I could use this in my life.)
- a change or reconfirmation of a feeling (I used to feel … but now that I understand … I now feel …)
- a richer vocabulary (Before I would have said ... but now I can say …)
- increased competence in a skill (Before I knew how to do/be … but now I know how to do/be …)
- an increased confidence. (Before I could/would say and do … but now I feel I am able to say and do …)

We can confirm their self-assessment: through our own observations of how they demonstrate an increase in knowledge and understanding; through their responses to questions or the increasing accuracy or complexity of their explanations; by listening to and watching them appropriately and confidently apply their expanding vocabulary; and by observing the quality of their behaviours and the richness and equity of their interactions with others.

Assessment in PSHE education is not 'testing' (although there are times when a test, perhaps reframed as a 'quiz', to assess acquisition of new knowledge may be appropriate) nor is it 'judging a young person's worth'.

Although a variety of different groups have legitimacy in supporting assessment in PSHE education, for example peers, significant adults or visitors to the classroom, teacher and self-assessment are likely to be the main means of assessment.

> **Personal activity**
>
> Think about a module or theme from a PSHE education programme in a school with which you are familiar.
> How are baseline, formative assessment for learning and summative assessment of learning assessment built in? If they are not, then how could they be?

What evidence could we gather to help with our assessment?

Although the learning each individual child takes from a PSHE lesson will be unique to them, there is still an important place for the teacher assessing learning against the learning objectives. Examples of evidence that can assist with assessment might include:

- responses to challenges or questions
- pieces of written work, including diaries or personal 'learning logs'
- revisiting draw and write activities (see Chapter 4) and other techniques illustrated below
- 'testing' knowledge and understanding (can the child obey instructions? Do they know how to avoid hazards previously pointed out? Can they say why hazards need to be avoided? etc.)
- observation of pair and group activity, their interchange of ideas, their ability to work together and the quality of the work produced
- video, audio recordings or photographs taken by individual or groups
- drama projects (including both people and puppets)
- posters or displays
- presentations to a class or group.

There may be times when you want to assess the general progress of a group or class, and the examples in this list could also be used in these contexts.

It is essential not to confuse the learning outcomes from PSHE education with those from other curriculum subjects. A child may demonstrate a high degree of learning in PSHE through a piece of written work that is poorly spelt or poorly constructed grammatically. Their drawing may not be easily recognisable and their (sound) explanation hesitantly offered. They may have grasped the learning within a poorly designed or presented poster or display or through the use of weak drama skills. While it may be appropriate to provide feedback on these, it is vital that the assessment of learning within PSHE education is not diluted or lost during this process.

First principles

Let us return to first principles of assessment. You can only 'assess' against something else. For example, if we assess someone as 'being tall' there has to be someone to compare him or her against. If they were the only person in the world then they couldn't be 'tall', they would simply be what they were. Some of our descriptions are factual (e.g. 'He or she has black hair'), or we can measure someone against a scale to give us data in the form of a figure (for example metres and centimetres). However, once we make a judgement about someone, 'he is fat' or 'she is thin', our descriptions are actually comparisons with others.

We recommend the combination of ipsative assessment with reference to external criteria. Some pros and cons of each strategy are set out in Table 13.1 overleaf.

May we remind you here of the statement at the start of the chapter: that the teacher will be solely responsible for assessment in whatever form and for whatever purpose, until the pupils are old enough to contribute to the process themselves.

The stages of assessment

First, you need to establish and record the learning objectives and intended outcomes so that you know, and the child knows, what you are assessing.

Assessment can take place at different times in the process of learning: at the beginning, during the learning process or at the end. Sometimes the end of one piece of learning (for example the end of a unit) is midway within a larger piece of learning, for example a whole year. The point in the learning at which you decide to assess needs to relate to the purpose of the assessment:

- Baseline assessment (sometimes known as learning-needs assessment) provides teachers and children with their starting points: the knowledge, values, beliefs, vocabulary and skills that children already possess and bring to the learning. In PSHE education this links to the principle of 'starting where children are' (see Chapter 4). Baseline assessment is not simply discarded at the start of new learning. It can be a powerful tool to support all types of further assessment as children's learning progresses. If you look at the examples offered later in this chapter you will see how older children are able to reflect on their own baseline assessment, which can enable them to monitor and critically reflect on their own progress and also prioritise their own future learning.
- The terms 'formative assessment' and 'assessment for learning' (AfL) have often been used interchangeably; however, recent work around assessment has differentiated them. Assessment for learning has been

described as 'any assessment for which the first priority in its design and practice is to serve the purpose of promoting students' learning' (Black et al., 2004: 10). This is a dynamic process that is concerned with the immediate future through the daily adjustment of teaching based on feedback such as questioning by the teacher in the classroom.

- Formative assessment, as its name suggests, enhances and shapes learning through modifying teaching and is therefore central to AfL. However, any element of it that leads to medium- and long-term modifications to teaching rather than having an immediate impact in adjusting teaching and learning is not, strictly speaking, AfL.

- Summative assessment, or assessment of learning, is the assessment that takes place at the end of a piece of learning. It tells us where the learner is at a given point in time, which is useful for celebrating success, monitoring achievement, reporting to parents and so on. However, the information it provides does not help the learner to improve as it does not tell us the cause of any learning difficulty or suggest strategies for improving.

If children are not learning it is important to reflect on where the deficit lies. Is it with the children or with the teaching? Through reflective practice it is important to consider if there are different ways to help children achieve the learning objectives.

> ### Consider
> A cycle of assessment in PSHE education should include a balance of baseline, formative and summative assessment. Evidence of learning can include teacher questioning and observation, written work, taped or videoed material, personal diaries or learning logs. What is important is to evidence learning outcomes and understand the purpose of the assessment.

Ideally responsibility for assessment is shared, because:

- There are times when, as the teacher, you will be making assessments both to inform future teaching and learning, and for reporting to others.
- There are times when the children will be assessing themselves to reflect on how they are developing. In PSHE education this is particularly

Table 13.1 Three common assessment strategies

Process	Comment	Pros	Cons
• **Norm referenced** – we assess young people by comparing their understanding or competence against one another. Basically we rank them.	While formally ranking pupils in PSHE education would seem unnatural, teachers are often sensitive to children who may, compared with others, have particular skills or additional learning needs.	Many teachers have found themselves noticing things like 'This child seems to know more about how exercise makes us healthy/a better negotiator than the rest.' Children also frequently compare their skills with others: 'He/she is much better at handling that sort of thing than me!', 'I wish I was confident like …'	At first glance does not seem useful, as hard to gauge absolute value. Who is to judge that the statements are the correct ones to achieve the learning needs of your children?
• **Criterion referenced** – young people's knowledge and skills are assessed against a set of predetermined criteria, often in the form of statement banks that describe certain demonstrations of knowledge or skill against a 'level descriptor'.	While ranking places children in an order, all children could theoretically be at the same level. Some statement banks have a unique statement for each level of progress while some are simpler, identifying young people who are 'working towards', 'working at' or 'working beyond' a narrower or even single range	External criteria are really useful starting points, especially for planning a progressive programme.	Teachers need to be able to fine-tune criteria to meet the unique needs of their young people.

Process	Comment	Pros	Cons
	of statements. Children have a combination of 'universal needs' that every young person of their age will have, and unique needs that are relevant to them in their personal context.		
• **Ipsative** – young people's current knowledge and skills are assessed against their own prior knowledge and skills.	A powerful model of assessment for PSHE. Links most closely to personalised learning and the skill of critical self-reflection. Because PSHE education starts from the learner, works inside their reality and encourages critical reflection, the learner is naturally at the heart of assessment.	Assessment, teaching and learning become one continuous process. Can be useful to combine ipsative assessment with criterion assessment, so the child reflects on their learning and identifies their personal progress, in turn held up against a common progression framework. This can help further inform pupils' next steps in learning.	Would leave stage of progress unclear unless there is some reference to exterior levels or statements.

important as some learning can be very 'private' and not appropriate to share immediately (or ever) with others.
- If well structured and undertaken in a safe environment, there are times when peers are the best people to assess each other's learning. (Parents, carers or significant others can also have an important place in assessment.)

Pulling it all together

'Assessment' and 'teaching' are not separate activities but part of one single continuous process. At all stages the teacher and pupils should be engaged in the assessment process. Remember, too, that pupils' involvement in their own assessment will become more realistic and more valid as an exercise as they develop, but will need support at young ages and as they become familiar over time with the self-assessment process. So adapting Shirley Clarke's wise guidance (2005), the sequence might become:

1. *Baseline assessment* to provide data that shows the learners their prior learning and shows you the next steps in the learning that you need to provide. What is already in place that you can celebrate? What is almost in place that you just need to 'nudge' a little? What is missing (is it okay that this is missing for their age group or readiness?) that you need to teach? And what is misunderstood that you need to gently challenge? Does the data show you that you need to plan to provide new knowledge, opportunities to gain new understanding, to help pupils recognise new responsibilities, to help them develop new or rehearse existing strategies or skills, to extend vocabulary, enrich language or explore and clarify values or beliefs? When the children are very young, they will need your help to share their prior learning. (See Chapter 4 on starting where children are.) At very young ages, baseline assessment is four-pronged: parental visits, observations of the child, earlier practitioners' records, and draw and tell – 'What I can do or say'. (Note, parents and carers are likely to have been the sole or key teachers of all the child has learned before attending nursery or school.)
2. You need to be mindful of any national guidance related to PSHE and defining expectations of what your pupils should know and be able to do at benchmark ages. Your assessment should be working to evidence these.
3. You set your PSHE *learning objectives* and the *learning outcomes* you want the children to demonstrate in order to provide evidence that the learning objectives have been met. You share these with the learners,

perhaps through language such as 'Today we are going to learn about ...', 'How could you show me (we show each other) that we have learnt this?' It is an opportunity for you to share your expectations, 'What I am looking for is ...', and an opportunity to explore why this learning is really important: 'Why do we think it is really important that we know this/can do this?'

4. You select and plan (or you could work with your children to plan) an *assessment activity* that will enable *all* pupils to have a realistic opportunity to demonstrate that they have achieved your PSHE learning outcomes. It is essential that the *process* of assessment facilitates rather than inhibits all pupils in demonstrating their new learning. You may need to offer a variety of different assessment opportunities in order to ensure all pupils have an equal opportunity to demonstrate their learning. For example, some children may find it easy to provide written evidence; some may prefer to verbally describe (which could be taped); some may find it easier to draw a diagram or picture or act out a scenario with puppets (which could be videoed) and then talk about it.
5. You set, or the pupils and you jointly set, the 'success criteria' that describe what 'good' looks like. 'How could you show me (we show each other) that you are really good at this?', 'What would a really good ... look like ... have in it?'
6. *Assessment for learning* enables your pupils and you to 'fine-tune' the learning as it progresses.
7. *Summative assessment* data seeks evidence that pupils have achieved the learning outcomes, showing where your objectives have been met.
8. If your pupils are successful in meeting the learning outcomes you can therefore *evaluate* this as an effective lesson/unit as a means of meeting your learning objective. (You are acting as a reflective practitioner, helping yourself to constantly refine and improve your practice.) If not, what do you need to do differently next time or revisit and reinforce in a subsequent lesson?
9. Summative assessment becomes your new baseline.
10. Formative assessment data now informs your future teaching.

Now the cycle repeats. Every time a child answers a question or offers a contribution there is an opportunity for assessment and fine-tuning the next step in learning. Each time a child answers a question, contributes their opinion or enters into a dialogue with us, they are learning more about our subject and we are learning more about them.

The most important people to reflect on what they are learning and how they are changing are the young people themselves, and as they grow older you will help them become more familiar and more effective at such reflection. Simply looking at what they thought, knew or felt before a session or module and what they think, know and feel now can be illuminating.

- Have I learned a lot or a little?
- Has the 'lot' I learned been important for me?
- Has the 'little' I learned been a useful piece of learning, the one thing that could really make a difference?
- Have I been reminded of things or strategies I already knew or that I may have forgotten, not previously thought relevant, or not thought might be transferable to this new situation?

If we are going to ask young people to assess their own learning we need to help them assess their starting points. Surprisingly, simply asking people to put themselves on a scale can offer an insight into their perceptions of their existing skills and knowledge. As we learn, our assessment of ourselves may prove overly optimistic, accurate or overly pessimistic.

- Use a suitable scale for the child's age, for example:
  - a scale of 1–5
  - a more simple three-point scale: 'not at all', 'a little' and 'very'
  - or a smiley face, a neutral face or a sad/worried face.
- Then refer to the scale to help them assess, for example:
  - 'If I asked you how confident do you feel you are to deal with … where would you put yourself?'
  - 'If someone asked for your advice concerning … would you feel very, a little or not at all confident that you could help them?'

We could offer a character from a story who knows or can do something and invite children to consider if 'That's a lot like me', 'That's a little like me' or 'That's not much like me'.

At the end of a module or session you simply invite the pupils to see if they feel they have moved on the scale. Moving downwards is not necessarily negative. It can mean that a pupil now understands that an issue or skill is more complex than they first believed.

However, a word of warning: If PSHE education really starts from where children are, really respects and builds on their current understanding, and seeks to be relevant, there are times when it is best that you abandon your learning objective and allow the children to take you where they need to go.

Be sensitive to any apparent undercurrent indicating a need to explore in depth something you were going to gloss over. Be ready to gloss over something that seems to underestimate the knowledge, confidence or experience of the class. And be flexible enough to change tack when it seems from the children's responses that this would be more useful to them. Always use your judgement about what is appropriate, but don't be blind or deaf to the clues that may help you decide when to vary your direction or focus. The younger the children, the more sensitive you may need to be to pick up any signs that you need to exercise your flexibility. Gentle questions – such as 'Is anyone not clear ...? Or still worried ...? Does anyone want to ask something about this? Can anyone tell us how you would explain this to someone in another class?' – can often shine light on where the children are, and where to take them (or let them take you).

One of the skills of effective PSHE education is knowing when to allow the learners to take over the direction of their learning and when you need to pull them back to your chosen path. There is no point in rigidly following your lesson plan if it is becoming obvious that your learning objective is no longer relevant, or that a more relevant or valuable learning objective is evolving.

The early years

Teachers of children aged five to six years will be building on work undertaken in the children's early years. The 'Early Learning Goals' published in England in 2012 (DfE, 2012) define the personal, social and emotional development of children prior to the age of five years as:

> *Self-confidence* and *self-awareness*: children are confident to try new activities, and say why they like some activities more than others. They are confident to speak in a familiar group, will talk about their ideas, and will choose the resources they need for their chosen activities. They say when they do or don't need help. (DfE, 2012: 8)

The child makes choices within their environment and expresses their preferences. The child tries new things, explores resources and tools, and shares their experiences with others including adults, peers or within a group. The child plays independently, expressing their ideas and innovations, and asks for support when needed.

Managing feelings and behaviour: children talk about how they and others show feelings, talk about their own and others' behaviour, and its consequences, and know that some behaviour is unacceptable. They work as part of a group or class, and understand and follow the rules. They adjust their behaviour to different situations, and take changes of routine in their stride. (DfE, 2012: 8)

The child responds appropriately to experiences, communicating his or her needs, views and feelings. The child is aware of the consequences of words and actions and adapts his or her behaviour accordingly. When playing as part of a group, the child takes turns and shares. The child knows the expectations and routines of the setting, applies strategies to respond to changes of routine and offers explanations as to why these are necessary. The child is usually able to adjust his or her behaviour to reflect this understanding.

Making relationships: children play co-operatively, taking turns with others. They take account of one another's ideas about how to organise their activity. They show sensitivity to others' needs and feelings, and form positive relationships with adults and other children. (DfE, 2012: 8)

The child plays co-operatively in a group, sharing and taking turns. When playing together with others, the child usually responds in a friendly and kind way, listening to other children's ideas and points of view. The child interacts positively with other children and adults.

In English schools a profile of children's learning is created using a scale of 'emerging', 'expected' and 'exceeding' and should be passed to the child's Year 1 teacher (teaching ages five and six years). This will have drawn on:

- practitioners' knowledge of the child
- materials which illustrate the child's learning journey, such as photographs, observations of day-to-day interactions, video/tape/electronic recordings
- the child's view of his or her own learning
- information from parents and carers; and information from other relevant adults.

Much of this assessment will be through observation and teachers working with children to help them to recognise their progress.

Into practice

So how do we do all this? Let's start with baseline assessment. You could think of this as a form of classroom research and invite the children to think of themselves as your 'research assistants'. It is also true even with the very youngest! Helping you gather data can be affirming.

Drawing/writing/annotating (non-traditional forms of pencil and paper assessment)

Below are listed some simple classroom techniques that help to 'illuminate' pupils' prior learning about a variety of issues. They are limited only by your imagination. It is important to think about what data you want to gather because these work equally well for children working individually and then perhaps sharing in groups or as group activities. If you want children to have individual baseline data to enable you to monitor their progress then ask them to work alone, but if you are comfortable with a class baseline then group work can be very effective. (If you are going to ask children to share their work with their peers it is ethically essential that they know this in advance.) Preparing some of these techniques does not need any artistic talent. They actually work far better if the drawings are very simple. 'Pin people' work really well because they can be either gender, any culture or any age. The simpler the drawings are, the better.

> *Draw and write* and *draw and tell* – These are two techniques that are explored in greater detail elsewhere in this book (see Chapter 4). They are two of the most powerful baseline assessment tools available to us and have the strength of being inclusive. For children who struggle with writing, the teacher can act as scribe. For very young children, draw and tell invites children to first draw and then talk about their drawings. To an adult they may simply appear as marks on the paper but to the child they have meaning and with encouragement they can share this with us. Children's drawings and writing can be returned to them following the completion of a piece of work and they can be invited to add to or change their original work.
>
> *The little alien* – The teacher invites children to explain to a visiting alien (or someone from another class if speaking to an 'alien' is too advanced an idea) a concept such as bullying, prejudice, money or debt. The little

alien has no understanding of this concept and needs the children's help. Their explanations offer a powerful insight into their starting points, and this technique also offers the opportunity for formative and summative assessment since the little alien can revisit the classroom, and children can be invited to add to or change what they originally told the alien. Some teachers have found using 'A detective who is visiting our class needs our help in finding out …' also works well. We have included a photocopiable blank of the 'little alien' in Appendix 3.

Storyboard – This is a simple yet powerful technique to explore children's strategies for managing a situation or dilemma. We place the dilemma into the first of six squares; for example one child is saying to another child, 'Can you help me? I am being bullied.' The children are invited to draw and write the rest of the story that ends in the final square with the problem being successfully resolved. Once again the story can be revisited and revised in the light of new learning. The storyboard can also be extended further into the future to see what might be the consequences of a strategy that might at first glance seem appropriate but with further consideration might not be so good.

Park bench – This is a shorter version of storyboard but explores feelings, too. It is a simple sketch of two children sitting on a park bench. It could be on the board for all the class to see, or on paper if they're able to work in groups. The gender of the sketches need not be recognisable, though that could be explored if the situation needs it. Above each child draw a speech bubble and a thought bubble. Complete one child's speech bubble and invite the class either individually or as groups to consider what this person would be thinking and feeling. They (or you) could write this in the thought bubble. Explore what the second child might be thinking and feeling (or what *the class* think and feel about this fictitious friend's situation). Write ideas in. The friend's speech bubble is either for what the class think the friend might be saying, or for any advice the class think would help the first child.

Bubbles – If you are worried about your design skills one of the simplest techniques is simply to draw a face with a speech bubble and place the dilemma inside, then draw another face with an empty speech bubble, two thought bubbles and an empty rectangle, all suitably labelled. Again one sketched child speaks the dilemma and your class consider what they would be thinking, feeling, saying and doing.

Bus-stop people – This is a slightly different tool. We know that children can misunderstand the views of their peers, often believing themselves to be unique in their views, fears or anxieties. They may overestimate the behaviours of their peers, especially any risky behaviours, and so feel 'the odd one out'. In this technique pupils are given a sheet with some drawn figures of children waiting by a bus stop with speech and thought bubbles over their heads. Tell the children, 'A group of children from our school have met up at the bus stop. They are all thinking and talking about ... (Add what it is you want to explore. Maybe it's about how noisy everyone is at lunchtime, or what they get up to on the way home). What do you think they are thinking, feeling and saying?' If they asked you for your opinion, how would you feel? What would you say? *Bus-stop people* is a powerful technique for exploring what children think others are thinking. Sharing this can be very reassuring, as children find their behaviours and feelings are often very similar to those of others their own age. Of course you can vary this. Perhaps they are a little older, a lot older, younger or much younger. You could change them to 'parents' or 'people who live round here'. It all depends on what you want to explore.

In many of these techniques it can be fascinating to explore with children why what they (or the children on *park bench* or *bus-stop*) are thinking and feeling may be different from what they are saying and doing. Might something be holding them back from saying or doing what they feel they want to or ought to say or do?

> **Consider**
> How could you help your class to explore how to be good judges of what to say when they think and feel a certain way? It would probably be best to provide, or encourage them to think of, one or more concrete situations in which to explore this idea. What endings could be added to the sentence starting 'What could you say when ... and you felt ...?' that would elicit the children's ideas you are seeking? Substitute a fictitious character's name in place of 'you' to create a safe distance if you need to.

Younger children – This can also be a useful technique and is similar to the little alien. Tell the children, 'My friend is a teacher who works with children a little younger than you and she needs our help.' Again from this point the exercise is limited only by your imagination. Perhaps she needs to explain a complex concept to them, like 'being fair', 'why turn taking is important', 'negotiation' or 'bullying'. But it could also be more focused: 'There is a railway/farm/busy road nearby. What do you think she should warn them about? Which do you think might be most important? What could my friend's class do to keep themselves and others safe?'

Brain-storm or *first thoughts* – This exercise is perhaps the simplest technique, where a class is invited to literally 'dump' everything that they know about something onto a sheet of paper or interactive whiteboard and save for later comparison. A long sheet of wallpaper and lots of pens can be an active way of doing this with a whole class who are ready to write, and it also can increase anonymity as all the children are working at the same time.

Now imagine each child was completing one of these activities. If it is an individual piece of work, it could be placed into an envelope with the child's name on it. If it is the product of a group it could be put away somewhere safe, again with all their names on it. Now imagine bringing this out at intervals as their learning progresses, to review and amend.

Imagine the little alien came back to our classroom; what would we say now that we wouldn't have said (didn't say) before?

In our storyboards we thought these were good strategies. Now we have learnt ... do we think there are other ideas that could be better?

At the start of this work we would have thought ... felt ... said ... and done. Now we have learnt about ... we think, feel and would say and do ...

Before, the advice we would have given them would have been ... but now we would tell them to ...

We can add in a knowledge component to any of these, for example by simply adding to *park bench*, 'Suppose they asked you why they should take your advice. Do you know enough to persuade them?' As their learning progresses we could ask the pupils if they could now offer more reasons to take their advice.

In this way baseline assessment respects the children's starting points. It can become a powerful teaching resource and support both formative and eventually summative assessment. Because children's development is so great between commencing and finishing primary schools, enabling them to reflect on the extent of their learning over, perhaps, six years can be both powerful and affirming.

Using sentence stems

Below are some unfinished statements that can help structure the critical reflection that lies at the heart of assessment in PSHE education. Because the age range covered in primary schools is so great these are only offered to be helpful and you should select the ones you feel are most appropriate. There are far too many to be used in one go and they would need to be reworked for different ages.

- One thing/Things I know now that I didn't know before is/are …
- Some new words I have learnt to use to describe 'things' are …
- Some new words I have learnt to describe my 'feelings' are …
- One question/Questions I still have is/are …
- Something/Some things I want to find out more about is/are …
- One thing/Things this lesson has made me think about is/are…
- Something/Some things this lesson made me think about again/reminded me of is/are …
- Something/Some things I will remember to do/say is/are …
- One thing/Things I feel differently about is/are … (because …)
- One thing/Things that have really surprised me is/are …
- One thing/things I would want everyone else to know is/are …
- One thing/Things I am now concerned about is/are …
- One thing/Things I would like to change in myself/my school/my community/my world is/are …
- One thing/Things I am going to do/say differently now is/are …
- One thing/Things I really enjoyed is/are …
- Something/Some things I will say now that I wouldn't have said before is/are …
- Something/Some things I now feel more confident about is/are …
- Something/Some things I would like to learn more about is/are …
- Something/Some things I need to find out more about is/are …
- Something/Some things I feel clearer about is/are …
- Something/Some things I now feel confident I could advise others about is/are …

Here are some statements that encourage reflection on what the children feel willing to share and what they want to keep inside themselves:

- Something/Some things I am happy to share with others is/are…
- Something/Some things I want to keep private to me is/are…

But beware the invitation to disclose the very things they want to keep private!

Using Circles of Feeling

Use the class 'Circle of Feelings' (see p. 89) to add to the cumulative record of the words the children feel ready to use to describe how they or a fictional character in a story feel. Once the children can, they can be invited to record them in the circle themselves.

We may want children to reflect not only on *what* they have learnt but *how* they learnt. Some questions that reflect on the process, if group work was involved:

- We worked well together because ...
- We could have worked better if ...
- I helped my group by ...
- It was really helpful when ... did ...
- I found it hard to say when I disagreed with the others' views about ...
- I felt safe to say what I thought even when I thought others in the group wouldn't agree ...

And some sentence stems that offer feedback on the learning to the teacher to help with evaluation:

- If I could have changed something in this session it would have been ... because ...
- One thing I would like the teacher to know is ...
- I really found ... useful/helpful/interesting
- When we did ... it really helped me to ...

Peer and external assessment

While developing the skills of self-evaluation and self-assessment are at the core of PSHE education the children also need to have opportunities to check out 'how *others* perceive me' and 'how *others* feel I am growing and changing'. This checking-out can involve adults such as teachers, their parents/carers and each young person's own trusted peers.

It takes time to teach a class how to give and receive feedback to and from one another but these abilities go far beyond simply supporting assessment in PSHE education. Developing the ability to provide, and to receive, constructive feedback is a fundamental life skill and is a critical skill for maintaining all sorts of healthy relationship.

Peer feedback is very powerful and needs a clear structure and ground rules to avoid a child being emotionally hurt by (fair) criticism. There also needs to be clarity about exactly what the focus of any feedback should be. It should normally only occur when one child seeks it from another, or accepts a trusted offer. You will need to make this very clear to the children. Even sensitively offered criticism may be uncomfortable enough to be unacceptable if it is not wanted.

The child offering feedback needs to be insightful and focused in gathering their views and opinions about their fellow student and sensitive and supportive in offering feedback.

As a general rule feedback should either validate the positive or offer positive alternatives to areas that could be developed. However, sometimes it is important to know when our comments or actions have challenged (which may be a very positive outcome) or even distressed others (which may be less so). Feedback is of no use at all unless there is a willing recipient! The following tips may be useful.

Giving feedback

The following advice is equally valid for children and grown-ups! Start with the positive because launching straight in with even gentle criticism may be hard for the receiver to take, and may make them feel defensive. Point out things that can be changed, and give examples because there's no point mentioning things the recipient can do nothing about – like their height, or where they live! Mentioning a specific example can help focus on behaviour that might be improved or usefully reflected on. Try to say in what way something was (supportive, unhelpful, thoughtless, etc.) rather than just 'good' or 'bad'.

These prompts can help:

- I liked it when you … because …
- I thought it was good when you … because …
- I found it helpful when you said …
- I found it helpful when you did …
- Your presentation was helpful because …
- I would have found your presentation even more helpful if you had …
- I would like to have known more about …
- I found it really interesting when you said/asked/did …
- I found it difficult when you said/did …
- When we work in groups I find it helpful the way you …
- I think you showed this skill when you …
- I think it might have been more helpful if you had …

For younger children, just being encouraged to get into the habit of saying 'Thank you for … (doing, saying)' can provide appreciative feedback;

and 'I'm sorry I ...' when they have hurt, offended or otherwise upset someone else can pave the way for the sorts of responsibility that come into sharper focus when they are older and more ready for structured feedback.

Receiving feedback

Children receiving feedback need to learn to listen. Feedback, particularly criticism, can feel uncomfortable, but it can be very helpful. It may be useful to listen carefully rather than jumping in with defence or argument. If it seems mistaken, they need to have a chance to say so. If necessary, the receiver can ask the giver to explain and expand, to make it (and the reasons for it) clearer.

They can be encouraged to check it out! Okay, so it's one person's view. Checking with others can help you discover whether your giver's feedback is a minority view, or is generally shared. If they want feedback on something particular, encourage them to ask for it.

If any criticism seems right to its receiver, encourage them to decide what to do about it. Can they change? Do they want to? How will things be different if they do? Can they do this on their own or do they need a little help? Who can help them?

If children have had honest feedback, genuinely given and meant, they need to thank the giver, even if it was hard for them to hear. Then the giver may offer feedback again. But if the receiver seems not to appreciate it, it may be harder to get feedback next time they want it. Note, though, appreciating the feedback being given isn't quite the same as agreeing with it! Even positive feedback can be hard for some children to receive.

We recommend that the skills of offering feedback be developed within the entire PSHE education programme, and that recipients be encouraged to say how helpful they find their peers' comments. This is part of a genuine, reflective 'learning community'.

Helping children to record their learning

There are many ways of helping children record and celebrate their learning and progress in PSHE. For example:

Treasure chest

This is simply a picture of an open treasure chest. Children write inside all of the things they have learnt to do well or now know that they didn't before. Outside of the chest, on the same page, they can record those things they have yet to learn or that they need to practise more.

Targets

This involves a picture of an archery target with a large bull's-eye to record learning that has been achieved or skills that have been mastered. The bull's-eye records 'things I know and can do really well', the middle rings can record 'things I can almost do' or 'things I am getting better at' or 'things I need to improve (or learn)', and the outermost ring, 'things I need to begin to learn'.

Looking back, looking forward

This is a versatile reflective tool that can be used for more than assessment of a single piece of learning or even module. The Roman god Janus looked both ways in time. A piece of paper is divided in half and a Janus head with two faces, one facing left and one right, is placed in the middle of the sheet. Now put lots of thought bubbles beside the faces. Now you can put 'prompts' above each bubble.

For example, looking back:

- One thing I really enjoyed learning was …
- One thing I did really well was …
- One thing I would have done differently is …
- The most important thing I learnt was …
- One thing I tried really hard at was …
- Something I got better at is …

And for looking forward:

- One thing I am curious to know more about is …
- Something I want to get better at is …
- Something I will try harder at is …
- Something I am interested in learning is …
- A question I still have is …

This can also be a powerful tool to use at transitions, perhaps between phases within a school or between schools, demonstrating the links between PSHE education and wider pastoral issues. We could think of this as 'big assessment' in which case looking back we could add:

- Something I will miss is …
- Something I won't miss is …
- Someone I will miss is …
- Something I am really proud of is …

And looking forward:

- Something I am excited about is …
- Something I want to try out is …
- Something I am a bit nervous about is …
- Something I am *really* nervous about is …
- Something I would like everyone to know about me is …
- Something I want my new teacher, *but nobody else*, to know about me is …

You will know what kind of language to use that will fit the age group you work with.

Again this activity is limited only by your imagination, but this is powerful data and can help a teacher or school reflect on their own practice and ease a child through transitions by recognising and addressing their anxieties as well as celebrating their achievements.

Encouraging a habit of reflection in the classroom

Away from the formal assessment of the learning undertaken, there are lots of opportunities to encourage a 'habit of reflection'. At the end of any lesson, series of lessons or even at the end of a school day we suggest asking a few questions that encourage young people to reflect on how they feel about their learning.

Invite them to think, then share with someone else, then perhaps to share in fours and finally invite any contributions from the fours to the whole group.

These are offered simply as a way of closing and perhaps crystallising some of the learning both in terms of the outcomes and the process. While not intended as a formal 'assessment' process it might be useful to record some of the answers you get to help reflect on your session. They would need to be adapted for different ages, abilities and circumstances. A very few questions are often enough to gauge general feelings and specific responses. This is intended to be a fast activity. For example:

- Who has learnt something new today?
- Who can do something now that they couldn't do at the start of the day? Who has got better at something?
- Who learnt something really surprising – perhaps something they didn't expect? How does that feel?

- Who got stuck? What did you do next?
- Who has worked with someone else? How did you get on?
- Who has helped someone else to learn something today? What did you do that helped?
- Who mucked something up/made a real mess of something? Is it something you can go back to and put right?
- Who tried really hard today? At everything?

More searching questions can sometimes be useful:

- Who felt like giving up? What stopped you from giving up? Who helped you? What did they say or do?
- Who had an 'ah-ha' moment – one of those times when something confusing suddenly made sense? What does that feel like?
- Who said something to you today that made you feel really good? (Quickly tell them what they said and why it made you feel good!)
- Who still has a question that they haven't been able to answer? Who is still wondering about something?
- Think about what we have done today – any important questions that we could have asked but didn't?

Of course, the questions you select will depend on the nature of the lesson, the sort of feedback you want, and the children who you want feedback from.

Because so much of this learning is very personal we have to find ways to encourage children of all ages to make their own personal meanings out of their learning. What does this mean to me? How, when, where and with whom can I make use of this learning? How does knowing this reinforce or challenge what I believe?

It is important for children to own their own progress. It is easy for a child's progress to exist only in a teacher's mark book or evidence file.

In PSHE we have assessment *of* learning, we have assessment *for* learning but perhaps there is no subject where it is so vital to provide opportunities for assessment *as* learning.

Chapter summary

This chapter considers one of the most important aspects of PSHE, that of assessment. It offers a range of approaches to the assessment, makes a clear distinction between assessment and evaluation, and offers different techniques that can be used to assess learning in PSHE in a variety of contexts.

> **Further reading**
>
> Clarke, S. (2005) *Formative Assessment in Action: Weaving the Elements Together*. London: Hodder Education.
>
> Muijs, D. and Reynolds, D. (2011) 'Assessment for learning', in *Effective Teaching: Evidence and Practice*. London: Sage.
>
> These are two key texts that consider key aspects of general assessment.
>
> DrugScope and Alcohol Concern (2006) *Assessment in Drug Education*. London: DrugScope/Alcohol Concern. http://bit.ly/KyTRY1 (accessed 8 January 2014).
>
> This paper considers some of the key issues surrounding the assessment of drug education. The broad principles are transferable to the wider PSHE context.

References

Assessment Reform Group (1999) *Assessment for Learning: Beyond the Black Box*. Cambridge: Assessment Reform Group, University of Cambridge.

Black, P., Harrison, C., Lee, C., Marshall, B. and Wiliam, D. (2004) 'Working inside the black box: assessment for learning in the classroom', *Phi Delta Kappan*, 86 (1): 9–21.

Clarke, S. (2005) *Formative Assessment in Action: Weaving the Elements Together*. London: Hodder Education.

DfE (2012) *Statutory Framework for the Early Years Foundation Stage 2012*. London: Department for Education.

DrugScope and Alcohol Concern (2006) *Assessment in Drug Education*. London: DrugScope/Alcohol Concern. Available at: www.drugscope.org.uk/Resources/Drugscope/Documents/PDF/Education%20and%20Prevention/assessment-briefing.pdf (accessed 23 October 2013).

National Children's Bureau (2006) *A Whole-school Approach to Personal, Social and Health Education and Citizenship*. London: National Children's Bureau.

APPENDIX 1

PSHE EDUCATION AND SAFEGUARDING

Because PSHE education addresses many of the most sensitive issues in children's lives and draws on children's real life experiences it is inevitable that some pupils will reveal experiences that cause us concern. Any concern whatsoever that a teacher has about a child's personal safety should be shared immediately with the school's 'named' or 'responsible' person for safeguarding (sometimes referred to as child protection), usually the school's head teacher or deputy head. The rule for any adult working with children is 'If in doubt, shout'.

Personal activity

Ask to read the child protection or safeguarding policy of a school with which you are familiar. Consider the strategies, language and skills children would need in order to be able to alert adults that they, or one of their peers, needs help.

PSHE education is not the central focus for work around safeguarding but it can make a significant contribution. A planned programme of PSHE education can help children to reflect on their own safety, and to develop the skills, vocabulary and strategies that will help them keep themselves safe.

In the real world children may be unable to protect themselves, especially from adults. These may be adults that they love deeply and care about. Asking for help is not easy, even for adults. If a child is being abused they need to know that the abuse is wrong, that they have a right for it to stop, and that it can and should stop. They have to be able to share how they feel and what is happening to them. If the abuse is sexual they need an appropriate vocabulary that enables them to share and describe the nature of this abuse.

PSHE education also supports children in recognising the distress of their classmates and their responsibilities for helping others, and it provides them with the skills, strategies and language they need to get support for others they feel are at risk.

One day your children will be autonomous adults and will need the skills either to protect themselves or access support. This work also provides a foundation for later work in secondary schools. PSHE education encourages the development of positive relationships which may minimise abuse in future society. Examples of the contribution PSHE education can offer are embedded throughout this book.

There is key legislation covering all professionals' responsibilities with regard to the safeguarding of children, see the Children Act, 2004, this can be accessed at the following web address: http://www.legislation.gov.uk/ukpga/2004/31/pdfs/ukpga_20040031_en.pdf (last accessed 28 January 2014).

APPENDIX 2

PSHE EDUCATION AND THE SCHOOL POLICY FRAMEWORK

The vast majority of schools work within a clear policy framework that defines 'how we do things here'. While policies will often be drafted by members of the school's senior leadership team they are usually the responsibility of the school's governing body, academy trust or in the case of a private school the owner or board of trustees who ratify these drafts. Policies help to make the way schools work transparent to those people who need to know – the teachers, parents and carers, school governors, visitors to the school and external agencies.

In the case of primary schools, children will usually not be directly involved in the creation of policy; however, many schools consult with children about what is important to them through their student council, and this data informs the creation or review of many policies.

Policies can help keep all members of the school 'safe' by offering an agreed way of working. The best policies are formulated through consultation with all the different groups that will be affected by the policy, and many schools report that the process of constructing a policy is as valuable as the final document. Through consultation a common understanding emerges; there is clarity of purpose; and once this is in place, people can work independently, confident that they know the overall direction of work and the boundaries within which they can operate.

Policy is not the same as protocol. Protocols are the agreed procedures everyone agrees to follow should something happen. Protocols will be shaped by the individual school's policy.

The majority of schools will have an overarching mission statement – this tries to encapsulate in a sentence or two the overall purpose of the school. While these can seem a little like a 'marketing slogan', once again it is the process of trying to create a concise short statement that truly captures the school's overall purpose that is of value. The power of this process and the dialogue it generates, if undertaken in a truly inclusive 'whole school approach', should not be underestimated and can strengthen the whole school community (see Chapter 3 for more on the importance of the health promoting school).

Many schools then underpin their mission with a series of stated overarching aims (general statements of intent describing the direction in which the children will go in terms of what they might learn or what the teacher will provide) and objectives (more specific statements about what the learner should or will be able to do after attending the school). In the best schools decisions are always undertaken mindful of the school's mission, aims and objectives. Policies then contextualise the mission and aims into either subject policies (for example the school's PSHE education policy) or issue-based policies (for example safeguarding or child protection policy).

Since a school is a place of learning, any policy related to children should begin by exploring the contribution of the curriculum. For example, a school's anti-bullying policy should focus on how the curriculum reduces bullying behaviour and encourages and enables young people who either experience or fear bullying to be able to get help. The next level of the policy should consider how the school's overarching ethos can address bullying through either modelling appropriate behaviour or supporting children, and then finally how the school will respond to incidents of bullying.

PSHE education is taught within a wide policy framework. It will be shaped by the specific PSHE education policy, the school's sex and relationships policy, the school's drug policy, anti-bullying policy, health and safety policy and the school's equalities and inclusion policy. Just as with any other subject, PSHE education should be mindful of the school's assessment, reporting and recording policy.

As we have stated elsewhere, overarching all of these is the school's safeguarding or child protection policy with the guiding principle that 'The child's welfare is always paramount'.

We recommend keeping up to date with any changes in expectations at the national level by visiting the PSHE Association's website: www.pshe-association.org.uk.

APPENDIX 3

'LITTLE ALIEN' – PHOTOCOPIABLE ACTIVITY PLAN

Hello! I'm trying to find ... _____
_____

Can you help me?
Can you tell me what to look for?

INDEX

abstract conceptualisation, 26
academic subjects at school, 96
accidents, 148, 150
accountabilty: of adults, 55; of children, 96, 117, 215, 221
accreditation of learning, 247
action-based representation, 23
active experimentation, 26
active methodology in PSHE classes, 99–101, 105–10
affective input, 40
aims, educational 276
alcohol consumption, 212, 217
Aristotle and Aristotelianism, 19, 21
assertiveness, 173–4
assessment, 243–71
  common strategies for, 254–5
  coverage of, 250
  in the early years, 259–60
  and evaluation, 247–8
  evidence for, 251
  importance of, 249
  as learning, 271
  for learning and *of learning*, 246, 252–7, 271
  pupils' involvement in, 256
  shared responsibility for, 253, 256
  as a single continuous process with teaching, 256
  stages of, 252–6
  see also self-assessment
assessment activities, 257
Assessment Reform Group, 249
attainment as distinct from achievement, 60
attention deficit hyperactivity disorder,100
attention span, 100
auditory learning, 27

'backward mapping', 157, 166, 173–5, 214
Bandura, A., 25
Bar-On, R., 86
baseline assessment, 252, 256, 261, 264
behaviourism, 21, 29
bisexuals, 179–80
Black, P., 252–5
borrowing, 239
boundary-setting, 12, 138
brain development, 28–9
brainstorming, 108, 264
British Market Research Bureau, 178
Bronfenbrenner, U., 25, 31
Bruner, Jerome, 23–4
bubble dialogue, 76–7
bullying, 33, 190–205, 276
  bystanders' role in, 194–5
  definitions of, 191–2
  effects of, 192
  prevention of, 196, 202
  support group approach to, 204–5
  victims of, 183, 204–5
  whole-school and class policies on, 200
Burgher, M.S., 53
'Bus stop people' tool, 262–3

Cave, Kathryn, 203
child abuse, 33, 274
child-centred approach to learning, 24, 66
child development, 23–5, 29–31
child protection, 176, 273, 276
childbirth, children's explanations of, 169–70
childhood
  concept of and attitudes to, 30–2
  new sociology of, 31
'circle of feelings', 266
circle time, 76–7
circles, 89

Clarke, Shirley, 256
classical conditioning, 21
classroom climate, 101–6, 166, 175
Cleveland, M.J., 33
closed questions, 124
cognition, 21–2, 29
collaboration in educational governance, 54–5
communities, role of, 55
computer games, 240
conditioning, *classical* and *operant*, 21
confidentiality, 137–8
conforming, 37
constructivism, 7, 23–4, 151, 169, 237; *see also* social constructivism
contraception, 172–3
counsellors, 14, 16, 72
criterion referencing, 248, 252
cultural diversity, 177, 179
curriculum issues, 54, 276; *see also* hidden curriculum;spiral curriculum
cyber-bullying, 195

danger, sense of, 219–20
decision-making skills, 9
'deficit model' of the child, 23
democratic principles, 53
Dewey, John, 20
DiClemente, C.C., 41
Disclosure and Barring Service (DBS), 133
disclosure by children, 12, 265
discovery learning, 24
'distancing', 74, 110, 222
diversity (religious, cultural and physical), 131
drama, use of, 122–3
'Draw and talk' technique, 75–6, 261
'Draw and write' technique, 66–76, 102–4, 150–1, 158–9, 197, 237, 261
   in drug education, 213–14, 218, 221–8
   examples of, 72–5
   pros and *cons* of, 70–1
drug education, 33, 38, 73–6, 124–5, 208–32
   definition of, 210
   history of, 212–14
   need for, 210–13
   as part of safety education, 210–11
   purpose of, 210
   teachers' attitudes to, 221
drug education co-ordinators, 213
drug policies of schools, 225–6, 230
drugs
   attitudes to, 220–1
   definition of, 209

drugs *cont.*
   referred to in the classroom, 227
   risk factors and protective factors for abuse of, 230–2
DrugScope website, 218
'duty of care', 149–50
DVDs, use of, 114, 124

Early Learning Goals, 259
ecological theories of child development, 25
economics, children's understanding of, 6, 237–8
economic wellbeing, 235–6
education, nature of, 6–8
emotional bullying, 192
emotional health and wellbeing, 56, 83
emotional intelligence, 28, 83–6
   definitions of, 85–6
emotional literacy, definition of, 84
emotional quotient (EQ), 28
emotional 'zones', 111
empathy, 49, 174, 193; development of, 202–3
empowerment of young people, 54
environmental factors in children's learning, 25
equity principle, 53
ethos of a school, 48–50, 83–4, 276
European Network of Health Promoting Schools (ENHPS), 53
evaluation, 247, 257; *see also* self-evaluation
experiential learning, 26, 241

'facilitator' role for teachers, 97
faith schools, 177
families, partnership with, 178–9
fear, experiences of, 88–9
fear arousal, 35, 40
feedback, 266–8
feelings: importance of, 84; management of, 260
financial capability, development of, 241; *see also* personal finance education
Fine, Anne, 203–4
focus groups, 77–8
forest schools, 161
formative assessment, 252, 253, 257, 262
Formby, E., 147
Froebel, F.W.A., 24
functional magnetic resonance imaging (fMRI), 29
Furnham, A., 86

gambling, 239–41
Gardner, Howard, 28, 85
gender, definition of, 168
Ghodse, H., 217

Gill, Tim, 149
Gill, V., 38
Goleman, D., 28, 86
governing bodies of schools, 57
group work and group organisation in PSHE classes, 106–8

Hallam, S., 87
Haralambos, Michael, 50
Headstart programme, 25
health
  as an aspect of PSHE education, 6
  definition of, 6
Health Action Model, 38–41
Health Belief Model, 34–6, 39
health-promoting schools, 52–5, 59–62
  principles of, 53–5
health-related behaviour, 33–41
healthy eating, 10, 12, 52, 56, 87, 229
'healthy school' concept, 11, 40–1, 59, 196; see also National Healthy Schools Programme
Hemingway, Ernest, 112
hidden curriculum, 50–1
homosexuality, 179–80
Hunter, Judy, 120

image-based representation, 23
images, use of, 120
imitation of behaviour, 25
injury prevention, 147–8
injury rates, 149
insight learning, 22
intelligence, forms of, 27–8
interactive work, 101
interpersonal intelligence and skills, 5, 28, 85
intrapersonal intelligence and skills, 5, 85
ipsative assessment and ipsative referencing, 248, 252
IQ tests, 27
Ironside, Virginia, 120
issue-based policies, 276

James, Allison, 31
Jenkins-Pearce, Susie, 203

Kansas Safe School Resource Center, 193
Key Stages 1 and 2, 228–9
kinaesthetic learning, 27
Kohlberg, L., 23
Koizumi, H., 30
Kolb, David, 26

language, development of, 29–30
language-based representation, 23

learning
  definitions of, 6, 18
  as distinct from education, 30
  methods of assessment of, 246–7
  philosophical approach to, 19–20
learning agreements or contracts, 12
learning needs assessment, 252
learning objectives, 90–3, 247–9, 252, 256–9
learning outcomes, 249, 251–2, 256
learning situations, 121
learning styles, 26–9, 131
learning theories, 19–22
listening skills, 100
'Little alien' technique, 261–2
Locke, John, 19
locked-in syndrome, 29
'Looking back, looking forward' tool, 269

McKee, David, 120
McWhirter, J., 157–8
magneto-encephalography (MEG), 29
Maines, Barbara, 204–5
Mayer, J.D., 85
medicines, 211–12, 219
Meighan, Roland, 50
menarche and menstruation, 170–1
mental maps, 22
micro events and micro interactions, 51, 59
mirroring, 49
mission statements, 276
Misuse of Drugs Act, 212
modelling of behaviour, 25, 49, 276
money, learning about, 236–41
Montessori, Maria, 24
Moon, Alysoun, 150
Moore, Inga, 203
moral reasoning, theory of (Kohlberg), 23
moralistic attitudes, 36
Moran-Ellis, J., 32
Mosley, J., 89
Moss, Steven, 149
motivational interviewing, 36
Muijs, D., 24
multiple intelligences, 28, 85

National Healthy Schools Programme (NHSP), 55–6
neuroscience, 29–30, 192
norm referencing, 248
normative approach to drug education, 38
norms see social norms
Northern Ireland, 226

objectives, 276; *see also* learning objectives
Office for Standards in Education (Ofsted), 150, 155
Olweus, D., 192
'one off' sessions in PSHE classes, 133, 140
open-ended questions, 98, 124, 130
operant conditioning, 21
optical topography (OT), 29
'optimistic bias' in young people, 35–6
organisational psychology, 26

paired discussion, 79
'Park bench' tool, 262–4
Pavlov, Ivan, 20–1
peer assessment, 249
peer feedback, 266
peer mediators, 56–7
peer pressure, 37–8, 195, 220–1
peer support, 190–1, 204
personal finance education, 235–42
personal nature of PSHE education, 4–5, 10–12
personal and social development (PSD), 48, 50, 196
Personal, Social, Health and Economic (PSHE) education
 aims of, 8–9
 alternative terminology for, 4
 definition of, 4, 20
 as distinct from personal and social development, 48
 importance of, 8
 in relation to other school subjects, 9–11
 special nature of teaching in, 96–9
 ten principles of, 42, 66
 see also PSHE Assocation
personalised learning, 20
Petrides, K.V., 86
Phillips, Stella, 120
photography, use of, 79
physical activity in school, 56
Piaget, Jean, 23–4, 152
picture books, 112–13
Planned Behaviour, Theory of, 36–9
'play leaders', 56
Plutchik, R., 85
pocket money, 238
primary emotions, 85
prior learning, 256, 261
'processing', 125
Prochaska, J.O., 41
promises of co-operation in class, 102–4
protective factors for children, 32–3, 217, 231–2
protocols, 138, 276
Prout, Allan, 31

PSHE *see* Personal, Social, Health and Economic education
PSHE Association, 4, 18, 20, 41, 66, 276
puberty, 167, 170, 180, 187
pupil responsibility and the pupil voice, 56–7
puzzles, 123

quizzes, 76, 123

recording of learning by children themselves, 268–70
reflection in the classroom, 5, 10, 61–2, 100, 265, 270–1
reflective observation, 26
reflective practice and reflective practitioners, 253, 257
reinforcement, *positive* and *negative*, 21
relationships, learning about, 5–6, 90, 167, 170, 260, 274
research, classroom-based, 71–2, 200, 237, 261
resilience in children, 25, 33
resources for PSHE education, 128–33
responsibility *see* accountability
Reynolds, D., 24
risk
 definition of, 155
 high levels of, 219–20
risk assessment, 155–6, 161
risk competence, 157
risk education, 160–1
risk factors for children, 32–3, 217, 230–1
road safety, 157
Robinson, George, 204–5
roles, taking on, 122–3
Rousseau, Jean-Jacques, 19–20, 24
Royal Society for the Prevention of Accidents (RoSPA), 147–8, 155
rules of behaviour, 102, 175
Ruskin, John, 20

safeguarding of children, 138, 176, 273–4, 276
safety education, 147–55
 relevance to other school priorities, 153–4
same-sex marriage, 180
saving, 239
'scaffolding' of learning, 23
schema, 23
school policies, 137–8, 275–6; on drugs, 225–6, 230; on sex and relationships education, 177–80
Scotland, 226
self-assessment, 249–50, 256, 258
self-awareness, 259
self-confidence, 89–90, 259

self-efficacy, 25, 40
self-esteem, 89–90
self-evaluation, 266
sensitive issues in school, 73–5, 110, 148, 212, 222
sentence completion, 105
sentence stems, 265–6
'settings' approach to education, 52
sex, definition of, 168
sex education, biological, 73, 167, 180–7
Sex Education Forum, 179
sex and relationships education (SRE), 165–6, 171–87
  dreaded questions, 176–7
  example of a programme, 181–6
  undertaken by parents, 178
  withdrawal from, 179
sexuality and sexual orientation, 168, 179–80
Singer, W., 29
skills, application of, 219
Skinner, B.F., 21
smoking, 9–10, 19, 217
social aspects of PSHE education, 5
social constructivism, 24, 31
Social and Emotional Aspects of Learning (SEAL) programme, 28, 86–8
social isolation of some children, 56
social networking, 195
social norms, 37–8; perceived, 38
social psychology, 25
social sciences, 33
Socrates, 19
'soft skills', 5
solvent-sniffing, 217
spiral curriculum, 23, 153, 157
'stage theory' of children's cognitive development, 23
stereotypes, 131
stimulus–response (S-R) learning, 22
stories for children, 88, 100–1, 110–21, 203, 222, 258; creation of, 121; deconstruction of, 114–20; selection of, 113
storyboards, 262
student councils, 57–8, 275
subject policies, 276

success, measurement of, 54
success criteria, 257
summative assessment, 253, 257, 262
Sure Start programme, 25
sustainability of educational practice, 55
synaptic connections, 29

'Targets' tool, 269
teacher training, 54
TeachFind website, 88
teaching styles, 131
television programmes, 124
textbooks, 129
thankyous, 267
Tolman, C.T., 21
transgender relationships, 168
'Treasure Chest' tool, 268–9

unconscious learning, 50

values, 130–1, 196, 239
visitor sessions in school, 124–5, 129, 133–40, 147–8, 161
vivid stimulus, 108
volatile substance abuse (VSA), 217
vulnerable young people, 32–3, 36, 138, 217
Vygotsky, L.S., 23–4, 31

Wales, 226
'walking buses', 147
Webley, Paul, 237–8
wellbeing of children, 32; *see also* emotional health and wellbeing
Wetton, Noreen, 67, 97, 120, 130
'What Money Means' project, 238–9
whole-school approach to PSHE education, 11, 33, 40–1, 52, 190, 200, 276
Williams, Trefor, 150–1
Wolke, D., 192–3
workbooks and worksheets, 129–30
'working disassociated', 110
World Health Organisation (WHO), 83

zone of proximal development, 24